Oxford Smart

Key Stage 3 Science

Activate
Teacher handbook
2

Curriculum Editor: Dr Andrew Chandler-Grevatt

Alyssa Fox-Charles • Anna Harris • Jo Locke

OXFORD
UNIVERSITY PRESS

Contents

Contents	ii–iii
Introduction	iv–ix
Your Teacher Handbook and Kerboodle	x–xiii

Metacognition and self-regulation	2
1.1 Strategies for effective learning	2
1.2 Using strategies effectively	4

Working scientifically Unit Opener — 6

2.1	Planning investigations 2	8
2.2	Presenting data 2	10
2.3	Analysing and evaluating 2	12
2.4	Communicating scientific information	14
2.5	Using evidence and sources	16
2.6	Development of scientific understanding	18

Biology 2 Unit Opener — 20

Chapter 1: Health and lifestyle — 22
1.1	Nutrients	24
1.2	Food tests	26
1.3	Unhealthy diet	28
1.4	Digestive system	30
1.5	Bacteria and enzymes in digestion	32
1.6	Drugs	34
1.7	Alcohol	36
1.8	Smoking	38

Chapter 1 Checkpoint Lesson: Health and lifestyle — 40

Chapter 2: Biological processes — 42
2.1	Photosynthesis	44
2.2	Leaves	46
2.3	Plant minerals	48
2.4	Aerobic respiration	50
2.5	Anaerobic respiration	52

Chapter 2 Checkpoint Lesson: Biological processes — 54

Chapter 3: Ecosystems and adaptation — 56
3.1	Food chains and webs	58
3.2	Disruption to food chains and webs	60
3.3	Ecosystems	62
3.4	Competition	64
3.5	Adapting to change	66

Chapter 3 Checkpoint Lesson: Ecosystems and adaptation — 68

Chapter 4: Inheritance — 70
4.1	Variation	72
4.2	Continuous and discontinuous	74
4.3	Inheritance	76
4.4	Natural selection	78
4.5	Extinction	80

Chapter 4 Checkpoint Lesson: Inheritance — 82

Chemistry 2 Unit Opener — 84

Chapter 1: The Periodic Table — 86
1.1	Three elements	88
1.2	Physical properties of metals and non-metals	90
1.3	Chemical properties of metals and non-metals	92
1.4	Groups and Periods	94
1.5	The elements of Group 1	96
1.6	The elements of Group 7	98
1.7	The elements of Group 0	100

Chapter 1 Checkpoint Lesson: The Periodic Table — 102

Chemistry 2 Unit Opener (Cont.)

Chapter 2: Separation techniques		104
2.1	Pure substances	106
2.2	Mixtures	108
2.3	Solutions	110
2.4	Solubility	112
2.5	Filtration	114
2.6	Evaporation and distillation	116
2.7	Chromatography	118
Chapter 2 Checkpoint Lesson: Separation techniques		120
Chapter 3: Metals and other materials		122
3.1	Metals and acids	124
3.2	Metals and oxygen	126
3.3	The reactivity series	128
3.4	Metal displacement reactions	130
3.5	Extracting metals	132
3.6	Ceramics	134
3.7	Polymers	136
3.8	Composites	138
Chapter 3 Checkpoint Lesson: Metals and other materials		140
Chapter 4: The Earth		142
4.1	The Earth and its atmosphere	144
4.2	Sedimentary rocks	146
4.3	Igneous and metamorphic rocks	148
4.4	The rock cycle	150
4.5	The carbon cycle	152
4.6	Global heating	154
4.7	Climate change	156
4.8	Recycling	158
Chapter 4 Checkpoint Lesson: The Earth		160

Physics 2 Unit Opener — 162

Chapter 1: Electricity and magnetism		164
1.1	Charging up	166
1.2	Circuits and current	168
1.3	Potential difference	170
1.4	Resistance	172
1.5	Changing the subject	174
1.6	Series and parallel	176
1.7	Magnets and magnetic fields	178
1.8	Electromagnets	180
1.9	Using electromagnets	182
Chapter 1 Checkpoint Lesson: Electricity and magnetism		184
Chapter 2: Energy		186
2.1	Food and fuels	188
2.2	Energy resources	190
2.3	Energy adds up	192
2.4	Energy and temperature	194
2.5	Energy transfer: particles	196
2.6	Energy transfer: radiation	198
2.7	Energy transfer: forces	200
2.8	Energy and power	202
Chapter 2 Checkpoint Lesson: Energy		204
Chapter 3: Motion and pressure		206
3.1	Speed	208
3.2	Motion graphs	210
3.3	Pressure in gases	212
3.4	Pressure in liquids	214
3.5	Pressure on solids	216
3.6	Turning forces	218
Chapter 3 Checkpoint Lesson: Motion and pressure		220

Student Book answers	222	Imprint	242
Index	239		

Introduction

About the series

The *Oxford Smart* Activate has been updated to align with the principles of the *Oxford Smart* Curriculum for Science. It is designed to match the Key Stage 3 Programme of Study, with careful consideration of the transitions from Key Stage 2 and onto Key Stage 4 to help prepare students for success at GCSE and equivalent qualifications.

Oxford Smart Activate is flexible to suit your preferred route through Key Stage 3. The Programme of Study is covered in *Oxford Smart* Activate 1 and 2, making it a perfect match for a two-year course. *Oxford Smart* Activate 3 offers consolidation and extension of core concepts through application of knowledge and practice in the skills needed for success at Key Stage 4.

Across the Student Books, Teacher Handbooks, and Kerboodle courses, *Oxford Smart* Activate allows you to track students' progress using reliable assessment and learning resources. Our expert author and editor teams all have teaching experience, and our curriculum editor is a school-assessment expert. You can be confident that *Oxford Smart* Activate provides the best support for your students and teachers.

About your Teacher Handbook

This Teacher Handbook aims to save you time and effort by offering lesson plans and guidance on differentiation and assessment with a page-by-page match to the Student Book.

Unit openers provide context for students and show the prior knowledge required for a topic at a glance. The chapter openers include tips for delivering the content and the checkpoint lessons support students who have yet to grasp a secure knowledge of the outcomes. Lesson plans are written for 55-minute lessons but are flexible and fully adaptable.

About the *Oxford Smart* Curriculum for Science

The *Oxford Smart* Curriculum for Science has been built to address what research shows to be the most pressing considerations for teachers and learners. It connects content, methods, assessment, insight, and evaluation to deliver a holistic learning experience. Using data, insights, and research, it equips teachers to deliver personalised learning for all students.

Designed with an explicit egalitarian purpose to enable teachers and students to experience the joy and wonder of learning, the *Oxford Smart* Curriculum for Science's intent is based on the following six pillars. More information on each pillar can be found in the CPD and Research hub on Kerboodle.

Six Pillars

Provide clear and coherent pathways

The well-researched progression and sequencing support transition from Key Stage 2, through Key Stage 3, and onto GCSE or equivalent qualifications. The pathways are described in the Curriculum narratives documents and embedded throughout *Oxford Smart* Activate. Unit and chapter openers clearly show the learning journey for students and highlight the common misconceptions identified by our research.

Coherence

Hold high expectations, aspirations, and ambitions for all learners

Oxford Smart Activate identifies strengths, opportunities for challenge, and addresses learning 'gaps'. Expectations are clearly defined using the Developing, Secure, and Extending assessment framework. Challenge and scaffolding are provided in the resources through opt-in, rather than task-based, differentiation.

High expectations

Enable responsive teaching and learning that continually evolves and improves

Regular opportunities for formative assessment are provided through in-book questions, reactivate questions, mini-checkpoint tests, and checkpoint assessments, with embedded checkpoint follow-up lessons and recommended next steps allowing for easy intervention. Regular spaced practice is included to help students retain concepts.

Responsive teaching and learning

Support engaged, self-regulated, and metacognitive learning

The *Oxford Smart* Activate equips learners to succeed with the ability to understand and use learning strategies effectively, facilitating independence and resilience. Learners develop metacognitive skills with scaffolded resources and reflection plenaries for every lesson, while professional development and targeted resources support teachers in modelling metacognitive strategies and self-regulation in the classroom.

Metacognitive learning

Promote development of learner identity and identification with science

Oxford Smart Activate reflects diversity and promotes a sense of belonging for students. The Trigger interest activities and unit openers demonstrate where science impacts our world, enabling learners to make connections with other subjects and their everyday lives.

Learner identity

Stimulate fascination, awe, and wonder in discovery of self and the world around us

Oxford Smart Activate promotes the awe and wonder of science through a wide range of hands-on practical activities and hooks for each topic. The unit openers and Trigger interest sections of lessons provide suggestions to spark curiosity and amazement.

Awe and **wonder**

Research and CPD

The *Oxford Smart* Curriculum for Science and supporting resources and assessment in *Oxford Smart* Activate are based on a sound corpus of pedagogical research, and will generate its own evidence and impact from educators, experts, and real learning and assessment. Over time, this portfolio of evidence will in turn inform and inspire future curriculum evaluation and development.

What to expect from the research library

A Research library is available on Kerboodle. Here, we have collated the key pedagogical research and evidence that has been used to develop the *Oxford Smart* Curriculum for Science and *Oxford Smart* Activate, including a summary of the research that supports each pillar, references, and further reading.

In addition to the research used to shape the *Oxford Smart* Curriculum for Science are additional summaries of pedagogical literature that may impact the classroom now and in the future, including science-specific summaries and applications of the research.

The Research library will continue to be updated as the body of research grows to support the implementation of effective pedagogy in the classroom.

Impact

The *Oxford Smart* Activate has been trialled with 30 pioneer schools. Their feedback has informed the development of the curriculum, resources, and assessment.

Our pioneer schools have reported that some of the highlights of *Oxford Smart* Activate have been:

- the reduced planning time required for lessons
- the improved metacognitive practices from the embedded curriculum structure
- the enhanced student engagement from the range of lesson activities and practicals.

Continuing professional development

Alongside the Research library on Kerboodle, we are building a bank of CPD resources to support teachers as they implement *Oxford Smart* Activate.

These resources include blogs, articles, and videos that will cover:

- the six pillars of the *Oxford Smart* Curriculum for Science, how they are implemented in *Oxford Smart* Activate, and practical support for the classroom
- topic-focused support to help teach tricky topics or to approach a new topic for ECT and non-specialists
- targeted support for common misconceptions and how to address them.

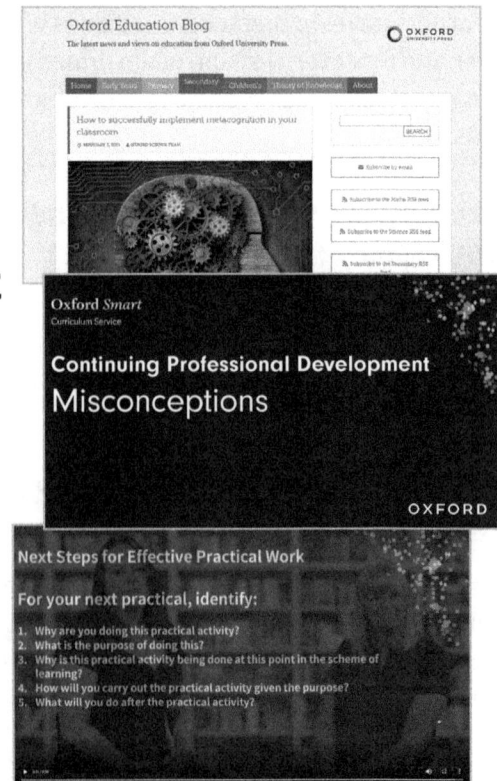

Curriculum narratives

The Curriculum narratives are overarching domain narratives, that provide a macro-level view of a learner's journey through the curriculum for each domain of science. They give a broad picture of the scope and progression of learning within the curriculum and articulate the rationale for the inclusion of content.

Working together with experienced, subject-expert teachers and reviewers, the Curriculum narratives were created using research and data mapping every part of the content to its prerequisite knowledge from the start to end of secondary education.

They have helped us ensure effective and coherent sequencing of learning for each science domain through the curriculum, informing on all resources. They also been of crucial importance in ensuring the KS3 curriculum content seamlessly follows on from primary science content and aligns with student and teacher needs at GCSE.

All the Curriculum narratives can be found in the Research hub on Kerboodle.

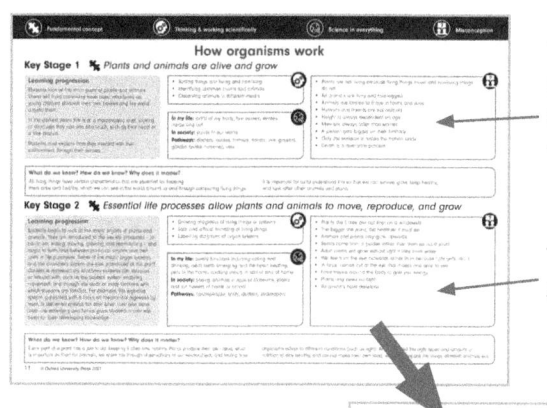

The Key Stage 1 and 2 information sets Key Stage 3 learning in the context of prior content covered and can help you to understand what knowledge and misconceptions students may bring into secondary education.

The narrative follows the same structure for each key stage.

The **Fundamental concept** section is a short summary of the core substantive knowledge for the domain at each key stage.

Opportunities for students to practice **thinking and working scientifically**.

The **Science in everything** section gives relevancies of the domain content to learners' personal lives, wider society, and future pathways.

The **Learning progression** section details how the domain's substantive knowledge is introduced to learners, explored, and developed, from Key Stage 1 (where appropriate) to the end of Key Stage 4.

Some of the most common and key **misconceptions** learners may have about the domain's knowledge.

The **What do we know? How do we know? Why does it matter?** section addresses the rationale behind the knowledge in the domain and its importance to society and our understanding of the world.

The Key Stage 4 information sets Key Stage 3 learning in context of what learning is still to come and how students' understanding will develop.

vii

Assessment and reporting

About the Curriculum Editor and Assessment Expert

Dr Andrew Chandler-Grevatt has a doctorate in school assessment and a passion for science teaching. Having worked as a teacher for ten years, Andy has a real understanding of teaching in the classroom. This stays at the front of his mind during all of his work in education. Alongside his research in school assessment, Andy is a teaching fellow on the PGCE course at the University of Sussex and a successful published assessment author.

Welcome from the Curriculum Editor

Welcome to your *Oxford Smart* Activate 2 Teacher Handbook. The Teacher Handbooks, together with Kerboodle, and the Student Books, provide comprehensive assessment that is coherent with the rest of the *Oxford Smart* Curriculum for Science. Our assessment is built in across the curriculum and will help your school to monitor progress against a clear framework. Throughout *Oxford Smart* Activate, formative assessment has been made easy and we have followed a set of guiding principles.

Oxford Smart Activate assessment principles

Assessment in *Oxford Smart* Activate aims to:

- inform teaching and/or learning directly (have a formative function)
- assess agreed and shared objectives
- provide opportunities for peer- and self-assessment
- provide opportunities for specific feedback to be given to individual students
- provide usable data that informs teachers of class and individual progress.

I have been working closely with our expert author teams across all components of the *Oxford Smart* Curriculum for Science, meaning you can be confident when using *Oxford Smart* Activate to monitor your students' progress.

Andy Chandler-Grevatt

Assessing the curriculum

The *Oxford Smart* Activate assessment model is based on bands: the middle band indicates that students have a secure grasp of the knowledge or skills specified in the curriculum. The band working towards 'secure' is 'developing', and the band moving past 'secure' is 'extending'.

All the lesson outcomes are differentiated. Support sheets are provided to help developing students to access the lesson activity or practical, while extension tasks and resources can be found on the Lesson presentations and Kerboodle.

The Summary Questions and End-of-Chapter Questions in the Student Book are ramped. The level of demand of each question is indicated by the number of dots shaded in by the question number.

Activate Bands	Developing	Secure	Extending
What it looks like – content	Demonstrates knowledge and understanding by recall and simple descriptions	Demonstrates secure knowledge and understanding of the learning objective	Demonstrates knowledge and understanding beyond secure
What it looks like – application	Able to apply knowledge and understanding only in highly scaffolded, familiar situations	Able to apply knowledge to familiar situations	Able to apply knowledge and understanding in unfamiliar situations

The checkpoint system

Our assessment model combines regular formative and traditional summative assessments. An additional element is regular, low-stakes quizzing aimed at interrupting the forgetting curve and helping students retain new concepts.

The formative assessment comprises the checkpoints and mini-checkpoints on Kerboodle. Regular mini-checkpoint assessment tracks progress through the chapter and there is a checkpoint assessment following each chapter. These are all automarked and will help determine if students have a secure understanding of the chapter.

Following each checkpoint or mini-checkpoint, students are offered personalised next steps. They can consolidate their knowledge where they are at a developing level and challenge themselves where they have demonstrated secure knowledge.

At the end of each year, there is a summative assessment, available as a digital or paper-based assessment, to evaluate understanding of the whole unit.

Reporting and insights

The formative assessment data will feed online reporting on Kerboodle and give insights into students' strengths and weaknesses.

The curriculum breaks each science into the Curriculum narrative domains and then splits them into related themes that run through all key stages. The themes are divided into sub-themes to enable targeted interventions.

The reporting will support you in diagnosing learner strengths and weaknesses, and to identify misconceptions so you can adapt your teaching.

Follow assessment with learning

Oxford Smart Activate has been designed with responsive teaching in mind. There are opportunities embedded throughout the course to use the formative assessment data to inform your teaching.

The data from the mini-checkpoints and checkpoints can be used to inform which follow-up activities for students to target their weaknesses and to support all students towards working at a secure level.

Extension resources are available on Kerboodle to help students at a secure level move towards extending.

The Metacognition chapter has information on building in student reflection, and this can be useful before and after an assessment.

Your Teacher Handbook

Unit opener

Overview

This provides a summary of the unit (biology, chemistry, or physics), how it links to Key Stage 2 and 4, ideas for how a teacher could put learning into context, and inspire awe and wonder with information related to the corresponding Student Book unit opener.

Introduction
An overview of the chapters in this unit.

Curriculum links
The National Curriculum subject and Working scientifically statements that link to this unit.

Learning journey
An overview of the unit, the Key Stage 2 topics that lead up to it and the later topics that it builds to.

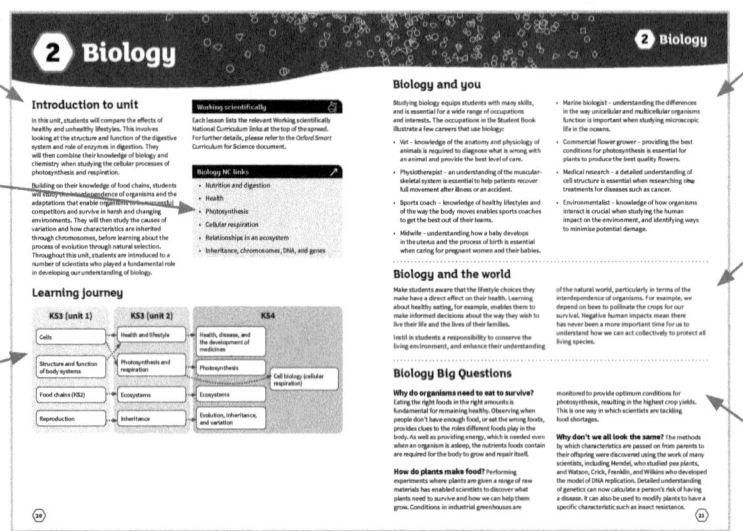

Science and you
Suggestions for how to inspire awe and wonder.

Science and the world
Ideas for how to provide context for the unit and make it relevant to students' lives.

Big questions
The Student Book features three fundamental questions that science aims to answer that link to the unit. This section provides further details and guidance on leading discussions around these.

Chapter opener

Overview

The chapter opener provides teacher-focussed preparation for the chapter content to ensure all teachers are prepared and confident to teach the content.

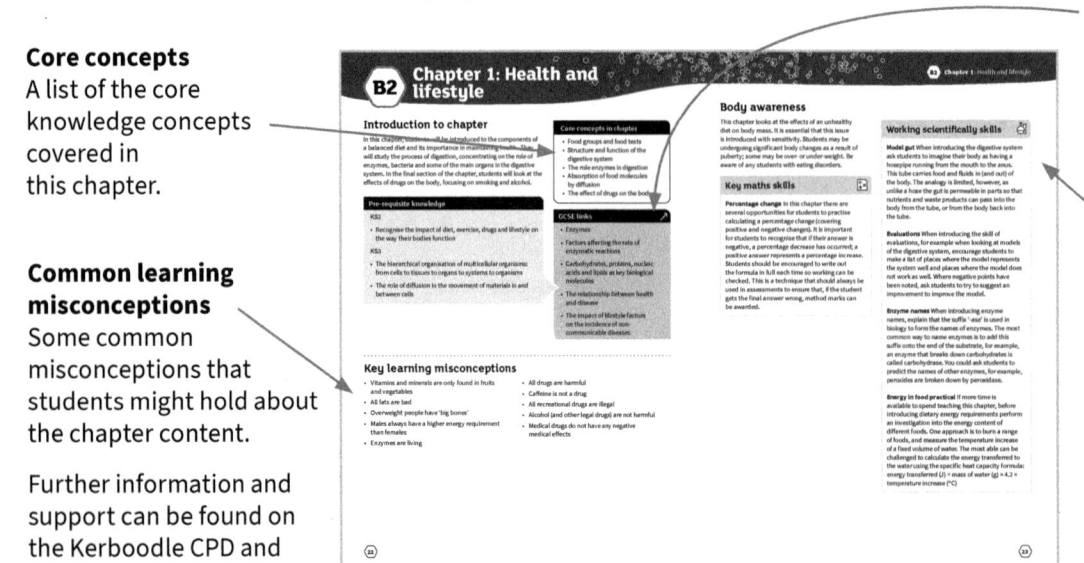

Core concepts
A list of the core knowledge concepts covered in this chapter.

Common learning misconceptions
Some common misconceptions that students might hold about the chapter content.

Further information and support can be found on the Kerboodle CPD and Research hub.

Curriculum links
The prerequisite knowledge for the chapter content (Key Stage 3 or primary) and links to GCSE content.

Teaching preparation
Tips and information to consider when teaching the chapter.

These will vary, but may include further information on misconceptions, suggestions for tackling key skills, and useful strategies for teaching particular content.

x

Lesson

Differentiated outcomes
This table shows the lesson outcomes, which are ramped and divided into three ability bands.

Vocabulary
Tier 2 vocabulary includes words that are more academic in nature and operate across different contexts. Tier 3 key words are subject-specific. Words in italics have multiple meanings and misconceptions may arise due to this.

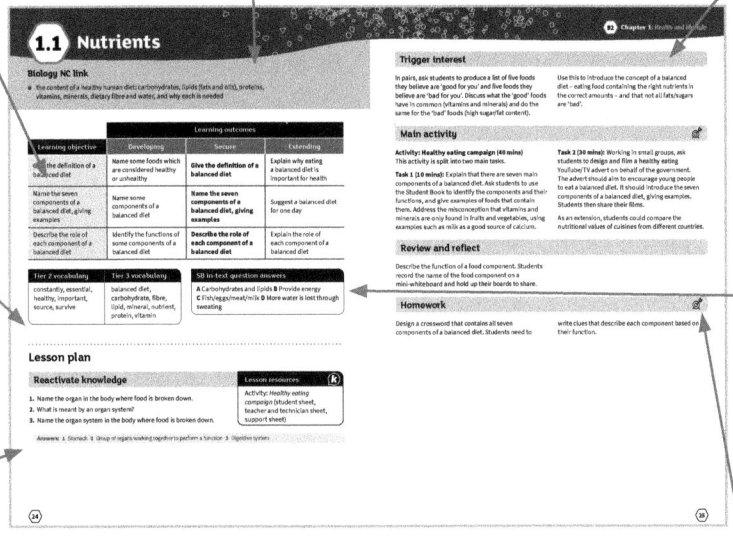

Reactivate knowledge
The retrieval questions from the Student Book are included here, along with the answers and any suggestions for discussions of key prerequisite knowledge.

Core concepts
The theme and sub-theme indicate the area of the *Oxford Smart* Curriculum for Science that this lesson focusses on. Students' understanding can be monitored with the curriculum reports. Links to the National Curriculum are also given here.

Skills
These symbols indicate where different skills have been embedded in the lesson.

🧪 Working scientifically   🎯 Literacy   ➕ Maths

These skills are ramped through *Oxford Smart* Activate and divided into the three bands. A progression grid and learning outcomes are supplied on Kerboodle.

Suggested lesson plan
A suggested route through the lesson is provided, including ideas for support and homework. The structure has been carefully designed using cognitive science research.

Answers
Answers to the Student Book in-text questions can be found here. The answers to all other questions from the Student Book are found at the back of the Teacher Handbook, except for the Maths, Working scientifically, and Literacy activities and chapter openers, which are supplied on Kerboodle.

Checkpoint lesson

Overview

The checkpoint intervention lesson is a suggested follow-up after students complete the automarked checkpoint assessment on Kerboodle. The activities aim to move all students from developing to secure on the key assessment learning objectives.

Checkpoint secure learning outcomes
A list of all of the secure learning outcomes covered in the checkpoint assessment.

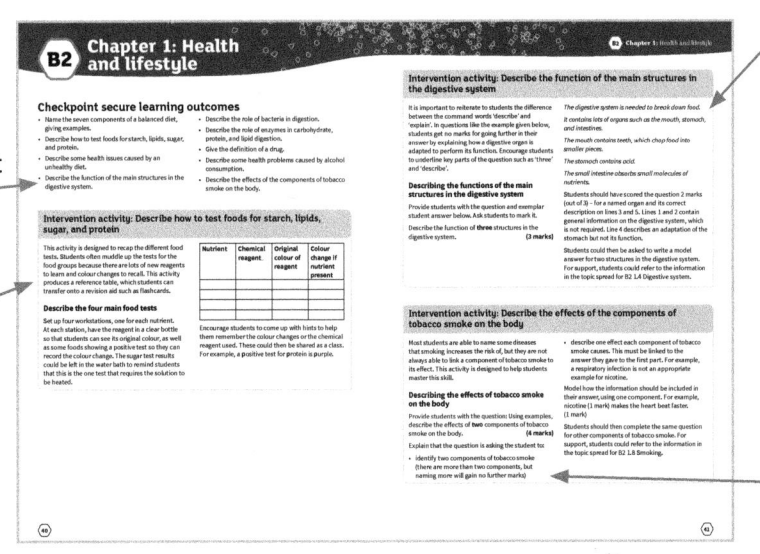

Student reflection
This section suggests how to help students to reflect on their learning over the chapter.

Additional strategies to aid reflection can be found in the Metacognition chapter or in the Research hub on Kerboodle.

Intervention activities
Guidance on possible missing information or misconceptions and an intervention activity for each core learning outcome from the checkpoint assessment with the aim to ensure that all students are at a secure level.

These activities are flexible so you can select the most appropriate one(s) for your class.

Extending students
Further resources are available on Kerboodle for classes or students where moving from secure to extending would be appropriate.

xi

Kerboodle

Oxford Smart **Activate Kerboodle** provides hundreds of engaging lesson resources, as well as a comprehensive assessment package. They are regularly updated, intuitive, and customisable. Resources include lessons and associated resources, automatically marked assessments, books, and the CPD and Research hub.

You can adapt many of the resources to suit your students' needs or your own scheme of work, with all non-interactive activities available as editable Word documents. You can also upload your existing resources so that everything can be accessed from one location.

Kerboodle is online, allowing you and your students to access the course anytime and anywhere. You can set homework and assessments through the Assessment system and track progress using the Markbook.

Kerboodle Book

The *Oxford Smart* Activate Kerboodle Book provides a digital copy of the Student Book for use at the front of the classroom.

Teacher access to the Kerboodle Book is automatically available as part of the Lessons, Resources, and Assessment package. You can also purchase additional access for your students.

A set of tools is available with the Kerboodle Book so you can personalize your book and make notes.

Like all other resources offered on Kerboodle, the Kerboodle Book can also be accessed using a range of devices.

Use different tools such as sticky notes, bookmarks, and pen features to personalise each page

Navigate around the book quickly with the contents menu, key word search, or page number search.

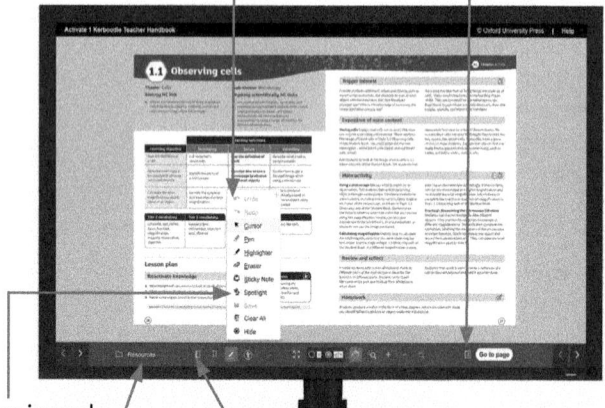

Zoom in and spotlight text

All the associated resources can be viewed on each spread.

Every teacher and student has their own digital notebook for use within their Kerboodle Book. You can choose to share your notes with students or hide them from view – all student notes are accessible to themselves only.

Lessons

Click on the 'Lessons' tab to access the *Oxford Smart* Activate Lesson Plan and Presentation (with accompanying notes).

There is a lesson plan to complement every spread in the Teacher Handbook and Student Book. Each plan is accompanied by teachers' notes on that lesson and links to the resources required for the lesson, including the Lesson presentation.

Each lesson comes with a presentation that features *Reactivate* question starters, lesson objectives, *Trigger Interest* content, activity guidance, key diagrams, extension questions, plenaries, and homework suggestions. You can further personalise these by adding in your own resources and notes.

Resources are built into each lesson plan so that associated interactive content, presentations, practical, or activity worksheets are ready to launch from one location.

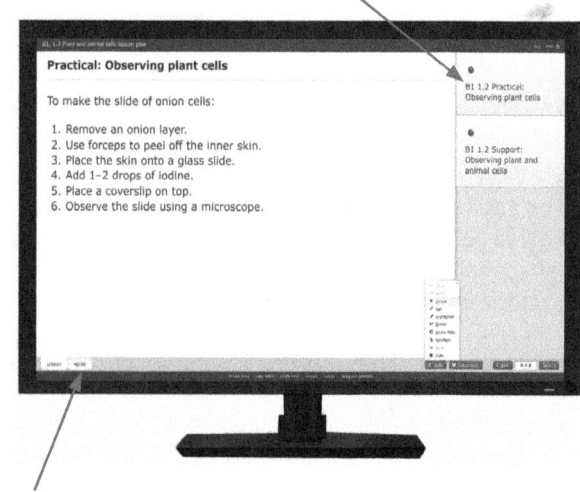

Every lesson is accompanied by teacher notes that provide additional support and extension opportunities to fully support lesson delivery.

Resources

Click on the 'Resources' tab to access the full list of *Oxford Smart* Activate lesson resources.

The resource section includes:

- **Practicals and activities** Fully-editable resources to use in class. In addition to an activity sheet and a support sheet, which are accessible by pupils, a teacher and technician sheet provides further ideas on differentiation, answers and a list of resources required by technicians.
- **Maths and Working scientifically skill sheets and interactives**
- **Videos and animations**
- **PowerPoints**
- **Extension resources**
- **Knowledge organisers**
- **Checklists**
- **Glossaries**
- **Webquests**
- **Metacognition support**

Navigation panel and search bar allow for easy navigation between resources by book, unit, and chapter.

Resources can be made visible or hidden to students and a link will take you to the corresponding Student Book spread.

Set single or multiple assignments for your classes using the Assignment basket.

Existing resources and links can be uploaded onto the platform using the My Resources section.

Resources matching every lesson in the *Oxford Smart* Activate series are shown here.

Assessment and Markbook

All the assessment material in Kerboodle has been quality assured by our assessment expert. Click on the Assessment tab to find a range of materials to help you deliver a varied, motivating, and effective assessment programme.

It's easy to import class registers and create user accounts for your students. Once your classes are set up, you can assign them assessments to do at home, individually, or as a group.

A Markbook with reporting function helps you to keep track of your students' results. This includes both automarked assessments and work that needs to be marked by you.

In the Assessment tab, you can find mini-checkpoints for each lesson, checkpoints for each chapter, and end-of-unit assessments for each unit.

Different follow-up tasks are available to students after they complete the checkpoints and mini-checkpoints, depending on how well they did.

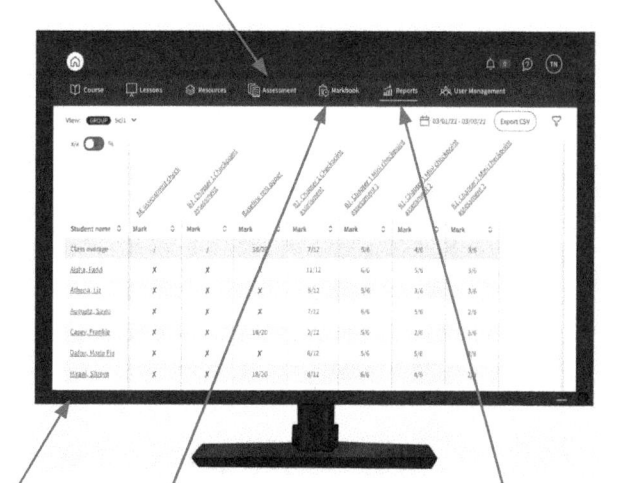

A Markbook and reporting function helps you track your students' progress.

Reports can be generated using data from the checkpoints and mini-checkpoints.

xiii

Strategies for effective learning

Metacognition: A review

Metacognition refers to the understanding a student has about their own learning processes. This includes their knowledge of tasks that they may face and the strategies they have available to use, as well as knowledge of themselves as a learner.

The seven-step approach

The Education Endowment Foundation suggests the following seven-step approach to teaching metacognitive skills.

1. Activate prior knowledge
2. Explicit strategy instruction
3. Modelling of learned strategy
4. Memorisation of strategy
5. Guided practice
6. Independent practice
7. Structured reflection

This approach allows a student to learn about a strategy in relative isolation. If you were introducing students to the EVERY method which is outlined in the student book, you would do it in the context of a very simple calculation. You would also use an example that they are very familiar with. This removes the extra cognitive load of unfamiliar science content.

A key aspect of this approach is modelling. Metacognitive modelling is where the focus is on demonstrating how an expert learner would approach a task by verbalising your inner thought processes. For example, you could answer a question 'live' in front of the class. This helps students because they are learning about how an expert learner plans, monitors, and evaluates their own learning.

A question tree is a tool which can complement the modelling process. For example, when completing circuit calculations, it is common for values to be placed on a circuit diagram and students then need to choose which values are needed for a calculation. The question tree shown in Figure 1 could be used to summarise how they should approach the task.

What type of circuit is it?

Series:
Review circuit rules:
- **Current** is the same at all points
- Total **potential difference** of power supply is shared between components
- Total **resistance** is the sum of all components

Parallel:
Review circuit rules:
- **Current** is split between each branch
- **Potential difference** is the same across each branch
- Total **resistance** is less than the smallest resistance value

What type of calculation do you need to complete?

Whole circuit calculation
You will need to use:
- Supply **voltage**
- **Current** at supply
- Total **resistance**
$V = I \times R$

Component calculation
You will need to use:
- **Potential difference** across component
- **Current** at component
- Component **resistance**
$V = I \times R$

Branch calculation (*Parallel circuits*)
You will need to use:
- Supply **voltage**
- **Current** on branch
- Total **resistance** of the branch
$V = I \times R$

▲ Figure 1 A question tree for completing circuit calculations

What does this look like in practice?

Scenario: You would like to introduce some independent study strategies and think graphic organisers would be appropriate.

When you could use it	Examples	
grouping, classifying, or summarising your ideas	Spider diagram	Concept map
sequencing events or ordering ideas	Cycle circle	Flow chart
making links between ideas	Fishbone	Bridge
making comparisons	Venn diagram	T chart

▲ **Figure 2** Some graphic organisers, as seen in the Student Book

Seven step approach: A summary of a seven-step approach to introduce independent study strategies is given below.

1. Activate prior knowledge	The teacher reviews key content relating to the topic with the class using low stakes quizzes, topic maps, and some independent reading.
2. Explicit strategy instruction	The teacher explores the variety of graphic organisers and examples of when each would be used. They talk through the table in the student book and start to ask the students about what scientific content each one could be useful for. They explore why graphic organisers are useful in each case.
3. Modelling of learned strategy	Teacher identifies a topic to translate into a graphic organiser and models how they approach condensing the information and selecting the key information for their chosen graphic organiser. At all points the teacher is explicitly explaining why they are doing what they are doing.
4. Memorisation of strategy	The students are given time to note down the strategy and then the teacher circulates the room questioning students to see if they understand how to use the strategy and why it is effective.
5. Guided practice	The class is then given a partially completed graphic organiser and some topic information to fill it with. When finished the class then compare it to a WAGOLL (what a good one looks like) on the board.
6. Independent practice	In the next lesson, students are given time to create a different type of graphic organiser so that they can practice the skill of translating the scientific content into the simplified structure.
7. Structured reflection	At the end of the lesson, the group reflects on whether the graphic organisers they have made are effective. They also reflect on their use of the graphic organisers and how they can use it for revision at home.

▲ **Figure 3** A seven-step approach that could be used when introducing independent study strategies

Using strategies effectively

Metacognitive regulation: A review

Metacognition refers to the knowledge a student has about their own learning processes. A key part of this is metacognitive regulation. This is where students are able to regulate themselves through planning, monitoring, and evaluating their own learning.

An expert learner will naturally follow a cycle like this when they tackle a new task. By explicitly teaching students about this cycle, they will be able to adopt a similar thought process, and this will help them build confidence to successfully complete new and challenging activities.

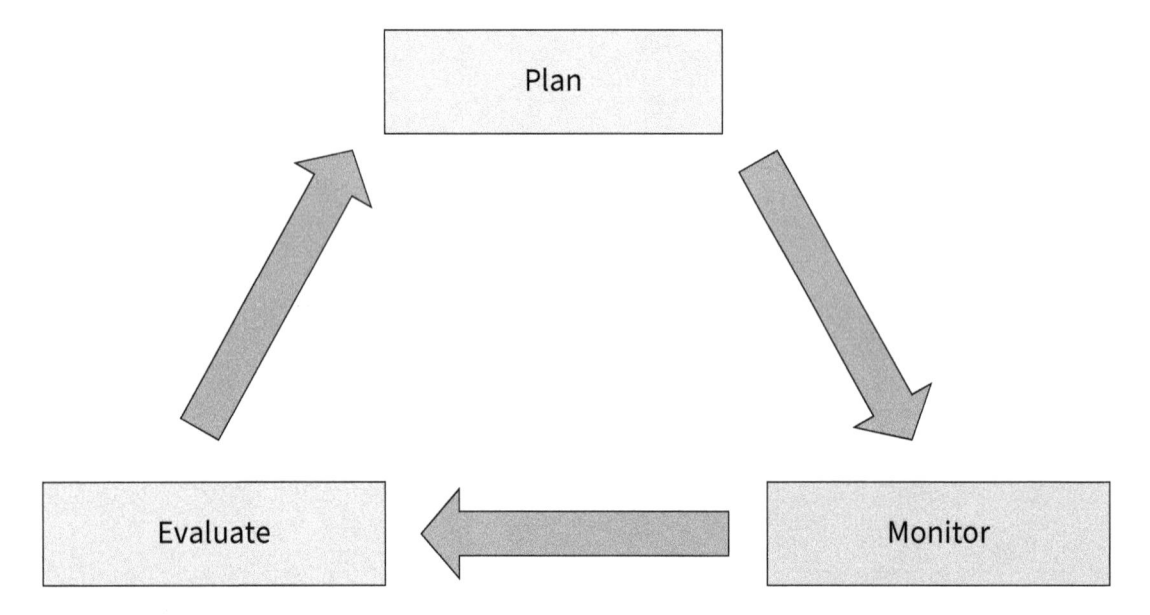

Plan → Monitor → Evaluate → Plan

The planning phase

This takes place before the task. An expert learner would plan their approach carefully by thinking about what strategies they could use and what scientific knowledge is relevant. They would also reflect on whether they have completed something similar before and apply this experience to the new task.

The monitoring phase

This takes place during the task. An expert learner would regularly pause and check back to make sure their chosen approach is still right. They would also have the confidence to stop and start again if needed.

The evaluation phase

This takes place at the end of the task. An expert learner would reflect on their performance and carefully consider any areas for improvement. They would plan for how they would use what they have learnt in the future so that they can be successful when doing similar tasks again.

Supporting students to plan, monitor, and evaluate

Once students are familiar with the strategies they have available to them, this part of the student book then aims to help them use these strategies effectively. It outlines what they should be doing when planning, monitoring, and evaluating their learning. But what does this look like in the classroom?

When introducing a new strategy using the seven step approach students will have an opportunity to complete independent practice. At this point they could use a checklist to help them to regulate their learning. This is a series of questions which guide students through each of the plan, monitor, and evaluate phases. When first introducing the checklists, it may be more appropriate to focus on one of these phases rather than the whole checklist. Or it may be appropriate to have the whole class reflect on the questions as a group when completing their independent practice, rather than them each reflecting on the questions individually.

If we take the example of using the seven step approach to teach the use of graphic organisers from the previous spread, here are some examples of the types of regulatory checklists that you could use with students when they are completing independent practice:

Plan
- How do you feel about completing this task? Confident or unsure?
- Do you have a good understanding of the scientific content you are reviewing? If not, what can you do to change this?
- Which type of graphic organiser suits the information you need to summarise?
- Have you done a graphic organiser like this before? What did success look like?
- Have you identified what key bits of information need to be included in your graphic organiser?

Monitor
- Am I doing well?
- Do I still think the graphic organiser I have chosen is the correct one?
- If not, which one would be more appropriate?
- Do you need to make any changes to what you have done? Do you need to start again?
- Are there any sections of the information that I am unsure how to summarise? If so, what resources do I have to help me work it out?

Evaluate
- How do you feel now that you have completed the task? Confident or unsure?
- Did you summarise all of the correct information? If not, what did you miss?
- What were your strengths when completing this task?
- What would you do differently next time?

Whilst this is just one example of how we can use a regulatory checklist to help our students to plan, monitor, and evaluate their learning. Any of these questions can be adapted to suit any task that they complete. Over time the need for a structured checklist will reduce and these types of questions will naturally form the thoughts and discussions the students will have when completing a new task.

2 Working scientifically

Introduction to unit

In this unit, students revisit the planning of investigations, focusing on collecting precise, reproducible data, and writing risk assessments to ensure their safety and the safety of those around them.

They will extend their focus on analysing data through looking at how to plot a pie chart and a histogram, along with how to identify the median and mode averages in a data set. They will identify linear and directly proportional relationships, and use lines of best fit to interpolate and extrapolate data. Students will also use secondary data to improve confidence in their conclusions.

Finally, students will study how our understanding of science develops over time, the importance of peer review, and how scientists communicate information with different audiences.

The Working scientifically skills required for success in KS3 Science, aligning with the UK National Curriculum, have been sequenced to ensure effective development for learners and to accompany the course's scientific knowledge. Further details of the skills covering in Years 7, 8, and 9 can be found in the *Oxford Smart Curriculum for Science* and in the Research and CPD hub on Kerboodle.

In addition to this unit, Working scientifically skills have been embedded within lessons. Each lesson spread includes the relevant Working scientifically National Curriculum links.

Working scientifically and you

Working scientifically skills are essential for a wide range of occupations, as well as their wider interests. The occupations in the Student Book illustrate a few careers that use working scientifically skills:

- Microbiologist – being able to write and follow a risk assessment is essential when working with bacteria and viruses.
- Astronaut – being able carry out experiments independently is essential when doing research in space.
- Engineer – engineers need practical skills in the workplace and knowledge of how to analyse data.
- Meteorologist – communication skills are required when explaining scientific phenomena to the public about weather forecasts.
- Nutritionist – understanding possible bias in health claims about food is essential when advising on diet.
- Geologist – an understanding of staying safe is required when monitoring tectonic activity.

Working scientifically and the world

Regularly remind students that we all have responsibility to protect and enhance the living world and the physical environment. The ability to think like a scientist is critical to ensure that they can listen to the evidence (e.g., about climate change), take account of what it says, and then act in a way which is the most beneficial to the planet.

Discuss with students that the collective actions of many people make an enormous difference, and are critical in ensuring a stable, sustainable future, not only for human beings, but for all species on Earth.

At the same time, explore with students misinformation and 'fake news', which is often shared via social media. Compare this with the rigorous process of peer review prior to scientific research being released. Reinforce with students that they should always interrogate information in the following way: Who does this information come from? Why was it published? What is the basis for any claims made?

2 Working scientifically

Big questions

How do scientists keep safe? Before carrying out a scientific investigation, a risk assessment is performed. This identifies the hazard (what could hurt you), the risk (how it could hurt you), and control measures to ensure no one is harmed. By thinking about risk before an activity is started, scientists ensure that their work is safe, even when working with hazardous substances and equipment.

How can you trust a scientific claim? Scientists learn how to spot bias and check the reliability of a source. For a piece of research to be valid, it should be produced without bias. Students should be aware that scientific research is often funded by business, which may lead to an undue focus on the positive aspects of a product, potentially ignoring or side lining any negative impacts.

Why do scientists change their minds about how things happen? The development of new technology, including artificial intelligence, carrying out different experiments, and new ways of thinking, can all provide new evidence. This can result in scientists needing to amend a previous idea or change their thinking entirely. Science is an ever-evolving subject. For example, some teachers may be teaching science to students that wasn't even known when they started their teaching career!

Learning journey

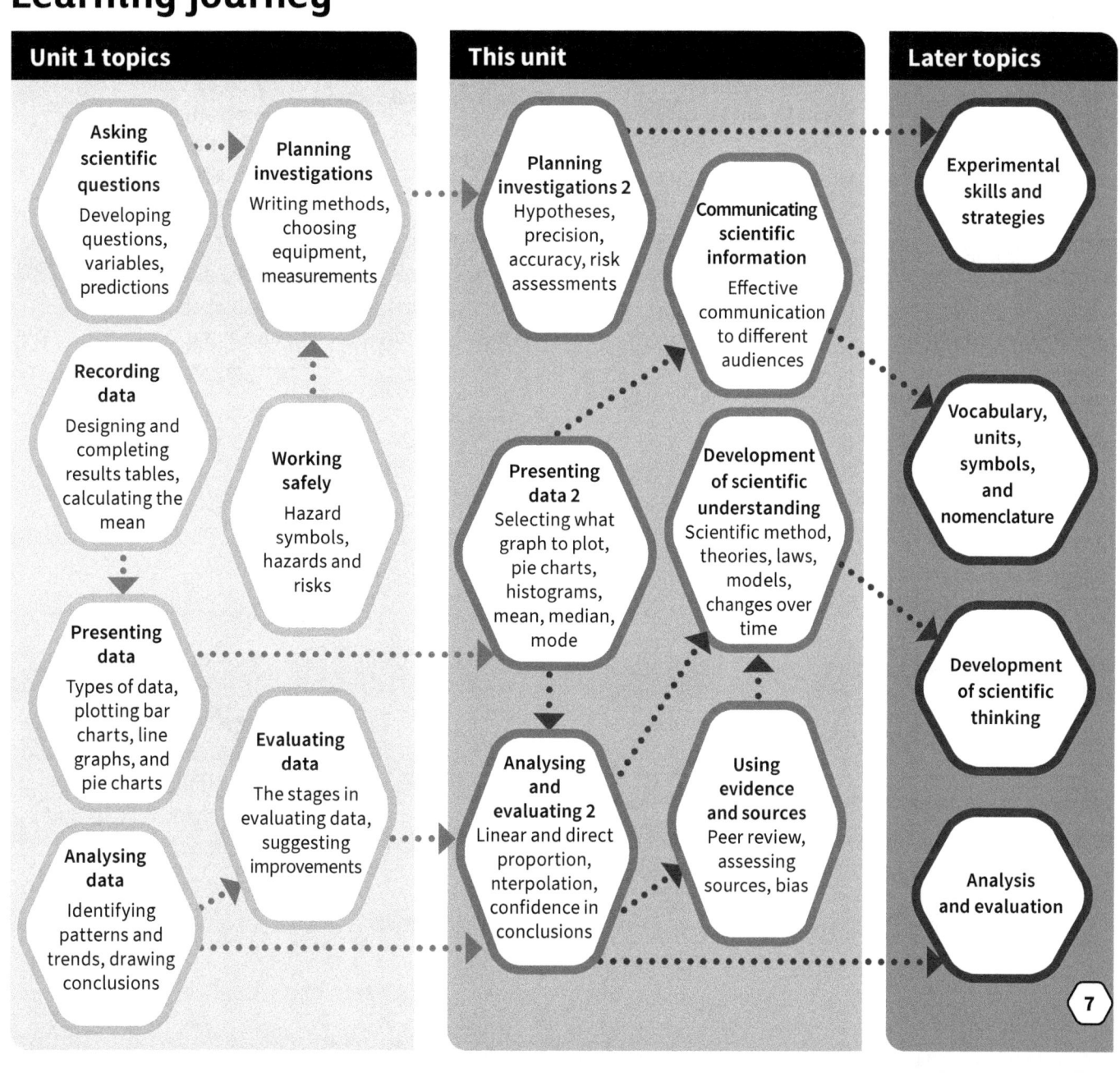

Unit 1 topics

- **Asking scientific questions**: Developing questions, variables, predictions
- **Planning investigations**: Writing methods, choosing equipment, measurements
- **Recording data**: Designing and completing results tables, calculating the mean
- **Working safely**: Hazard symbols, hazards and risks
- **Presenting data**: Types of data, plotting bar charts, line graphs, and pie charts
- **Evaluating data**: The stages in evaluating data, suggesting improvements
- **Analysing data**: Identifying patterns and trends, drawing conclusions

This unit

- **Planning investigations 2**: Hypotheses, precision, accuracy, risk assessments
- **Communicating scientific information**: Effective communication to different audiences
- **Presenting data 2**: Selecting what graph to plot, pie charts, histograms, mean, median, mode
- **Development of scientific understanding**: Scientific method, theories, laws, models, changes over time
- **Analysing and evaluating 2**: Linear and direct proportion, interpolation, confidence in conclusions
- **Using evidence and sources**: Peer review, assessing sources, bias

Later topics

- Experimental skills and strategies
- Vocabulary, units, symbols, and nomenclature
- Development of scientific thinking
- Analysis and evaluation

7

2.1 Planning investigations 2

Working scientifically NC links

- pay attention to objectivity and concern for accuracy, precision, repeatability, and reproducibility
- make predictions using scientific knowledge and understanding
- select, plan, and carry out the most appropriate types of scientific enquiries to test predictions, including identifying independent, dependent, and control variables
- use appropriate techniques, apparatus, and materials during fieldwork and laboratory work, paying attention to health and safety

Learning objective	Learning outcomes		
	Developing	Secure	Extending
Write a hypothesis for a scientific investigation	Write a prediction for a scientific investigation	**Write a hypothesis for a scientific investigation**	Write a hypothesis using detailed scientific knowledge
Describe the difference between precise and accurate data	State what is meant by accurate data	**Describe the difference between precise and accurate data**	Categorise data into being accurate and/or precise
Write a risk assessment for a scientific investigation	State what is meant by a hazard and a risk	**Write a risk assessment for a scientific investigation**	Write a detailed risk assessment that identifies and controls all possible hazards

Tier 2 vocabulary	Tier 3 vocabulary	SB in-text question answers
accurate, extension, hazard, investigation, minimise, precise, prediction, repeatable, reproducible, risk, *spread*, uncertainty	control measure, dependent variable, hypothesis, independent variable	**A** Force applied/original length of elastic/material of elastic **B** Burns/setting hair alight

Lesson plan

Reactivate knowledge

1 What is a prediction?
2 What information helps you to keep safe during an investigation?
3 What is accurate data?

Answers: 1 What you think will happen in an investigation **2** Risk assessment **3** Data that is close to the true value

Lesson resources

Practical: *Investigating bungee cords* (practical sheet, teacher and technician sheet, support sheet)

Trigger interest

Show students Figure 1 in the Student Book of the person bungee jumping. How do they think the person could be injured? What safety equipment can they see? What safety precautions may have been taken that they can't see?

Use the students' answers to introduce the main components of a risk assessment.

Exposition of main content

Discuss with students the factors they think are important when choosing which bungee cord to use in a jump. Explain that in today's activity they are going to look at how the thickness of elastic affects how much it stretches. Ask them to predict what they think will happen. Then introduce the students to the difference between a hypothesis and a prediction by asking them to introduce an explanation to today's prediction. This can be repeated for a range of questions if required.

Ask students what is meant by accurate data (data that is close to the true value of what you are trying to measure). Then introduce the concept of precise data (getting similar results if you repeat a measurement). You may need to remind students that the spread of data refers to the difference between the smallest and largest results. Precise data therefore has a small spread. Illustrate the difference between accurate and precise data using the images of archery targets in Figure 3 in the Student Book.

Explain that precise data is also referred to as repeatable. Discuss the difference between repeatable and reproducible data. (Reproducible data: when similar results are achieved by other people carrying out the same experiment, or through using different equipment.)

Introduce the three main components of a risk assessment – hazard, risk, and control measure – using the example of broken glass as shown in Figure 4 in the Student Book. Ask students to create a risk assessment for using bleach (hazardous chemical, could damage skin/eyes, wear gloves/goggles).

Main activity

Practical: Investigating bungee cords (40 mins)
Students investigate the relationship between the thickness of an elastic band and how much it stretches.

Before they complete the practical, they write a hypothesis and complete a risk assessment. Once they have collected their data, they need to decide if their data is repeatable, and by looking at other students' results whether it is reproducible. (Students need to keep their data for WS2.5 Activity: *Using evidence and sources* for further analysis.)

Review and reflect

State a number of different hazards, such as worn carpet, heating a test tube, or using a sharp knife.

Students record the risk and control measures on their whiteboards and hold them up.

Homework

Students produce a risk assessment for carrying out three routine activities of their choice, such as making a cup of tea.

2.2 Presenting data 2

Working scientifically NC links

- apply mathematical concepts and calculate results
- present observations and data using appropriate methods, including tables and graphs
- undertake basic data analysis, including simple statistical techniques

Learning objective	Learning outcomes		
	Developing	Secure	Extending
Select the appropriate graph to display data	Describe the difference between discrete, categorical and continuous data	**Select the appropriate graph to display data**	Justify the graph chosen to display a set or sets of data
Present data as a pie chart or a histogram	Draw a pie chart when given section angles	**Present data as a pie chart or a histogram**	Draw a histogram using different class widths
Calculate the mean, mode, and median of a set of data	Calculate the mean	**Calculate the mean, mode, and median of a set of data**	Identify which is the most appropriate average to calculate for a set of data

Tier 2 vocabulary	Tier 3 vocabulary
average, bar chart, data, line graph, *mean*, measurement, percentage, pie chart	categorical, continuous data, *discrete*, histogram, median, *mode*

SB in-text question answers
A Bar chart or pie chart **B** 60+ **C** 18–29

Lesson plan

Reactivate knowledge

1 What is continuous data?
2 What is discrete data?
3 What are some different ways data can be presented?

Answers: 1 Data that can have any value within a range **2** Data that can have only whole-number values **3** Bar chart, line graph, pie chart

Lesson resources

Activity: *Displaying data* (activity sheet, teacher and technician sheet, support sheet)

Working scientifically

Trigger interest

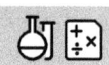

Show students Figure 1 from the Student Book. What different charts do they recognise? How do they differ? Remind students that bar charts or pie charts are used to represent discrete or categorical data, and that line graphs are used to represent continuous data. To check understanding further, ask students to give some examples of continuous, discrete, and categorical data. This knowledge is essential when choosing which type of graph they should plot.

Exposition of main content

Show students Figure 2 of the pie chart from the Student Book which represents the age range of people. What are its main features? What can they remember about how to plot a pie chart? They should be familiar with how to use a protractor to plot given angles.

Introduce how to calculate the angle of each section of the pie chart by working through the worked example on the Lesson player. Students then complete task 1 of the Activity: *Displaying data*, which requires them to draw their own pie chart from raw data.

Introduce students to a histogram using the example in the Student Book. Talk through its key features and how it differs from a bar chart. Introduce how the data the histogram was drawn from is recorded using a frequency table with grouped categories. Pick a couple of mass values and ask students to decide which category the data would fit into.

Explain that histograms are plotted against frequency density as it is the area of the bar that represents the number of people with a particular mass. Introduce the algebraic symbols '<' and '≤'. Then work through the example of how to calculate frequency density. Ask students to calculate one or two examples on the remainder of the chart. Students then complete task 2 of the Activity: *Displaying data*, which requires them to draw their histogram.

Discuss what is meant by an average and ask students to explain how to calculate a mean. Introduce the mode and median averages, and demonstrate how to identify these using the worked example.

Main activity

Activity: Displaying data (45 mins)
For task 1, students draw their own pie chart from raw data. Encourage students to check that their angles total 360° before starting to plot their pie chart.

For task 2, students draw a histogram.

Allow extra time at the end of the activity to discuss the different kinds of average.

Review and reflect

Choose five students in the class and ask them for their shoe size. Ask students to calculate the mean, mode, and median values. For extension, students could be asked to explain which is the most appropriate average to use (unlikely to be the mean as this will usually result in a size that doesn't exist).

Homework

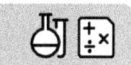

Students produce a Venn diagram to compare the similarities and differences between a line graph and a histogram.

For support, students could be provided with a list of features to categorise.

11

2.3 Analysing and evaluating data 2

Working scientifically NC links

- present observations and data using appropriate methods, including tables and graphs
- interpret observations and data, including identifying patterns and using observations, measurements, and data to draw conclusions
- present reasoned explanations, including explaining data in relation to predictions and hypotheses

	Learning outcomes			
Learning objective	**Developing**	**Secure**	**Extending**	
Identify linear and directly proportional relationships	Describe a simple trend shown in data	**Identify linear and directly proportional relationships**	Describe inversely proportional relationships	
Take readings from a graph using a line of best fit	Draw a line of best fit	**Take readings from a graph using a line of best fit**	Extrapolate data from a graph using a line of best fit	
Describe how to improve confidence in a conclusion	Write a simple conclusion	**Describe how to improve confidence in a conclusion**	Describe the level of confidence in a set of data	

Tier 2 vocabulary	Tier 3 vocabulary
artificial, extension, investigation, measurements	dependent variable, directly proportional, independent variable, investigation, line of best fit, linear relationship, secondary data

SB in-text question answers
A 20 m **B** It will pass through the origin **C** 4 cm

Lesson plan

Reactivate knowledge

1. What does a line of best fit show?
2. What shape should a line of best fit be?
3. Which type of average identifies the middle value in a data set?

Answers: 1 The pattern/trend in data **2** Curved or straight (going through/close to as many points as possible) **3** median

Lesson resources

Activity: *Is the bungee safe?* (activity sheet, teacher and technician sheet, support sheet, homework sheet)

Working scientifically

Trigger interest

Show students Figure 1 of the man about to bungee jump. Ask them to make a list of all the data the organisers may need to collect/refer to when adjusting the bungee cord to ensure the jump is safe.

Explain that data the organisers refer to, which they haven't collected themselves, is called secondary data.

Exposition of main content

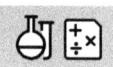

Show students the graph on the Lesson player and ask them to spot the mistake (the line of best fit should be a curve). Remind them what a line of best fit shows and that later in the lesson, they will use a line of best fit to predict values for which they have taken no data (interpolation).

Introduce linear relationships using the graph in Figure 2 from the Student Book of the extension of the bungee rope versus its composition. In this type of relationship, increasing the independent variable causes an increase in the dependent variable, so in this example the more artificial rubber the bungee rope contains, the more the rope extends. Students should be made aware that when plotted, these graphs are always straight (explain that this example shows a positive correlation, but linear relationships can also show a negative correlation).

Then introduce direct proportion using the graph in Figure 3 from the Student Book of bungee rope extension against starting length. Explain that this is a special type of linear relationship where doubling the independent variable causes a doubling of the dependent variable. It can be recognised on a graph by a straight line of best fit that goes through the origin.

Use the graph in Figure 4 of the Student Book of Tom and Katie's investigation into how the thickness of a wire affects the amount it extends to show how to take measurements using the line of best fit. Explain that this allows the extension of a cord to be determined without having to physically measure every thickness of elastic that may exist.

Explain that unless the relationship between two variables is linear, it is hard to predict with any confidence values for data above or below the graph's extremes. In the same way, Katie and Tom are only confident that their prediction is true for elastic that has a thickness of approximately 1–6 mm. Introduce the role of secondary data in providing more evidence for a conclusion and therefore increasing your confidence that you are correct.

Main activity

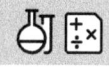

Activity: Is the bungee safe? (30 mins)
Students calculate the mean values of a set of data on the strengths of different bungee cords before plotting a graph and adding a line of best fit. They then write a conclusion, using data from the graph to improve its validity.

Review and reflect

Show students a range of graphs. Students hold up a different coloured card to identify if they show a linear relationship, a directly proportional relationship, or a non-linear relationship.

Homework

Students complete the homework sheet on how a planet's year length is affected by its distance from the Sun.

2.4 Communicating scientific information

Working scientifically NC links

- develop use of scientific vocabulary, including the use of scientific nomenclature and units and mathematical representation
- present observations and data using appropriate methods
- present reasoned explanations, including explaining data in relation to predictions and hypotheses

Learning objective	Learning outcomes		
	Developing	Secure	Extending
Describe the key features of effective communication	Describe what is meant by concise and coherent writing	**Describe the key features of effective communication**	Identify places where writing is not clear, concise, or coherent and explain why
Describe how to adapt communication for different audiences	Name some examples of audiences	**Describe how to adapt communication for different audiences**	Explain the differences in writing for a scientific journal and a scientific magazine

Tier 2 vocabulary	Tier 3 vocabulary
audience, coherent, concise, investigation, third person	

SB in-text question answers

A For example, peers, teacher, younger students, general public **B** Prediction: what you think will happen; hypothesis: also includes scientific reasoning **C** Real-life examples/vivid words

Lesson plan

Reactivate knowledge

1. How can you display data visually?
2. What should you include in observational drawings?
3. Name three sections which should be included in a scientific investigation.

Lesson resources

Activity: *Same idea, different audience* (activity sheet, teacher and technician sheet)

Answers: 1 Using line graphs, pie charts, bar charts, and histograms **2** Clear labels (and where relevant, magnification/scale) **3** For example, hypothesis, method, results table, graph, conclusion

Working scientifically

Trigger interest

Show students the photo of different types of literature from Figure 1 in the Student Book or provide them with real-life examples to look through. Ask them in small groups to make a list of all the different audiences a scientist might need to write for to share information and the different styles of writing that could be used. Discuss findings as a class.

Encourage students to think about writing scripts; for example, for a TV advertising campaign for public health, for a media interview, or for digital forms of communication, such as social media.

Exposition of main content

Ask students in pairs to think about features of effective communication (a list of features can be found in the Student Book for reference). What makes something easy to understand, especially when reading or hearing about a new topic for the first time? Use students' ideas to produce a class list, which can be added to throughout the lesson. If not identified by students from the Student Book, introduce them to the idea of 'the 4 Cs' – coherent, concise, clear, and correct.

Show students the cartoon of Katy and Tom from Figure 2 in the Student Book discussing what they think should be included in a scientific report for a teacher/fellow student. Ask students to write down what should be included in a report and key features they should include, for example, a method should be written in steps and contain an annotated diagram of the equipment set-up.

Share ideas and then discuss how this may be reported for a different audience, such as a newspaper article: Is the method still needed? Or a results table? How will the article grab attention?

Main activity

Activity: Same idea, different audience (40 mins)
Students are provided with the outline of an experiment and data relating to it. They can use the genuine data given on the activity sheet, or use any other data you wish, even some from a novel situation, such as the discovery of organic material on Mars or the discovery of exoplanets.

Students produce a piece of writing about the experiment in a style of their choice, such as a newspaper article, the storyboard for a children's television programme, or a summary for a science journal. Students need to ensure their writing is concise, coherent, clear, and correct.

At the end of the activity, ask students to share their pieces of writing. Discuss with students the specific features of the style of writing chosen.

Review and reflect

Students match key terms to their definitions in the Lesson player to describe four key features of effective communication.

Homework

Students choose a piece of writing from a newspaper, magazine, or the internet on a scientific topic of their choice. They produce a checklist based on the content of the lesson and use it to assess the article in terms of effective communication.

As an extension, ask students to identify any parts of the writing that are not clear, concise, coherent, or correct and explain why.

2.5 Using evidence and sources

Working scientifically NC links

- pay attention to objectivity and concern for accuracy, precision, repeatability, and reproducibility
- understand that scientific methods and theories develop as earlier explanations are modified to take account of new evidence and ideas, together with the importance of publishing results and peer review

Learning objective	Learning outcomes		
	Developing	Secure	Extending
Describe what peer review is	State where scientists publish their research	**Describe what peer review is**	Explain why peer review enables a finding to be accepted
Describe how to assess sources of evidence	Name some sources of scientific evidence	**Describe how to assess sources of evidence**	Assess a source of evidence for how reliable it is
Identify possible sources of bias	State what bias is	**Identify possible sources of bias**	Explain the effect of bias in unfamiliar situations

Tier 2 vocabulary	Tier 3 vocabulary	SB in-text question answers
anecdotal, evidence, funder, peer review, reliability, research, review, scientific journal		**A** Journal **B** Any three from: who wrote it/where was it published/is it up-to-date information/might the information be biased/is there enough data to form conclusions/is there other research that backs up these findings

Lesson plan

Reactivate knowledge

1 How do you collect data?
2 What is repeatable data?
3 What is reproducible data?

Answers: 1 Through measurements and observations **2** Very similar measurements when repeated by the same person, using the same equipment and method **3** Very similar measurements when repeated by a different person using different equipment and/or methods

Lesson resources

Activity: *Peer review* (activity sheet, teacher and technician sheet, support sheet)

Working scientifically

Trigger interest

Show students the quote from the Student Book on smoking and cancer. Ask them to discuss whether they think this is evidence. What different kinds of evidence can scientists collect to prove or disprove statements such as this? Explain that this statement is referred to as anecdotal evidence. You cannot reason from this one example that smoking doesn't cause cancer.

Exposition of main content

Explain that before a scientist can publish the results of an investigation, other scientists check the research to make sure that the results and conclusions are correct. This is called peer review. The investigation can then be published in a scientific journal.

Hand out some examples of scientific journals and ask students to make a list of things that are common to the articles in the journal, such as an abstract, evidence/data/graphs, conclusion, and references (they can refer to this during the activity).

Explain that when you look for evidence to back up your own findings, you need to check if it is reliable. The more reliable it is, the more valid the information. Discuss ways you interrogate sources to check for reliability using the table in the Student Book for reference. Explain that it is best to look for more than one source, especially when looking at the internet, to check for consistency.

Lead the discussion on to the sources of funding for scientific research – government, companies, or charities – and how this may end up with results being presented in a biased way.

Main activity

Activity: Peer review (40 mins)
Students use their data from the elastic band experiment in WS2.1 Practical: *Planning experiments 2* in conjunction with secondary data to write a paper for a scientific journal. Students then peer review each other's articles and decide if they should be published.

Review and reflect

Show students the statements on possible sources of bias. Students decide which examples may contain bias. Encourage them to explain how and why this may affect the results for their chosen statements.

Homework

Students produce a list of questions they can refer to to check the reliability of a source of evidence. Challenge students to then use this checklist to assess the reliability of a piece of evidence of their choosing.

2.6 Development of scientific understanding

Working scientifically NC link

- understand that scientific methods and theories develop as earlier explanations are modified to take account of new evidence and ideas, together with the importance of publishing results and peer review

Learning objective	Learning outcomes		
	Developing	Secure	Extending
Describe what is meant by the scientific method	State what is meant by a hypothesis	**Describe what is meant by the scientific method**	Explain how a theory is developed using the scientific method
Describe the difference between a theory, law, and model	State what is meant by a theory, model, and law	**Describe the difference between a theory, law, and model**	Use examples to describe the differences between a theory, law, and model
Describe how our understanding of science changes over time	State some ways new evidence can arise	**Describe how our understanding of science changes over time**	Use examples to describe how our understanding of science changes over time

Tier 2 vocabulary	Tier 3 vocabulary
astronomer, conclusion, development, evidence, explanation, *law*, model, rejected, representing, *theory*	conclusion, hypothesis, law, scientific method, theory

SB in-text question answers
A A theory provides an explanation whereas a law is a statement of fact **B** Planets in correct order **C** Planets in same order; planets have circular orbits

Lesson plan

Reactivate knowledge

1. Give some examples of scientific evidence.
2. What is a hypothesis?
3. Where do scientists publish the results of their research?

Answers: 1 Measurements, observations **2** A description of what you think will happen, backed up with scientific reasoning **3** Scientific journals

Lesson resources

Activity: *What's the evidence?* (activity sheet, teacher and technician sheet, support sheet)

Working scientifically

Trigger interest

Show students the image of the bacterium *Vibrio cholerae* in Figure 1 in the Student Book. Tell them that people thought that infectious diseases were caused by a poisonous vapour known as miasma that came from decaying matter. What do they think this is an image of? How do they think it was created? How does it support the idea that disease is not caused by miasma?

Explain that it is an image of the bacterium that causes cholera. Bacteria is spread through contaminated water sources. The image was developed using information gained through a microscope. This introduces the concept that scientific ideas are constantly revised when new evidence is gained.

Exposition of main content

Talk through the main steps in the scientific method using the flow diagram in Figure 2 in the Student Book. Focus on how the discovery of new evidence can lead to a scientific idea having to be changed, and that this is very much a part of science: not everything is yet known! Explain the difference between a model, law, and theory, discussing examples of each.

Recap that for a theory to be accepted, there has to be a lot of evidence to support it. Discuss how new evidence can arise through new technology, other scientists carrying out different investigations, and new ways of thinking. This can lead to a theory or model having to be revised.

Main activity

Activity: What's the evidence? (40 mins)
In small groups, students select a theory, law, or model, and research what it shows and the original evidence that led to its development. They also need to find out about at least one previous theory/model that was used to explain the same phenomenon and why this has since been discounted/amended.

Allow time at the end of the activity for groups to feedback on their findings, summarising their theory and how it has changed from previous ideas as a result of new evidence.

Review and reflect

Students write one sentence to define each of the following key terms – model, law, theory.

Homework

Students select a law that is named after a person. For example, Hooke's law. They then research what the law states and the evidence for it.

2 Biology

Introduction to unit

In this unit, students will compare the effects of healthy and unhealthy lifestyles. This involves looking at the structure and function of the digestive system and role of enzymes in digestion. They will then combine their knowledge of biology and chemistry when studying the cellular processes of photosynthesis and respiration.

Building on their knowledge of food chains, students will study the interdependence of organisms and the adaptations that enable organisms to be successful competitors and survive in harsh and changing environments. They will then study the causes of variation and how characteristics are inherited through chromosomes, before learning about the process of evolution through natural selection. Throughout this unit, students are introduced to a number of scientists who played a fundamental role in developing our understanding of biology.

Working scientifically

Each lesson lists the relevant Working scientifically National Curriculum links at the top of the spread. For further details, please refer to the *Oxford Smart Curriculum for Science* document.

Biology NC links

- Nutrition and digestion
- Health
- Photosynthesis
- Cellular respiration
- Relationships in an ecosystem
- Inheritance, chromosomes, DNA and genes

Learning journey

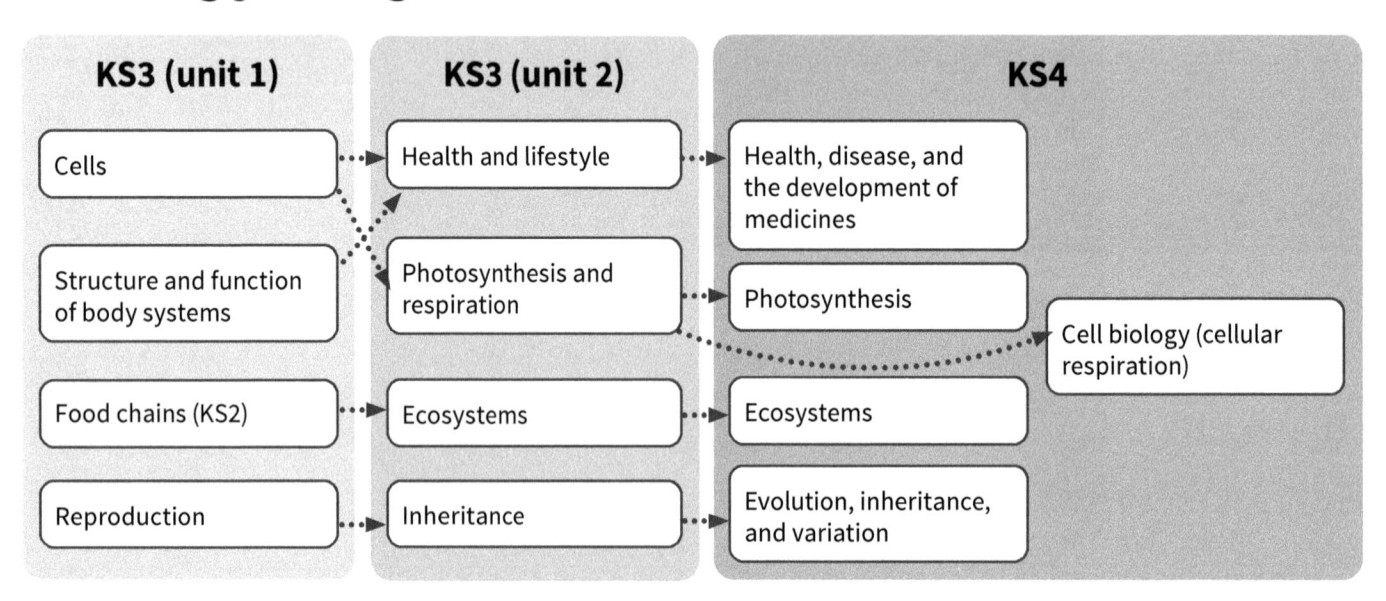

KS3 (unit 1)	KS3 (unit 2)	KS4
Cells	Health and lifestyle	Health, disease, and the development of medicines
Structure and function of body systems	Photosynthesis and respiration	Photosynthesis
		Cell biology (cellular respiration)
Food chains (KS2)	Ecosystems	Ecosystems
Reproduction	Inheritance	Evolution, inheritance, and variation

2 Biology

Biology and you

Studying biology equips students with many skills, and is essential for a wide range of occupations and interests. The occupations in the Student Book illustrate a few careers that use biology:

- Vet – knowledge of the anatomy and physiology of animals is required to diagnose what is wrong with an animal and provide the best level of care.
- Physiotherapist – an understanding of the muscular-skeletal system is essential to help patients recover full movement after illness or an accident.
- Sports coach – knowledge of healthy lifestyles and of the way the body moves enables sports coaches to get the best out of their teams.
- Midwife – understanding how a baby develops in the uterus and the process of birth is essential when caring for pregnant women and their babies.
- Marine biologist – understanding the differences in the way unicellular and multicellular organisms function is important when studying microscopic life in the oceans.
- Commercial flower grower – providing the best conditions for photosynthesis is essential for plants to produce the best quality flowers.
- Medical research – a detailed understanding of cell structure is essential when researching new treatments for diseases such as cancer.
- Environmentalist – knowledge of how organisms interact is crucial when studying the human impact on the environment, and identifying ways to minimise potential damage.

Biology and the world

Make students aware that the lifestyle choices they make have a direct effect on their health. Learning about healthy eating, for example, enables them to make informed decisions about the way they wish to live their life and the lives of their families.

Instil in students a responsibility to conserve the living environment, and enhance their understanding of the natural world, particularly in terms of the interdependence of organisms. For example, we depend on bees to pollinate the crops for our survival. Negative human impacts mean there has never been a more important time for us to understand how we can act collectively to protect all living species.

Big questions

Why do organisms need to eat to survive?
Eating the right foods in the right amounts is fundamental for remaining healthy. Observing when people don't have enough food, or eat the wrong foods, provides clues to the roles different foods play in the body. As well as providing energy, which is needed even when an organism is asleep, the nutrients foods contain are required for the body to grow and repair itself.

How do plants make food? Performing experiments where plants are given a range of raw materials has enabled scientists to discover what plants need to survive and how we can help them grow. Conditions in industrial greenhouses are monitored to provide optimum conditions for photosynthesis, resulting in the highest crop yields. This is one way in which scientists are tackling food shortages.

Why don't we all look the same? The methods by which characteristics are passed on from parents to their offspring were discovered using the work of many scientists, including Mendel, who studied pea plants, and Watson, Crick, Franklin, and Wilkins who developed the model of DNA replication. Detailed understanding of genetics can now calculate a person's risk of having a disease. It can also be used to modify plants to have a specific characteristic such as insect resistance.

B2 Chapter 1: Health and lifestyle

Introduction to chapter

In this chapter, students will be introduced to the components of a balanced diet and its importance in maintaining health. They will study the process of digestion, concentrating on the role of enzymes, bacteria and some of the main organs in the digestive system. In the final section of the chapter, students will look at the effects of drugs on the body, focusing on smoking and alcohol.

Prerequisite knowledge

- Recognise the impact of diet, exercise, drugs and lifestyle on the way their bodies function (KS2)
- The hierarchical organisation of multicellular organisms: from cells to tissues to organs to systems to organisms
- The role of diffusion in the movement of materials in and between cells

Core concepts in chapter

- Food groups and food tests
- Structure and function of the digestive system
- The role enzymes in digestion
- Absorption of food molecules by diffusion
- The effect of drugs on the body

GCSE links

- Enzymes
- Factors affecting the rate of enzymatic reactions
- Carbohydrates, proteins, nucleic acids and lipids as key biological molecules
- The relationship between health and disease
- The impact of lifestyle factors on the incidence of non-communicable diseases

Key learning misconceptions

- Vitamins and minerals are only found in fruits and vegetables
- All fats are bad
- Overweight people have 'big bones'
- Males always have a higher energy requirement than females
- Enzymes are living
- All drugs are harmful
- Caffeine is not a drug
- All recreational drugs are illegal
- Alcohol (and other legal drugs) are not harmful
- Medical drugs do not have any negative medical effects

B2 Chapter 1: Health and lifestyle

Body awareness

This chapter looks at the effects of an unhealthy diet on body mass. It is essential that this issue is introduced with sensitivity. Students may be undergoing significant body changes as a result of puberty; some may be over- or under-weight. Be aware of any students with eating disorders.

Key maths skills

Percentage change In this chapter there are several opportunities for students to practise calculating a percentage change (covering positive and negative changes). It is important for students to recognise that if their answer is negative, a percentage decrease has occurred; a positive answer represents a percentage increase. Students should be encouraged to write out the formula in full each time so working can be checked. This is a technique that should always be used in assessments to ensure that, if the student gets the final answer wrong, method marks can be awarded.

Working scientifically skills

Model gut When introducing the digestive system ask students to imagine their body as having a hosepipe running from the mouth to the anus. This tube carries food and fluids in (and out) of the body. The analogy is limited, however, as unlike a hose the gut is permeable in parts so that nutrients and waste products can pass into the body from the tube, or from the body back into the tube.

Evaluations When introducing the skill of evaluations, for example when looking at models of the digestive system, encourage students to make a list of places where the model represents the system well and places where the model does not work as well. Where negative points have been noted, ask students to try to suggest an improvement to improve the model.

Enzyme names When introducing enzyme names, explain that the suffix '-ase' is used in biology to form the names of enzymes. The most common way to name enzymes is to add this suffix onto the end of the substrate, for example, an enzyme that breaks down carbohydrates is called carbohydrase. You could ask students to predict the names of other enzymes, for example, peroxides are broken down by peroxidase.

Energy in food practical If more time is available to spend teaching this chapter, before introducing dietary energy requirements perform an investigation into the energy content of different foods. One approach is to burn a range of foods, and measure the temperature increase of a fixed volume of water. The most able can be challenged to calculate the energy transferred to the water using the specific heat capacity formula: energy transferred (J) = mass of water (g) × 4.2 × temperature increase (°C)

1.1 Nutrients

Theme: Health and disease　　**Sub-theme:** Health and diet

Biology NC link

- the content of a healthy human diet: carbohydrates, lipids (fats and oils), proteins, vitamins, minerals, dietary fibre and water, and why each is needed

Learning objective	Learning outcomes		
	Developing	Secure	Extending
Give the definition of a balanced diet	Name some foods which are considered healthy or unhealthy	**Give the definition of a balanced diet**	Explain why eating a balanced diet is important for health
Name the seven components of a balanced diet, giving examples	Name some components of a balanced diet	**Name the seven components of a balanced diet, giving examples**	Suggest a balanced diet for one day
Describe the role of each component of a balanced diet	Identify the functions of some components of a balanced diet	**Describe the role of each component of a balanced diet**	Explain the role of each component of a balanced diet

Tier 2 vocabulary	Tier 3 vocabulary
balanced diet, carbohydrate, constantly, essential, fibre, mineral, nutrient, protein, source, survive, vitamin	lipid

SB in-text question answers

A Carbohydrates and lipids B Provide energy
C Fish/eggs/meat/milk D More water is lost through sweating

Lesson plan

Reactivate knowledge

1. Name the organ in the body where food is broken down.
2. What is meant by an organ system?
3. Name the organ system in the body where food is broken down.

Answers: 1 Stomach 2 Group of organs working together to perform a function 3 Digestive system

Lesson resources

Activity: *Healthy eating campaign* (student sheet, teacher and technician sheet, support sheet)

B2 Chapter 1: Health and lifestyle

Trigger interest

In pairs, ask students to produce a list of five foods they believe are 'good for you' and five foods they believe are 'bad for you'. Discuss what the 'good' foods have in common (vitamins and minerals) and do the same for the 'bad' foods (high sugar/fat content).

Use this to introduce the concept of a balanced diet – eating food containing the right nutrients in the correct amounts – and that not all fats/sugars are 'bad'.

Main activity

Activity: Healthy eating campaign (40 mins)
This activity is split into two main tasks.

Task 1 (10 mins): Explain that there are seven main components of a balanced diet. Ask students to use the Student Book to identify the components and their functions, and give examples of foods that contain them. Address the misconception that vitamins and minerals are only found in fruits and vegetables, using examples such as milk as a good source of calcium.

Task 2 (30 mins): Working in small groups, ask students to design and film a healthy eating YouTube/TV advert on behalf of the government. The advert should aim to encourage young people to eat a balanced diet. It should introduce the seven components of a balanced diet, giving examples. Students then share their films.

As an extension, students could compare the nutritional values of cuisines from different countries.

Review and reflect

Describe the function of a food component. Students record the name of the food component on a mini-whiteboard and hold up their boards to share.

Homework

Design a crossword that contains all seven components of a balanced diet. Students need to write clues that describe each component based on their function.

1.2 Food tests

Themes: Chemical analysis, Health and disease

Sub-themes: Health and diet, Identifying substances

Biology NC link
- simple food tests for starch, simple (reducing) sugars, protein, and lipids

Working scientifically NC links
- use appropriate techniques, apparatus, and materials during fieldwork and laboratory work, paying attention to health and safety
- make and record observations and measurements using a range of methods for different investigations
- interpret observations to draw conclusions

Learning objective	Learning outcomes		
	Developing	Secure	Extending
Name the chemicals used to test foods for starch, lipids, sugar, and protein	Identify some of the chemicals used for food tests	**Name the chemicals used to test foods for starch, lipids, sugar, and protein**	Determine which chemical(s) would produce a positive test result for a named food sample
Give the positive result for each food test	Identify the positive result for each food test	**Give the positive result for each food test**	Identify the nutrients present in a food based on the outcome of the four food tests
Describe how to test foods for starch, lipids, sugar, and protein	Describe what is meant by a food test	**Describe how to test foods for starch, lipids, sugar, and protein**	Explain some safety precautions to be taken for the four food tests

Tier 2 vocabulary	Tier 3 vocabulary	SB in-text question answers
irritant, nutrient, protein, *solution*, starch, *sugar*, translucent	Benedict's solution, biuret solution, distilled water, food test, iodine, lipids	**A** Blue-black **B** Rub some food onto a piece of filter paper. If the paper becomes translucent, then the food contains lipids **C** boiled sweets **D** If you add biuret solution, it turns purple

B2 Chapter 1: Health and lifestyle

Lesson plan

Reactivate knowledge

1. Name the nutrient that is used for growth and repair.
2. What is the main function of carbohydrates?
3. What is meant by a balanced diet?

Lesson resources

Practical: *Food tests* (student sheet, teacher and technician sheet, support sheet)

Answers: 1 Protein **2** Provide energy **3** Eating food containing right nutrients in right amounts

Trigger interest

Show students the photo of chips on the Lesson presentation. Ask them which food group the chips contain that they can see evidence for.

Hopefully, they will recognise that fatty foods leave grease marks on paper. Demonstrate that this is a test for fats by rubbing some cheese/butter on a piece of filter paper and showing that the paper has gone translucent. Explain that scientists need clear results to tell us whether a food contains a chemical or not.

Main activity

Practical: Food tests (40 mins) Demonstrate the food tests for starch, lipids, sugar, and protein. Discuss the safety precautions that must be followed such as the use of eyewear and washing skin immediately upon contact, as some of the chemicals are irritants. Explain also how a food solution is required for three of the tests, and how this has been produced for them. Students should then complete the summary table on their practical sheet, which states the chemical used for each test and how to determine a positive result.

Ask students to work in small groups to carry out a circus activity where they will test for themselves, during their allocated time at each station, the presence of starch, lipids, sugar, and protein in the foods provided. Give students the opportunity to test for all four chemicals during this practical.

Students should then answer the questions that follow on the practical sheet.

Review and reflect

Hold up some test tubes of results from today's food tests. Ask students what each test result shows and what indicator has been used.

Homework

Students choose a packaged food product from their cupboard. They choose two food groups noted on the label, and describe how they would test the food product to confirm the presence of these groups.

1.3 Unhealthy diet

Theme: Health and disease
Biology NC links
- calculations of energy requirements in a healthy daily diet
- the consequences of imbalances in the diet, including obesity, starvation, and deficiency diseases

Sub-theme: Health and diet
Working scientifically NC links
- apply mathematical concepts and calculate results
- interpret observations and data, including identifying patterns and using observations, measurements, and data to draw conclusions

Learning outcomes

Learning objective	Developing	Secure	Extending
Describe some health issues caused by an unhealthy diet	List some health problems associated with an unhealthy diet	**Describe some health issues caused by an unhealthy diet**	Explain some health issues caused by an unhealthy diet
Give the definition of a vitamin or mineral deficiency	Name some examples of vitamins and minerals needed in a human diet	**Give the definition of a vitamin or mineral deficiency**	Describe examples of specific vitamin or mineral deficiencies
Compare the energy requirements of different people	Name some factors which affect a person's daily energy requirements	**Compare the energy requirements of different people**	Estimate and justify the energy requirements for different occupations

Tier 2 vocabulary	Tier 3 vocabulary	SB in-text question answers
deficiency, malnourishment, obese, requirements, starvation		**A** 2000 **B** Any three from: suffer health problems, poor immune system, lack energy, likely to suffer from a lack of vitamins or minerals (accept named condition) **C** Any three from: heart disease, stroke, diabetes, some cancers **D** Farmer

Lesson plan

Reactivate knowledge

1. Give one problem that may be caused by eating an unhealthy diet.
2. Name the two types of nutrient that provide the body with energy.
3. Name a good source of vitamins and minerals.

Answers: 1 Become overweight / lack energy / any other sensible suggestion 2 Lipids and carbohydrates 3 Fruits/vegetables

Lesson resources

Activity: *Energy requirements* (student sheet, teacher and technician sheet, support sheet)

B2 Chapter 1: Health and lifestyle

Trigger interest

Show students the image of Body Mass Index (BMI) on the Lesson presentation. Ask students to discuss what the image shows. How may the extremes be caused? (Be aware of students with a poor body image.)

Steer the discussion to explain that both extremes are caused by malnourishment – the people have eaten the wrong amounts or the wrong types of food.

Exposition of main content

Energy content of food: Introduce the idea that all the energy we require for life comes from food. Demonstrate the energy provided in food by sprinkling fine custard powder into a Bunsen flame using a funnel with some tubing (the screaming jelly baby experiment is also a classic option). This is a dramatic demonstration that creates a huge roaring flame. Keep students at a reasonable distance away from the experiment. Explain that energy is measured in joules (foods usually in kilojoules). The energy provided by a food source is listed on a food label.

Overweight vs underweight: Discuss what the body needs energy for – everything! Explain how eating foods with more energy than you use can result in weight gain. If the energy in the food you eat is less than the energy you use, you will lose body mass. This leads to you being underweight. These conditions both have associated medical issues. Show the list of common medical issues linked to being over- and under-weight. In pairs, students classify them into issues linked to being overweight, and those linked to being underweight. (Students are more likely to be aware of the issues linked to obesity.) Explain what is meant by a deficiency disease using examples from the Student Book.

Main activity

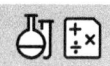

Activity: Energy requirements (20–25 mins)
Students compare the energy requirements of different people using the graph on the activity sheet. They answer the questions that follow.

Before students complete the task, explain how to calculate a percentage change by working through the example on the Lesson presentation.

Review and reflect

Play the 'higher or lower' game. State a job/gender/age – if the person has a higher energy requirement, students stand up; if lower, students sit down. Ask a student who identifies the answer correctly why this is the case.

Homework

Research a vitamin or mineral deficiency. Produce a fact sheet including the following information:

- name of disease/condition
- vitamin or mineral lacking
- symptoms of disease/condition
- examples of foods that are rich in the vitamin or mineral nutrient

1.4 Digestive system

Theme: Organisation
Sub-theme: Digestive system

Biology NC link
- the tissues and organs of the human digestive system, including adaptations to function and how the digestive system digests food (enzymes simply as biological catalysts)

Working scientifically NC links
- use models and analogies as a way of understanding things
- evaluate the effectiveness of a model

Learning objective	Learning outcomes		
	Developing	Secure	Extending
Describe the process of digestion	Give the definition of digestion	**Describe the process of digestion**	Explain the importance of digestion
Describe the functions of the main structures in the digestive system	Label the main structures in the digestive system	**Describe the functions of the main structures in the digestive system**	Explain the structural adaptations of the main structures in the digestive system

Tier 2 vocabulary	Tier 3 vocabulary
digestion, function, nutrient, protein, *stomach*	adaptation, anus, digestive system, faeces, gullet, large intestine, lipid, rectum, small intestine, villi

SB in-text question answers

A Smaller after digestion **B** Mouth → gullet → stomach → small intestine → large intestine → rectum → anus
C Muscles in the wall of the gut squeeze food along it

Lesson plan

Reactivate knowledge

1. What is the function of the digestive system?
2. Name some organs in the digestive system.
3. Name the food component that adds bulk to food.

Answers: 1 Break down food 2 Stomach/intestine/mouth 3 Fibre

Lesson resources

Activity: *Model of the digestive system* (student sheet, teacher and technician sheet, support sheet)

B2 Chapter 1: Health and lifestyle

Trigger interest

Show Figure 2 of the digestive system from the Student Book. Ask students to label as many organs as possible. (They should be familiar with some of the organs from KS2 and B1 2.1: *Levels of organisation*.)

Share students' answers. Use these to label a class diagram. Point out the main structural difference between the small and large intestines – the opening of the tube being wider. Add that if you unravelled your small intestine, it would be roughly four times taller than you – it is not very small!

Exposition of main content

Define the process of digestion and its purpose using Figure 2 in the Student Book to visually represent the process. Discuss the misconception that all digestion occurs in the stomach – digestion starts in the mouth, when the action of the teeth and the tongue break down food, as well as continuing in the small intestine.

Using an anatomical model of the human torso or Figure 2 in the Student Book, talk through each organ in the digestive system in turn and its role in digestion.

Use Figure 4 in the Student Book to introduce the role of the villi in the small intestine (increasing the surface area of the small intestine, thus maximising absorption). Enzymes should not be introduced at this point; refer to 'digestive juices' instead.

Model the movement of food through the digestive system by squeezing a nearly empty tube of toothpaste, or squeezing a pair of socks moving along a pair of tights.

Main activity

Activity: Model of the digestive system (30 mins)
Working in small groups, students produce a simple model of the digestive system using plastic tubing and a range of modelling materials to form the digestive organs. Students should label each key structure with a sticky note describing its function. Encourage students to also include any structural adaptations. When complete, get students to pour coloured liquid through their model to show the movement of food through the digestive system. The coloured liquid may stain, so perform this testing in bowls or near a sink.

Ask students to evaluate how well their model represents the digestive system. Allow time for students to share their thoughts and discuss any improvements as this will help with the homework task.

Review and reflect

Put the following structures in the order that food will pass through on its journey through the digestive system:

mouth   rectum   small intestine   stomach   large intestine   gullet   anus

Homework

Students evaluate their model by answering the following questions:

1. Describe one way your model helps make understanding the key features of the digestive system easier.
2. Describe one improvement you could make to your model.
3. Evaluate how well your model represents the key features of the digestive system.

Lower-ability students should complete questions 1 and 2.

1.5 Bacteria and enzymes in digestion

Themes: Bioenergetics, Organisation

Biology NC links
- enzymes simply as biological catalysts
- the importance of bacteria in the human digestive system

Sub-themes: Digestive system, Enzymes

Working scientifically NC links
- make predictions using scientific knowledge and understanding
- use appropriate techniques, apparatus, and materials during fieldwork and laboratory work, paying attention to health and safety
- make and record observations and measurements using a range of methods for different investigations

	Learning outcomes		
Learning objective	**Developing**	**Secure**	**Extending**
Describe the role of bacteria in digestion	List some facts about bacteria	**Describe the role of bacteria in digestion**	Explain the importance of bacteria in digestion
Give the definition of an enzyme	Identify the role of an enzyme in digestion	**Give the definition of an enzyme**	Explain the role of enzymes in digestion
Describe the role of enzymes in carbohydrate, protein, and lipid digestion	Identify the enzymes used to digest carbohydrates, proteins, and lipids	**Describe the role of enzymes in carbohydrate, protein, and lipid digestion**	Explain how bile supports the digestion of lipids

Tier 2 vocabulary	Tier 3 vocabulary
bacteria, bile, carbohydrate, digestion, protein, vitamin	carbohydrase, *catalyst*, enzyme, lipase, lipid, protease

SB in-text question answers

A Bacteria in the digestive system make vitamins **B** They speed up the reaction where large molecules are broken down

Lesson plan

Reactivate knowledge

1. What is meant by a unicellular organism?
2. What happens during digestion?
3. What food group does starch belong to?

Lesson resources

Practical: *Investigating enzyme action* (student sheet, teacher and technician sheet, support sheet)

Answers: 1 Organism made of only one cell 2 Breakdown of large food molecules into small molecules 3 Carbohydrates

B2 Chapter 1: Health and lifestyle

Trigger interest

Provide students with packaging from probiotic foods. Ask them to try to find out from the labelling what they are, what they contain, and why they are good for you.

Share students' ideas to determine that probiotic foods contain a range of bacteria that help digestion inside the human body. The bacteria live naturally in the large intestine on the fibre in your diet. They make important vitamins, such as vitamin K, which is needed for blood clotting and helping wounds to heal. These vitamins are then absorbed into your body and help to keep you healthy. This is a good opportunity to address the misconception that all bacteria are bad for you.

Exposition of main content

Introduce the role of enzymes in the body by showing the animation: *Digestion and enzymes*. Then use Figures 3–5 in the Student Book to reinforce the reactions catalysed by carbohydrase, protease, and lipase. Reinforce that enzymes are not living (they are proteins) and do not get 'used up'.

Main activity

Practical: Investigating enzyme action (30 mins)
Students carry out a practical to observe the action of carbohydrase on the breakdown of starch and answer the questions that follow.

Take time before the practical to discuss how enzyme action is being studied in this practical, so that students can complete their prediction.

You may wish to demonstrate the importance of timing in this practical and explain what results students are looking for. (For the colour change to stop occurring, showing that all the starch has been broken down.)

Wash anything that comes into contact with skin under a running tap, since iodine will stain skin and clothing. The pipettes should be labelled to prevent cross-contamination.

Review and reflect

Create sets of sort cards (one per group) with three arrow cards and the following words: carbohydrates, carbohydrase, sugar, proteins, proteases, amino acids, lipids, lipase, fatty acids, and glycerol.

Give each group of students a set of cards for them to explain enzymatic digestion. Students should then write the resulting word equations in their books.

(For support, have sets of cards where different colours are used to distinguish between substrates, enzymes, and products.)

carbohydrates → sugar (using carbohydrase)

proteins → amino acids (using proteases)

lipids → fatty acids and glycerol (using lipase)

Homework

Students construct a graphic organiser to summarise the role of enzymes and bacteria in aiding digestion.

1.6 Drugs

Theme: Health and disease
Sub-themes: Health and diet, Communicable diseases

Biology NC links

- the effects of recreational drugs (including substance misuse) on behaviour, health and life processes

Learning objective	Learning outcomes		
	Developing	**Secure**	**Extending**
Give the definition of a drug	Name some drugs	**Give the definition of a drug**	Describe some effects of drugs on the human body
Describe the difference between recreational and medical drugs	List some medicinal drugs and some recreational drugs	**Describe the difference between recreational and medical drugs**	Compare the health benefits and drawbacks of some common drugs
Describe what happens during drug addiction	Give the definition of an addiction	**Describe what happens during drug addiction**	Suggest some behavioural or societal impacts of drug addiction

Tier 2 vocabulary	Tier 3 vocabulary	SB in-text question answers
addiction, chemical reactions, drug, medicinal drug, medicine, recreational drug, risk, symptom, withdrawal symptoms		**A** A chemical substance that affects the way the body works **B** Treat symptoms of a condition/cure an illness **C** Any two from: for enjoyment, help relax, and stay awake **D** Any three from: heroin, cocaine, cannabis, and ecstasy

Lesson plan

Reactivate knowledge

1. Name two things you should do to stay healthy.
2. Name some medicines people take when they feel unwell.
3. Name the organ system that controls body reactions.

Answers: 1 Eat a balanced diet / exercise regularly / sleep well 2 E.g., cough medicine, aspirin, paracetamol 3 Nervous system

Lesson resources

Activity: *Drug research* (student sheet, teacher and technician sheet, support sheet)

B2 Chapter 1: Health and lifestyle

Trigger interest

Put a list of drugs on the board. Ask students to sort the drugs into medicinal and recreational drugs. Ask them to then further divide the recreational drugs into legal or illegal drugs. (This is an opportunity to gauge students' knowledge from Personal, Social, and Health Education (PSHE) or Citizenship sessions.)

Ensure students are clear about the difference between recreational and medicinal drugs. Explain that even if a drug is prescribed or legal, it can have side effects or negative effects on health.

Main activity

Activity: Drug research (35–40 mins) Ask students to produce a presentation about the different types of drugs that exist and the effects they have on the body. The presentation should be written in a style that could be shown to teenagers to educate them about the dangers of taking illegal recreational drugs.

Allow 20 minutes for students to research and plan their presentation, 10 minutes to produce their presentation, and then 10 minutes to share their presentation with at least one other student.

Review and reflect

Ask students to write definitions for the key terms 'drug' and 'addiction'. They then share their definitions with a partner, and then a four, to see if they can improve their definitions.

Homework

Students write a 4-mark exam-style question on one or more of: the types of drugs, addiction, and/or withdrawal symptoms. They should also provide a mark scheme illustrating where the marks are allocated.

1.7 Alcohol

Theme: Health and disease **Sub-theme:** Health and diet

Biology NC links

- the effects of 'recreational' drugs (including substance misuse) on behaviour, health, and life processes
- the effect of maternal lifestyle on the fetus through the placenta

Learning objective	Learning outcomes		
	Developing	Secure	Extending
Describe some effects of alcohol on the body	Name the drug present in alcohol	**Describe some effects of alcohol on the body**	Explain why a person should not drive after drinking alcohol
Describe some health problems caused by alcohol consumption	Name some health problems associated with alcohol consumption	**Describe some health problems caused by alcohol consumption**	Explain some health problems caused by alcohol
Describe some effects of alcohol consumption on conception and pregnancy	Identify some problems associated with alcohol consumption on conception and pregnancy	**Describe some effects of alcohol consumption on conception and pregnancy**	Explain some effects of alcohol consumption on conception and pregnancy

Tier 2 vocabulary	Tier 3 vocabulary	SB in-text question answers
addiction, aggressive, alcoholic, depressant, depressed, efficiently, pregnancy, premature	ethanol, placenta, unit of alcohol	**A** Ethanol **B** A person who is addicted to alcohol. **C** Any three from: stomach ulcers, heart disease, brain damage, or liver damage (cirrhosis) **D** Any three from: miscarriage, stillbirth, premature birth, low-birthweight babies, or Foetal Alcohol Syndrome (FAS)

Lesson plan

Reactivate knowledge

1. What is a drug?
2. What is a recreational drug?
3. What are withdrawal symptoms?

Answers: 1 Chemical substance that alters the way the body works 2 Drug taken for pleasure 3 Unpleasant symptoms an addict experiences when they stop taking a drug

Lesson resources

Activity: *Dangers of drinking alcohol* (student sheet, teacher and technician sheet, support sheet)

B2 **Chapter 1:** Health and lifestyle

Trigger interest

Show students a video clip of a drink-driving advert, or project a drink-driving poster on the board. Ask students to discuss in groups why these adverts are necessary. Ask students to then discuss the possible effects of alcohol on the body. (This is an opportunity to gauge students' knowledge from Personal, Social, and Health Education (PSHE) or Citizenship sessions.)

Introduce the fact that the drug present in alcoholic drinks is ethanol, which is a depressant (slows down the nervous system).

Exposition of main content

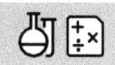

Provide students with some empty alcohol bottles, or images of bottles of alcohol. Working in small groups, ask students to place these in order, from strongest to weakest. Ask: *how much of each type of alcohol would count as a unit?* You could provide students with beakers to show visually what they think.

Share students' ideas, then show them what a unit of wine (75 ml), beer (250 ml), spirit (25 ml), alcopop (250 ml), and cider (225 ml) looks like, by pouring a coloured liquid into an appropriately sized glass. This could then be tipped into a beaker to compare with students' ideas.

Direct students to calculate the number of units in different common drinks, e.g., a pint of beer or a large glass of wine.

Explain that the government recommends that no adult should drink more than 14 units a week. Explain that this should be spread over a few days to prevent long-term harm to their body.

Discuss how people become alcoholics and why they find it difficult to stop drinking.

Main activity

Activity: Dangers of drinking alcohol (20–25 mins)
Ask students to read through the information in the Student Book on the dangers of drinking alcohol and to summarise the information. They should answer the questions that follow. If time allows, students can complete additional research into the effects of alcohol on the body and add this to their summary diagram.

Review and reflect

Provide two sets of coloured cards (green for true and red for false). Read out a series of statements such as 'alcohol is a stimulant' (F), and 'the drug present in alcohol is ethanol' (T). Include health problems caused by alcohol in the statements. Students hold up the appropriate card. For each false statement, choose a student to explain why it is incorrect.

Homework

Ask students to produce a health poster to be displayed in a doctor's waiting room encouraging pregnant women not to drink alcohol. The poster must fit onto one side of A4 paper and be clear and informative.

1.8 Smoking

Theme: Health and disease
Biology NC links

- the effects of 'recreational' drugs (including substance misuse) on behaviour, health, and life processes
- the effect of maternal lifestyle on the fetus through the placenta

Sub-theme: Health and diet
Working scientifically NC link

- record and interpret observations

Learning objective	Learning outcomes		
	Developing	**Secure**	**Extending**
Describe the effects of the components of tobacco smoke on the body	List some of the components of tobacco smoke	**Describe the effects of the components of tobacco smoke on the body**	Explain the effects of the components of tobacco smoke on the body
Describe some health problems caused by smoking	List some diseases linked with smoking	**Describe some health problems caused by smoking**	Explain some health problems caused by smoking
Describe some effects of smoking on pregnancy	Identify some problems associated with smoking and pregnancy	**Describe some effects of smoking on pregnancy**	Explain how smoking during pregnancy can cause serious illness in a foetus or miscarriage

Tier 2 vocabulary	Tier 3 vocabulary	SB in-text question answers
inflate, passive smoking, pregnancy, premature, stimulant, tobacco, toxic	alveoli, carbon monoxide, nicotine, *tar*	**A** Any three from: breathing conditions, cancer, strokes, or heart attacks **B** To prevent non-smokers from breathing in other people's smoke (and so having an increased risk of associated diseases) **C** Nicotine

Lesson plan

Reactivate knowledge

1. What do the lungs do?
2. What is the role of red blood cells in the body?
3. Name two problems linked to drinking alcohol whilst pregnant.

Answers: 1 Take in oxygen and remove carbon dioxide 2 Transport oxygen
3 Miscarriage/stillbirth/premature births/low birthweight/FAS

Lesson resources

Activity: *Chemicals in smoke* (student sheet, teacher and technician sheet, support sheet)

B2 Chapter 1: Health and lifestyle

Trigger interest

Working in pairs, give students 2–3 minutes to come up with as many harmful effects of smoking as possible. Share students' ideas to produce a class list – this can be added to throughout the lesson. (Examples include breathing problems such as bronchitis and pneumonia, 'smoker's cough', cancer, heart attacks, and strokes.) This is a good opportunity to gauge students' knowledge from PSHE or Citizenship sessions.

Exposition of main content

Light an incense stick in the centre of the room – a few seconds later, all students should be able to smell the incense (and potentially see the smoke). Use this to discuss the concept of passive smoking and how this increases a person's risk of developing circulatory and respiratory conditions. Babies and young children of parents who smoke are particularly at risk of respiratory illness, including bronchitis, pneumonia, and sudden infant death syndrome (SIDS – cot death).

Explain that, like alcohol, smoking increases the risk of miscarriage, affects foetal development, and increases the risk of a low birthweight.

Main activity

Activity: Chemicals in smoke (30–35 mins)
Demonstrate the smoking machine (in a fume cupboard) or show a YouTube clip of this procedure. Talk through each piece of equipment and what it is demonstrating. Demonstrate air being drawn through the equipment first before drawing air through a lit cigarette. (To demonstrate the effect further, the filter can be removed from the cigarette and the demo repeated.) Direct students to record the results of the demonstration as they watch.

Show students the results (tar deposited on the cotton wool, an acidic gas, and carbon dioxide present in tobacco smoke). Explain further, using the Student Book as required, the effects of the key components of tobacco smoke on health – tar (linked to respiratory illness and lung cancer), nicotine (addictive component), and carbon monoxide (affects red blood cells' ability to carry oxygen). Discuss the increased risk of respiratory infections, emphysema, and heart disease.

Review and reflect

Give the definitions of key words (such as 'nicotine' or 'stimulant') used in this lesson for students to write the correct key word on their mini-whiteboard, holding up their word as quickly as they can.

Homework

Give students an outline of a human body showing the main organs. Ask them to add annotations to describe how smoking can affect the body. They should add examples of smoking-related diseases. Encourage students to state which part of tobacco affects the organ. For example, nicotine makes the heart beat faster or tar causes lung cancer.

39

B2 Chapter 1: Health and lifestyle

Introduction to checkpoint intervention

This checkpoint intervention provides suggestions for a lesson to follow up the B2 1 Health and lifestyle checkpoint assessment. Depending on the outcomes of the assessment, these suggestions could move a class towards secure, to target specific learning outcomes, or to consolidate knowledge for students achieving secure outcomes. Use students' outcomes from the checkpoint assessment to address general misconceptions from the content covered. Be prepared to re-cover content as required; three key concepts from the chapter are covered in more detail below.

Checkpoint secure learning outcomes

- Name the seven components of a balanced diet, giving examples.
- Describe how to test foods for starch, lipids, sugar, and protein.
- Describe some health issues caused by an unhealthy diet.
- Describe the function of the main structures in the digestive system.
- Describe the role of bacteria in digestion.
- Describe the role of enzymes in carbohydrate, protein, and lipid digestion.
- Give the definition of a drug.
- Describe some health problems caused by alcohol consumption.
- Describe the effects of the components of tobacco

Student reflection

Encourage students to reflect on whether there were any checkpoint questions they found difficult or straightforward, as well as their preparation for the checkpoint assessment, including how they revised, the time spent on revision, and what areas they could improve on. For more strategies, see the Metacognition chapter or the Metacognition in Key Stage 3 Science guide on Kerboodle.

Intervention activity: Describe how to test foods for starch, lipids, sugar, and protein

This activity recaps the different food tests. Students often muddle up these tests because there are lots of new reagents and colour changes to learn. This activity produces a reference table, which students can transfer onto revision aids like flashcards.

Describe the four main food tests

Set up four workstations, one for each nutrient. At each station, have the reagent in a clear bottle so that students can see its original colour, as well as foods showing a positive test so they can record the colour change. The sugar test results could be left in the water bath to show that this is the one test that requires the solution to be heated.

Nutrient	Chemical reagent	Original colour of reagent	Colour change if nutrient present

Encourage students to come up with hints to help them remember the colour changes or the chemical reagent used. These could then be shared as a class. For example, a **p**ositive test for **p**rotein is **p**urple.

Intervention activity: Describe the function of the main structures in the digestive system

It is important to reiterate to students the difference between the command words 'describe' and 'explain'. In 'describe' questions, students get no marks for going further in their answer by explaining the thing they are describing. Encourage students to underline key parts of the question, such as 'describe'.

Describing the functions of the main structures in the digestive system

Provide students with the question and exemplar student answer below. Ask students to mark it.

Describe the function of **three** structures in the digestive system. **(3 marks)**

The digestive system is needed to break down food.

It contains lots of organs such as the mouth, stomach, and intestines.

The mouth contains teeth, which chop food into smaller pieces.

The stomach contains acid.

The small intestine absorbs small molecules of nutrients.

Students should have scored the question 2 marks (out of 3) – for a named organ and its correct description on lines 3 and 5. Lines 1 and 2 contain general information on the digestive system, which is not required. Line 4 describes an adaptation of the stomach but not its function.

Students could then be asked to write a model answer for two structures in the digestive system. For support, students could refer to the information in the topic spread for B2 1.4 Digestive system.

Intervention activity: Describe the effects of the components of tobacco smoke on the body

Most students can name some diseases that smoking increases the risk of, but they are not always able to link a component of tobacco smoke to its effect. This activity helps students master this skill.

Describing the effects of tobacco smoke on the body

Provide students with the question: Using examples, describe the effects of **two** components of tobacco smoke on the body. **(4 marks)**

Explain that the question is asking the student to:

- identify two components of tobacco smoke (there are more than two components, but naming more will gain no further marks)
- describe one effect each component of tobacco smoke causes. This must be linked to the answer they gave to the first part. For example, a respiratory infection is not an appropriate example for nicotine.

Model how the information should be included in their answer, using one component. For example, nicotine (1 mark) makes the heart beat faster. (1 mark)

Students should then complete the same question for other components of tobacco smoke. For support, students could refer to the information in the topic spread for B2 1.8 Smoking.

B2 Chapter 2: Biological processes

Introduction to chapter

In this chapter, students will study the process of photosynthesis, how leaves are adapted to maximise this process, and its importance for all life on Earth. They will then look at the effects of minerals on plant growth. The focus of the second half of the chapter is the process of respiration, beginning with aerobic respiration. Students will then compare this with anaerobic respiration in animals and fermentation in plants.

Core concepts in chapter
- The process and importance of photosynthesis
- The adaptation of leaves for photosynthesis
- The process of aerobic respiration in living organisms
- The process of anaerobic respiration in humans and microorganisms

Prerequisite knowledge
- The difference between producers and consumers
- The functions of the cell wall, cell membrane, cytoplasm, nucleus, vacuole, mitochondria, and chloroplasts
- The role of diffusion in the movement of materials in and between cells

GCSE links
- Photosynthesis as the key process for food production and therefore biomass for life
- The process of photosynthesis
- Factors affecting the rate of photosynthesis
- The importance of cellular respiration; the processes of aerobic and anaerobic respiration

Key learning misconceptions

- Breathing and respiration are the same thing
- Animals respire, plants do not (plants photosynthesise 'instead')
- Only organisms with lungs can respire
- Plants obtain water through their leaves when it rains
- Plant mass comes from the water and minerals from the soil
- Anaerobic respiration only takes place when there is no air

B2 Chapter 2: Biological processes

Key maths skills

Use of word equations to represent photosynthesis and respiration This may be the first time students have been introduced to word equations in Biology to represent chemical reactions. Link their use to students' prior work in Chemistry. Remind students that the reactants are always written on the left of the arrow, and the products on the right (the order on either side does not matter). In photosynthesis, light is required for the reaction, but is neither a reactant nor a product. 'Light' is therefore written above the arrow. Likewise, in respiration, we write 'energy transferred' in brackets within the word equation to differentiate it from the physical products formed.

Misconception

Plants do not respire Constantly reinforce the fact that plants also have to respire in order to transfer the energy from the glucose produced in photosynthesis to the plant cells, so that it can be used for growth. In the chapter, students look at the role of stomata in gas exchange for photosynthesis. You may wish to explain to higher-ability students that when a plant is photosynthesising, the net movement of gases is likely to be carbon dioxide into and oxygen out of the leaf, but some molecules will move the other way as a result of respiration.

Working scientifically skills

Photosynthesis practicals If more time is available to teach this chapter, there are a number of simple practical activities that could be included. For example, investigating the effect of light intensity on photosynthesis by counting the number of bubbles produced by pondweed such as *Elodea,* or testing leaves kept in the dark for the presence of starch by covering up parts of leaves on a tree. However, photosynthesis practicals are often season-dependent in terms of success, so this should be taken into account when planning the teaching of this chapter.

Fermentation If more time is available to teach this chapter, students could investigate the effect of different factors such as temperature and glucose concentration on yeast fermentation, by measuring the volume of carbon dioxide gas given off or counting the number of bubbles produced. This would provide a good opportunity for students to calculate a mean and then plot their results as a line graph, adding a line of best fit. The activities could be completed as a class exercise; for example, with each group responsible for collating the data for one temperature. The process of plotting and analysing the data could then be worked through together to aid mastering these important working scientifically skills.

2.1 Photosynthesis

Themes: Bioenergetics, Organisation

Biology NC links

- the reactants in, and products of, photosynthesis, and a word summary for photosynthesis
- the dependence of almost all life on Earth on the ability of photosynthetic organisms, such as plants and algae, to use sunlight in photosynthesis to build organic molecules that are an essential energy store and to maintain levels of oxygen and carbon dioxide in the atmosphere
- plants making carbohydrates in their leaves by photosynthesis

Sub-themes: Photosynthesis, Plant organ systems

Working scientifically NC links

- use appropriate techniques, apparatus, and materials during laboratory work, paying attention to health and safety
- evaluate risks
- interpret observations to draw conclusions

	Learning outcomes		
Learning objective	**Developing**	**Secure**	**Extending**
Describe the process of photosynthesis	Describe the difference between a producer and a consumer	**Describe the process of photosynthesis**	Explain the importance of photosynthesis to all organisms on Earth
Give the word equation for photosynthesis	Identify the substances that a plant uses for photosynthesis and the substances that it makes	**Give the word equation for photosynthesis**	Explain why plants require light to photosynthesise
Describe how to test a leaf for the presence of starch	Give the chemical test used to show the presence of starch	**Describe how to test a leaf for the presence of starch**	Predict the outcome of a starch test on a variegated leaf

Tier 2 vocabulary	Tier 3 vocabulary
chemical reaction, consumer, convert, digestion, photosynthesis, producer	algae, chlorophyll, chloroplasts, variegated

SB in-text question answers
A Consumer **B** Glucose **C** Chloroplast

B2 Chapter 2: Biological processes

Lesson plan

Reactivate knowledge

1. What substances does a plant need to grow?
2. Why are plants green?
3. Name three cell components only found in plant cells.

Lesson resources

Practical: *Testing a leaf for starch* (student sheet, teacher sheet, support sheet)

Answers: **1** Water, sunlight, carbon dioxide, minerals **2** Contain chlorophyll **3** Cell wall, vacuole, chloroplast

Emphasise to students that plants need minerals to grow.

Trigger interest

Before the lesson, set up some pondweed photosynthesising under a light with a test tube to collect the gas given off. Ask students which gas it is.

Show that it is oxygen by relighting a glowing splint.

Exposition of main content

Discuss the difference between consumers and producers. Then, building on students' previous knowledge, discuss the process of photosynthesis and introduce the word equation that summarises this process.

Explain that it is not just plants that photosynthesise by showing Figure 1 from the Student Book (some bacteria photosynthesise as well). Using the information in the Student Book, explain the differences between algae and plants.

Main activity

Practical: Testing a leaf for starch (30 mins)
Before introducing the practical, explain that plants store the glucose they make through photosynthesis as starch.

Ask students to follow the instructions on the practical sheet to carry out an experiment to test a leaf for starch.

They should write a risk assessment for the experiment and answer the questions that follow.

If time is available, students can compare observations from different types of leaves (variegated or coloured).

Review and reflect

Working on their own, ask students to write a description of photosynthesis. Ask them to then share their definition with a partner to see if they can improve it.

Homework

Students produce a flow diagram showing the main steps involved in testing a leaf for the presence of starch. (If required for support, students could be provided with the main steps in a muddled order to then rearrange.)

2.2 Leaves

Themes: Bioenergetics, Organisation

Biology NC links
- the reactants in, and products of, photosynthesis
- the adaptations of leaves for photosynthesis

Sub-themes: Photosynthesis, Plant organ systems

Working scientifically NC links
- use appropriate techniques, apparatus, and materials during laboratory work, paying attention to health and safety
- make and record observations

Learning objective	Learning outcomes		
	Developing	**Secure**	**Extending**
Describe the main adaptations of a leaf	List some features of a leaf	**Describe the main adaptations of a leaf**	Explain the main adaptations of a leaf
Describe the role of stomata	Give the definition of stomata	**Describe the role of stomata**	Explain how stomata allow gas exchange in a leaf
Describe how water is transported through a plant	Name the organs through which water passes within a plant	**Describe how water is transported through a plant**	Explain how plants obtain the reactants for photosynthesis

Tier 2 vocabulary	Tier 3 vocabulary
component, diffuse, evaporate, photosynthesis	adaptations, chloroplasts, chlorophyll, guard cells, stomata

SB in-text question answers

A Green/contain chlorophyll and large surface area
B Upper layer C To prevent water loss
D Carbon dioxide diffuses in and oxygen diffuses out

Lesson plan

Reactivate knowledge

1. What are the main organs of a plant?
2. Why are plants called producers?
3. What do plants need to photosynthesise?

Lesson resources

Practical: *Observing stomata* (student sheet, teacher sheet, support sheet)

Answers: **1** Root, leaf, flower, stem **2** They make their own food (photosynthesis) **3** Carbon dioxide, water, and sunlight

Chapter 2: Biological processes

Trigger interest

Provide students with a range of leaves from common plants. Ask them to make a list of the common features of the leaves. Can they explain why they have these features?

(Include at least one non-green leaf to address the misconception that all leaves are green. Red leaves, such as maple, contain anthocyanin, which provides the characteristic colour. The leaves also contain chlorophyll, but the anthocyanin levels are much greater.)

Exposition of main content

Through discussion, draw out the four main adaptations of a leaf as explained in the Student Book: green, thin, large surface area, and presence of veins.

Ask students to turn their leaves upside down. What do they notice? Explain that most sunlight hits the top of the leaf, so this is where the chloroplasts need to be to absorb as much sunlight as possible, so the upper surface is a darker green.

Provide students with waxy leaves to feel, such as privet. Explain that this layer prevents water loss by evaporation. Then introduce the movement of water through a plant to reach the leaves. Demonstrate, by sucking through a straw, that water being lost from the leaves draws water up the vessels. Take care to ensure students do not gain the misconception that plants 'suck' water in through their roots.

Show students Figure 2 of stomata from the Student Book. Explain their function in gas exchange and the role of guard cells.

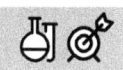

Main practical

Practical: Observing stomata (25–30 mins)
Ask students to produce an imprint of the underside of a leaf using nail varnish. They then observe stomata under the microscope (or a magnifying glass if it is easier) and answer the questions that follow.

Review and reflect

Working in pairs, ask students to sketch a diagram to show the movement of water through a plant, adding arrows and simple descriptions such as 'diffuses into the roots from the soil'.

Homework

Students produce a visual representation of how the reactants and products of photosynthesis enter, move through, and leave a plant.

2.3 Plant minerals

Theme: Health and disease

Biology NC link
- plants making carbohydrates in their leaves by photosynthesis and gaining minerals and water from the soil via their roots

Sub-theme: Plant diseases, deficiencies, and defence responses

Working scientifically NC links
- make and record observations and measurements using a range of methods for different investigations
- present observations and data using appropriate methods, including tables
- apply mathematical concepts and calculate results

Learning objective	Learning outcomes		
	Developing	Secure	Extending
Describe how a plant uses minerals for healthy growth	List some minerals required by plants	**Describe how a plant uses minerals for healthy growth**	Explain how minerals enable healthy growth in a plant
Describe the symptoms of plant mineral deficiencies	List some symptoms of unhealthy plants	**Describe the symptoms of plant mineral deficiencies**	Suggest and justify a mineral deficiency based on a plant's appearance
Explain why farmers use fertilisers	List some ways farmers can add minerals to the soil	**Explain why farmers use fertilisers**	Explain why using fertilisers enable land to be used for crop growth year after year

Tier 2 vocabulary	Tier 3 vocabulary	SB in-text question answers
absorb, artificial, deficiency, fertiliser, growth, harvest, healthy, proteins	amino acids, chlorophyll, magnesium, nitrates, phosphates, potassium	**A** Nitrates, phosphates, magnesium **B** Absorbed through root hair cells from soil (water) **C** Phosphorus **D** Manure/animal dung and fertilisers

B2 Chapter 2: Biological processes

Lesson plan

Reactivate knowledge

1. How does water get into a plant?
2. Why do leaves have stomata?
3. Give three adaptations of a leaf.

Lesson resources

Practical: *Investigating fertilisers* (student sheet, teacher sheet, support sheet)

Answers: 1 Through the roots (by diffusing into the root hairs) **2** To allow gases to diffuse into and out of the plant **3** Green/thin/large surface area/have stomata/have veins/waxy layer

Trigger interest

Provide the class with packaging from garden fertilisers or project an image of the contents of some fertilisers onto the board. Ask students to identify what chemicals are found in the fertiliser and explain why fertilisers are used.

Exposition of main content

Introduce the three minerals needed for plant growth described in the Student Book – nitrates, phosphates, and magnesium – and their specific functions. Use the photos to explain what can happen if the plant is deficient in this mineral (Link this to the concept of vitamin and mineral deficiencies in a human diet).

Discuss why fertilisers or manure are not needed for plants to flourish in natural areas, but are required in large quantities on farmland.

Main activity

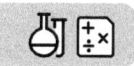

Practical: Investigating fertilisers (25–30 mins)
Give students two trays of seedlings (one treated with fertiliser, the other untreated) to compare. They should choose an appropriate variable for comparison, record results in a suitable table, calculate a mean, and answer the questions that follow.

Allow a few minutes at the end of this practical to discuss conclusions and the importance of calculating means in an experiment like this one.

Review and reflect

Provide students with three cards: nitrates, phosphates, and magnesium. Read out a series of statements such as *'needed to make chlorophyll'* or *'What might a plant be deficient in if its leaves are yellow?'*. Students hold up the appropriate card.

Homework

Students write the voice-over for an advert for a commercial fertiliser, naming the minerals involved and explaining how each mineral is important to the plant.

49

2.4 Aerobic respiration

Theme: Bioenergetics **Sub-theme:** Respiration

Biology NC links

- aerobic respiration in living organisms, including the breakdown of organic molecules to enable all the other chemical processes necessary for life
- a word summary for aerobic respiration

Learning objective	Learning outcomes		
	Developing	Secure	Extending
Describe the process of aerobic respiration	Name the chemical reaction where energy is transferred to cells	**Describe the process of aerobic respiration**	Explain why respiration is performed by all living organisms
Give the word equation for aerobic respiration	Identify the substances used for aerobic respiration and the substances produced	**Give the word equation for aerobic respiration**	Compare the processes of aerobic respiration and photosynthesis
Describe how the reactants and products of respiration are transported to and from cells	Identify the substances which move into and out of cells during respiration	**Describe how the reactants and products of respiration are transported to and from cells**	Explain how the reactants and products of respiration are transported to and from cells

Tier 2 vocabulary	Tier 3 vocabulary	SB in-text question answers
consume, diffuse, exhale, inhale, produce, transfer	aerobic respiration, glucose, haemoglobin, mitochondria, plasma	**A** Glucose and oxygen **B** Carbon dioxide **C** Diffusion **D** Carbon dioxide and glucose

Lesson plan

Reactivate knowledge

1. Where in the cell does respiration occur?
2. Name the structure in the lungs where gas exchange occurs.
3. What is the function of red blood cells?

Answers: 1 Mitochondria **2** Alveoli **3** Transport oxygen

Lesson resources

Activity: *Aerobic respiration* (student sheet, teacher sheet, support sheet)

B2 Chapter 2: Biological processes

Trigger interest

Give students 2 minutes to produce a list of everything you need energy for (everything!).

Ask students where this energy comes from (food) and how it is released to the body (respiration). This is another opportunity to address the misconception that 'respiration is breathing (ventilation)'.

Exposition of main content

Explain that, like photosynthesis, the process of respiration can be summarised in a word equation.

Main activity

Activity: Aerobic respiration (Task 1) (20 mins)
Put the blank word equation for aerobic respiration on the board. Then, as a class, deduce the word equation. Fill in the answers on the board and ask students to fill in their worksheets as each step is discussed/demonstrated.

1. What sugar is produced after food is broken down during digestion? (Glucose)
2. What gas do people breathe in? (Oxygen)
3. Give students a test tube of limewater. Using a straw, ask students to repeatedly breathe out into the water for 1 minute. What happens? Why? (Turns cloudy as respiration produces carbon dioxide.)
4. Give students a strip of cobalt chloride paper. Demonstrate that the paper, when placed in a test tube of water, turns from blue to pink. Ask students to repeatedly breathe on the strip. What happens? Why? (Turns pink as respiration produces water.) Note that cobalt chloride paper should not be handled without using tweezers.
5. Demonstrate burning food by sprinkling sugar or custard powder over a Bunsen burner. (This is dramatic! Even if used to introduce energy content of foods, students like to see it again. Alternatively, burn a crisp.) Discuss what happens in the reaction. (When glucose reacts with oxygen, energy is transferred thermally, representing energy being transferred to the cell. In the human body, the reaction is less energetic, but does release small quantities of thermal energy – generating warmth). Explain that energy is written in brackets as it is not a physical substance.
6. Students should complete Task 1 on their worksheet as each step is demonstrated.

Activity: Aerobic respiration (Task 2) (20 mins)
Using information from the Student Book, ask students to produce a visual summary of how the reactants of aerobic respiration enter the body and travel to the cell, and how the waste products of aerobic respiration leave the body.

Students then answer the questions that follow.

Review and reflect

Ask students to write down the ending of the following sentences and hold them up:

Aerobic respiration occurs in .... (mitochondria)

The purpose of respiration is to transfer .... (energy to the cell)

The products of aerobic respiration are carbon dioxide and .... (water)

The reactants of respiration are glucose and .... (oxygen)

Homework

Students write an exam-style question worth 3–4 marks, including a mark scheme, on aerobic respiration.

2.5 Anaerobic respiration

Theme: Bioenergetics   **Sub-theme:** Respiration

Biology NC links
- the process of anaerobic respiration in humans and micro-organisms, including fermentation, and a word summary for anaerobic respiration
- the differences between aerobic and anaerobic respiration in terms of the reactants, the products formed and the implications for the organism

Learning objective	Learning outcomes		
	Developing	Secure	Extending
Compare the processes of aerobic and anaerobic respiration	Give the definition of anaerobic respiration	**Compare the processes of aerobic and anaerobic respiration**	Explain why the body normally respires aerobically
Write the word equation for the process of anaerobic respiration	Identify the substances used for anaerobic respiration and the substances produced	**Write the word equation for the process of anaerobic respiration**	Explain what is meant by the term oxygen debt
Write the word equation for fermentation	Name some food products made using fermentation	**Write the word equation for fermentation**	Explain how the fermentation reaction is used to manufacture some food products

Tier 2 vocabulary	Tier 3 vocabulary
fermentation, strenuous, transfer	anaerobic respiration, ethanol, glucose, lactic acid, microorganism, oxygen debt

SB in-text question answers

A In the absence of oxygen **B** Aerobic respiration **C** Lactic acid is produced in humans, whereas ethanol and carbon dioxide are produced in fermentation **D** Bread, beer, wine

Lesson plan

Reactivate knowledge

1. What is the word equation for aerobic respiration?
2. Which part of the blood transports glucose?
3. Why do muscles need energy?

Answers: 1 Glucose + oxygen → carbon dioxide + water (+ energy) 2 Plasma 3 To contract (to cause movement)

Lesson resources

Activity: *Fermentation and food production* (student sheet, teacher sheet, support sheet)

52

B2 Chapter 2: Biological processes

Trigger interest

Show a video clip of a runner who becomes exhausted and pulls up in pain or show images of, for example, athletes/footballers who have cramp. Ask students to suggest what has happened to these sportspeople's bodies.

Introduce the idea of anaerobic respiration in short bursts to supply energy without the need for oxygen, making lactic acid as a by-product, which causes cramp. Explain that when you have finished exercising, you keep on breathing heavily. The extra oxygen you inhale breaks down the lactic acid. The oxygen needed for this process is called the oxygen debt.

Exposition of main content

Introduce the word equation for anaerobic respiration in animals. Write this next to the word equation for aerobic respiration. Then, working in pairs, ask students to write down a similarity and a difference between aerobic and anaerobic respiration. Share answers.

Ask students to give a reason why the body normally respires aerobically (to avoid cramp through lactic acid build-up). Go on to explain that aerobic respiration transfers more energy per glucose molecule than anaerobic respiration and, hence, is a preferable process for the body.

Main activity

Activity: Fermentation and food production (25–30 mins) Introduce the microorganism yeast using Figure 2 in the Student Book. Explain that when microorganisms respire anaerobically, the process is called fermentation and different products are produced. Show students a conical flask of yeast fermenting sugar with a tube passing through limewater to demonstrate that carbon dioxide is produced. Remove the bung from the conical flask and allow the students to smell the contents. There should be a noticeable 'alcohol' smell, which can be used to introduce the fact that ethanol is also produced. Represent fermentation using its word equation.

Ask students then to complete the activity to research a useful food or drink product made using fermentation, and produce a leaflet to explain how it is made.

Students then answer the questions on anaerobic respiration that follow.

Review and reflect

Issue cards with all the words and arrows necessary for the three equations for respiration (aerobic, anaerobic, and fermentation). Ask students to make the three equations by arranging the cards.

Homework

Students construct a Venn diagram to compare aerobic and anaerobic respiration in humans.

B2 Chapter 2: Biological processes

Introduction to checkpoint intervention

This checkpoint intervention provides suggestions for a lesson to follow up the B2 2 Biological processes checkpoint assessment. Depending on the outcomes of the assessment, these suggestions could move a class towards secure, to target specific learning outcomes, or to consolidate knowledge for students achieving secure outcomes. Use students' outcomes from the checkpoint assessment to address general misconceptions from the content covered. Be prepared to re-cover content as required; three key concepts from the chapter are covered in more detail below.

Checkpoint secure learning outcomes

- Describe the process of photosynthesis.
- Give the word equation for photosynthesis.
- Describe the role of stomata.
- Describe how a plant uses minerals for healthy growth.
- Give the word equation for aerobic respiration.
- Write the word equation for fermentation.

Student reflection

Encourage students to reflect on whether there were any checkpoint questions they found difficult or straightforward, as well as their preparation for the checkpoint assessment, including how they revised, the time spent on revision, and what areas they could improve on. For more strategies, see the Metacognition chapter or the Metacognition in Key Stage 3 Science guide on Kerboodle.

Intervention activity: Describe the process of photosynthesis

When asked to describe the process of photosynthesis, students often give a very simple answer such as 'the process by which plants make food'. Although correct, this lacks the detail necessary to score a high level on a longer answer question.

Describing the process of photosynthesis

On the board, produce a blank photosynthesis word equation:

_____ + _____ → _____ + _____
(in _____)

Invite students to share information to complete the word equation as a class, including mentioning light being absorbed by chlorophyll.

Ask students to complete this exam-style question:
Describe the process of photosynthesis. (4 marks)

Students should use the key information given in the word equation to structure their answer. They could tick off each key word as they use it.

B2 Chapter 2: Biological processes

Intervention activity: Describe the role of stomata

When looking at stomata, many students incorrectly label the guard cells as stomata, rather than the pore they control. To overcome this, show stomata in a range of different forms such as those in the Student Book and from a leaf cross section.

Describing the role of stomata

Show students some microscopic footage of stomata opening and closing. Discuss the purpose of stomata being open (to allow gases to diffuse into and out of a leaf). Then discuss the direction in which gases flow (net flow) for photosynthesis, and the reason why they are closed at night (the plant is not photosynthesising). Depending on the ability of the students, you could recap that water vapour is also lost through stomata. Thus, on a very hot day, stomata close to prevent water loss and the plant wilting.

Get students to divide their page in two. Ask them to sketch a stoma with its guard cells in an open state during the day (a sun could be added above) on one side, and in a closed state (a moon could be added above) on the other. Then ask them to add labelled arrows to show the (net) direction of gas flow.

Intervention activity: Give the word equation for aerobic respiration

In this topic, there are lots of similar equations for the students to learn, which often leads to them being stated incorrectly. This activity is designed to look at how they are similar and different to aid recall.

Recalling equations for respiration and photosynthesis

Provide students with six sticky notes on which they write a key term: carbon dioxide, water, glucose, oxygen, lactic acid, and ethanol. They should also have a seventh note, ideally a different colour, on which they draw an arrow.

Ask them to explain the purpose of respiration (to transfer energy from food to the cell). This should help them locate the glucose note. Then ask them to think about what gas we need in order to survive. This should lead them to locate the oxygen note. They should place these on the desk in front of them followed by the arrow. Discuss what we breathe out, to help them locate the carbon dioxide and water notes (get them to think about condensation on a window on a cold day, if required). They should then add these after the arrow. Discuss that it doesn't matter in which order they place the products or reactants. The students should then record this equation.

Place the sticky notes back in the original pile. Repeat the activity to recall the word equations for anaerobic respiration in both animals and microorganisms, and then photosynthesis.

Chapter 3: Ecosystems and adaptation

Introduction to chapter

In this chapter, students will begin by looking at the feeding relationships within food chains and webs, and how this can result in bioaccumulation. They will then study the interdependence of organisms by looking at what happens to the population of one organism when the population of another is changed; this is studied within food web diagrams, and graphically through predator–prey interactions. Students will then look in detail at the adaptations of a number of organisms that enable them to be successful competitors and survive in harsh and changing environments.

Core concepts in chapter

- Interdependence
- Plant and animal adaptations

Prerequisite knowledge

- Construct and interpret a variety of food chains, identifying producers, predators and prey (KS2)
- Recognise that environments can change and that this can sometimes pose dangers to living things (KS2)
- Identify how animals and plants are adapted to suit their environment in different ways and that adaptation may lead to evolution (KS2)
- The structural adaptations of some unicellular organisms
- The dependence of almost all life on Earth on the ability of photosynthetic organisms, such as plants and algae, to use sunlight in photosynthesis to build organic molecules that are an essential energy store and to maintain levels of oxygen and carbon dioxide in the atmosphere

GCSE links

- Levels of organisation within an ecosystem
- Some abiotic and biotic factors that affect communities; the importance of interactions between organisms in a community
- The role of microorganisms (decomposers) in the cycling of materials through an ecosystem
- Organisms are interdependent and are adapted to their environment
- Methods of identifying species and measuring distribution, frequency and abundance of species within a habitat

Key learning misconceptions

- In food chains, the arrows show what an organism eats so point at that organism
- Organisms that are higher in a food web eat all organisms that are lower in the food web
- Animals choose to adapt to suit their surroundings
- Adult animals do not change their appearance
- Camouflaged animals are brown or green
- Only predators can run fast
- Plants are prey organisms
- Predator and prey populations are similar in size

B2 **Chapter 3:** Ecosystems and adaptation

Misconception

Arrows in food webs At every opportunity when talking about feeding relationships between organisms, represent the relationships as food chains or webs (or parts of food chains or webs) so students continually practise drawing arrows showing where the energy/biomass is being transferred to. Use a range of diagrams such as producers being placed on the left of the diagram or at the base to ensure they understand what the arrows represent.

Misconception

Animals choose to adapt to their environment Students should be aware of the term adaptation from studying the adaptations of specialised cells and unicellular organisms in Activate 1. However, confusion arises from the everyday use of this term for how people adapt to changes, causing many students to believe that organisms choose to adapt to their environment. Reinforce the idea that organisms do not adapt quickly but that adaptation of a species is a slow change over time, by chance, where useful adaptations give an advantage so these organisms survive and reproduce. This serves as an introduction to evolution.

Working scientifically skills

Sampling ecosystems If more time is available to spend teaching this chapter, there are a number of simple practical activities that could be included for students to measure the abundance and distribution of organisms within an ecosystem. For example, using pooters and pitfall traps to investigate invertebrates. Students can then be introduced to the use of keys in identifying organisms. Sampling bias could also be introduced at this stage, and students taught how to compensate for it by using a random number generator to select a sample area. The data collected can be used to estimate population sizes.

Working scientifically/ maths skills

Predator-prey graphs If working with a less mathematically able class, you may wish to first introduce predator-prey graphs by sketching a coloured line on a blank graph showing a trend of increasing and decreasing in a repeating pattern. Discuss what this shows (over time, a population increases then decreases). Then add a second line in a different colour showing the same pattern with a time lag. Explain that the first line shows the prey population and the second line the predator population and that one is dependent on the other. Break the graph down into sections (as described in the SB) and ensure students understand what is happening to both populations at each stage and how the populations are interdependent. Then repeat this by looking at graphs with data.

This is also likely to be the first time that students have met graphs with different scales on the y-axis, so ask students to read relevant prey and predator numbers of a range of graphs so that they appreciate that prey numbers are always bigger than predator numbers.

3.1 Food chains and webs

Theme: Ecosystems and environment **Sub-theme:** Feeding relationships

Biology NC link

- the interdependence of organisms in an ecosystem, including food webs and insect-pollinated crops

Learning objective	Learning outcomes		
	Developing	Secure	Extending
Use relevant information to construct a food chain	State what is meant by a food chain	Use relevant information to construct a food chain	Explain why the Sun is the ultimate source of energy in food chains
Describe the feeding relationships between organisms within a food chain	Identify the producer and a consumer in a food chain	Describe the feeding relationships between organisms within a food chain	Explain why food chains rarely have more than four links
Describe the feeding relationships between organisms within a food web	State what is meant by a food web	Describe the feeding relationships between organisms within a food web	Explain why food webs describe feeding relationships more realistically than food chains

Tier 2 vocabulary	Tier 3 vocabulary	SB in-text question answers
bacteria, carnivore, consumer, decomposer, diagram, energy, nutrients, photosynthesis, predator, prey, producer, realistically, transfer	food chain, food web, fungi, herbivore	**A** Corn → mouse → owl **B** Predator **C** Impala

Lesson plan

Reactivate knowledge

1. What is a producer?
2. What is a consumer?
3. What is the word equation for photosynthesis?

Lesson resources

Activity: *Food chains and webs* (student sheet, teacher and technician sheet, support sheet)

Answers: 1 An organism that makes its own food by photosynthesis **2** An organism that eats plants or animals to gain energy **3** Carbon dioxide + water $\xrightarrow{light}$ glucose + oxygen

B2 Chapter 3: Ecosystems and adaptation

Trigger interest

Working in pairs, ask students to arrange the following organisms into a food chain: lion, acacia tree, and giraffe. Ask them to add as many key feeding relationship terms as possible, for example, producer, carnivore.

Food chains are covered in KS2. This activity will allow you to determine prior understanding. Check that all students have added arrows pointing in the correct direction. Explain that these represent the transfer of energy (through food). Discuss all the key terms: producer, consumer, herbivore, carnivore, prey, predator (and top predator).

Exposition of main content

Introduce the concept that most food chains do not have more than four or five links, due to less energy being transferred at each level. Ask students to come up with ways energy is **not** passed on. For example, leaves shed in winter/not all parts of an organism are eaten/energy is transferred to the environment as heat. (Reinforce the concept that energy is transferred to the environment; it is not 'lost'.)

Show this mathematically. First, look at the food chain example in Figure 2 of the Student Book.

Then complete the worked example on the Lesson presentation, calculating a 10% transfer each time. Finally, ask students to complete the same calculation using the question in the maths box.

Show the food web in Figure 3 from the Student Book. Explain how the two food chains studied earlier in the lesson link together. This diagram is therefore a more realistic representation of the feeding relationships present in an African grassland. Discuss various feeding relationships shown by the food web.

Main activity

Activity: Food chains and webs (25 mins)
Students make their own food webs using the organisms provided on the cards. They answer the questions that follow.

Review and reflect

Show students the food web on the Lesson presentation. Ask them a series of questions about the web, including identifying a food chain. Students record their answers on mini-whiteboards and hold them up.

Homework

Students construct a food web from a different environment of their choice. They include as many organisms as they can in their food web, before choosing one food chain from their food web to annotate using key words from the lesson.

As an alternative, lower-ability students could be asked to construct a food chain from their chosen environment, which they annotate.

59

3.2 Disruption to food chains and webs

Theme: Ecosystems and environment

Biology NC links
- the interdependence of organisms in an ecosystem, including food webs and insect-pollinated crops
- how organisms affect, and are affected by, their environment, including the accumulation of toxic materials

Sub-themes: Ecosystems, Interdependence and competition

Learning objective	Learning outcomes		
	Developing	Secure	Extending
Describe what is meant by the interdependence of organisms	Name some ways in which organisms depend on each other to survive	**Describe what is meant by the interdependence of organisms**	Use specific examples to explain why organisms are interdependent on each other
Suggest and justify how the change in population of one organism affects the population of another within a food web	List the food chains within a food web	**Suggest and justify how the change in population of one organism affects the population of another within a food web**	Suggest and explain the effect of a population change of one organism on a range of other organisms within a food web
Describe how toxic materials can accumulate in a food chain	Describe how the number of animals changes as you move through a food chain	**Describe how toxic materials can accumulate in a food chain**	Explain how bioaccumulation can lead to human health problems

Tier 2 vocabulary	Tier 3 vocabulary	SB in-text question answers
consumer, depend, interdependence, pollination, population, predator, prey, producer	bioaccumulation, food web, insecticides	**A** Bees and flowers/crops/named plant **B** It decreases **C** Build-up of chemicals inside organisms in a food chain

Lesson plan

Reactivate knowledge

1 What is a food web?
2 What is the first type of organism found in a food web?
3 What happens during pollination?

Lesson resources

Activity: *Factors affecting food chains and webs* (student sheet, teacher and technician sheet, support sheet)

Answers: 1 A series of linked food chains 2 Producer 3 Pollen is transferred from the anther to the stigma

Trigger interest

Ask students to think about how a bee and a flower depend on each other to survive (flower for pollination, bee for nectar). Then ask students to produce a list of other factors that organisms depend on each other for (e.g., shelter, food, mates). Use these discussions to introduce the concept of interdependence.

Exposition of main content (part 1)

Introduce the term 'population'. Ask students to think about a population of rabbits in a field. State a number of situations such as disease, a bumper crop, fire, foxes, new fencing. Ask students to raise their hands if the population increases and to point them to the floor if the population decreases.

Show students the food web in Figure 2 from the Student Book. Start by naming a few animals and ask what they eat. Then discuss what would happen to the numbers of different consumers if the grass died. Do the same for vole and thrush numbers if the caterpillar population decreased. Repeat this activity for other organisms until students have a good grasp of the concept. For each scenario, ask students to suggest what will happen to the population numbers, and to explain their reasoning for this.

Activity: Factors affecting food chains and webs (10–15 mins) Ask students to complete Task 1 on the activity sheet. They answer questions about the interdependence of organisms in a food web.

Exposition of main content (part 2)

Show students the **Animation: Bioaccumulation** to introduce the build-up of toxic chemicals in a food chain.

Activity: Factors affecting food chains and webs (10 mins) Ask students to complete Task 2 on the activity sheet. They rearrange a series of statements to describe the process of bioaccumulation of insecticides in otters. They then write a definition of bioaccumulation.

Review and reflect

Show students the food chain from Figure 3 of the Student Book, which illustrates the bioaccumulation of insecticides in polar bears. In pairs, ask students to write a description of bioaccumulation using this example.

Homework

Ask students to produce a poster to explain to farmers how the use of pesticides could lead to the unintended death of fish-eating birds, such as herons.

For support, provide students with a food chain illustrating the concept for them to describe.

3.3 Ecosystems

Theme: Ecosystems and environment
Biology NC link
- the interdependence of organisms in an ecosystem, including food webs and insect-pollinated crops

Sub-theme: Ecosystems
Working scientifically NC links
- apply sampling techniques
- interpret observations and data, including identifying patterns

Learning objective	Learning outcomes		
	Developing	Secure	Extending
Define the terms habitat, community, and ecosystem	Give an example of a habitat, and the plants and animals that live there	**Define the terms habitat, community, and ecosystem**	Describe the levels of organisation within a named ecosystem
Describe how different organisms co-exist within an ecosystem	Name some organisms that co-exist within a familiar ecosystem	**Describe how different organisms co-exist within an ecosystem**	Explain why different organisms within an ecosystem have different niches

Tier 2 vocabulary	Tier 3 vocabulary	SB in-text question answers
co-exist, community, compete, decomposer, depend, ecosystem, environment, habitat, location, niche, particular	microorganism, quadrat, transect line	**A** Forest **B** Any three named animals or oak tree, for example, bees, sparrows, earthworms **C** They have different food sources

Lesson plan

Reactivate knowledge

1 What is a population?
2 Name two things organisms depend on each other for.
3 What is the role of decomposers?

Lesson resources

Activity: *Investigating plant distribution* (student sheet, teacher and technician sheet, support sheet)

Answers: 1 The number of a particular type of plant/animal in an area **2** Food/shelter/mates/pollination **3** They break down dead plant and animal material

62

B2 **Chapter 3:** Ecosystems and adaptation

Trigger interest

Show students the image of the coral reef ecosystem in Figure 1 from the Student Book. Ask them to list the organisms present (explain that this is the community) and to describe the habitat (this is a term with which they should be familiar from KS2). Then explain that the term 'ecosystem' refers to both the community and the habitat found in an area.

Exposition of main content

Use the image of the oak tree ecosystem in Figure 3 from the Student Book. Ask students to describe the habitat and name some organisms present in the community.

Discuss how organisms can co-exist, because they fulfil different niches, by using the information in the Student Book. Look at the organisms present in different layers of the tree, and also within a layer.

Main activity

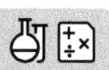

Show students a quadrat. Ask: *What do you think it is?* Talk about how sampling techniques are used to estimate the number of plants in a field, because the number within a whole field could not easily be counted. Explain to students that they will only be counting plants that lie completely within the quadrat. (If time allows, ask students to complete the maths box to estimate the number of daisies in a garden.)

Practical: Investigating plant distribution (30–35 mins) Students use sampling techniques to measure the abundance of a named plant on the school field (e.g., dandelions), and record their observations. Students then return to the classroom to answer the questions on their practical sheets.

Review and reflect

Ask students to write definitions of the terms habitat, community, and ecosystem on their mini-whiteboards, and then to show them.

Homework

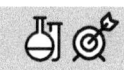

Ask students to research an ecosystem. They should produce an image of their chosen ecosystem, and select a number of different organisms within the ecosystem. Finally, they should write a short explanation on how the selected organisms are able to live together within the ecosystem.

3.4 Competition

Theme: Ecosystems and environment
Biology NC link
- the variation between species and between individuals of the same species meaning some organisms compete more successfully

Sub-theme: Ecosystems
Working scientifically NC link
- interpret observations and data, including identifying patterns and using observations and data to draw conclusions

Learning objective	Learning outcomes		
	Developing	Secure	Extending
Explain the resources that plants and animals compete for	Give some resources that plants and animals compete for	**Explain the resources that plants and animals compete for**	Compare the resources that plants and animals compete for
Describe the interaction between predator and prey populations	State what is meant by predator and prey organisms	**Describe the interaction between predator and prey populations**	Explain the interaction between predator and prey populations

Tier 2 vocabulary	Tier 3 vocabulary
competition, interdependence, photosynthesis, population, predator, prey, resources	

SB in-text question answers

A Food, water, space, and mates **B** Light, water, space, and minerals **C** Food

Lesson plan

Reactivate knowledge

1 What is a predator?
2 What is a prey organism?
3 What does interdependence mean?

Lesson resources

Activity: *Predator–prey relationships* (student sheet, teacher and technician sheet, support sheet)

Answers: 1 An animal that eats another animal **2** An animal that gets eaten by another animal **3** When one organism depend on another to survive

B2 Chapter 3: Ecosystems and adaptation

Trigger interest

Show students the photo in Figure 1 from the Student Book of birds fighting over food. Ask: *What are the birds competing for? What else do animals compete for?*

Exposition of main content

Ask students to make a list of what plants compete for. Share students' ideas to compose a class list. Discuss how this differs to what animals compete for.

Discuss the interdependence of predator and prey populations. Then use the graph in Figure 2 from the Student Book, showing the relationship between lynx and hare populations, to introduce the patterns shown on predator–prey graphs. Break the graph down into sections and ensure students understand what is happening to both populations at each stage. They should realise that the trendlines follow the same pattern, but with a time lag.

Main activity

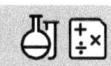

Activity: Predator–prey relationships (20–25 mins)
Students plot a graph to show the number of Canadian wolves in Quebec between 2001 and 2009. This graph is drawn on top of an existing graph, showing the number of caribou in the same period. Students then interpret the graphs to answer the questions that follow.

Review and reflect

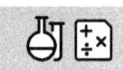

On a mini-whiteboard, ask students to sketch a predator–prey graph to show the interdependence between populations of zebra and cheetah. Encourage students to use different colours to represent the populations (or represent one population as a dashed line).

Describe certain situations – for example, a rise in the predator population. Ask students to point to where this is being represented on the graph.

Homework

Ask students to produce a Venn diagram to compare the similarities and differences between the factors plants and animals compete for.

They should then write a sentence to explain the differences.

3.5 Adapting to change

Theme: Ecosystems and environment

Sub-themes: Adaptation, Interdependence and competition

Biology NC link

- changes in the environment may leave individuals within a species, and some entire species, less well adapted to compete successfully and reproduce, which in turn may lead to extinction

Learning objective	Learning outcomes		
	Developing	Secure	Extending
Describe how organisms are adapted to their environment	Identify some adaptations of organisms that help them to survive	**Describe how organisms are adapted to their environment**	Explain how organisms are adapted to their environment
Describe how organisms adapt to environmental changes	Describe some seasonal changes that take place throughout the year	**Describe how organisms adapt to environmental changes**	Use examples to explain how organisms adapt to environmental changes

Tier 2 vocabulary	Tier 3 vocabulary	SB in-text question answers
camouflage, competition, habitat, hibernation, maximise, migration, predator, seasons, survival	adaptation, surface area	**A** Any two from: large body heats up slowly/does not sweat/moves around at night (when cooler) to feed/concentrated urine/dry faeces **B** Widespread root systems **C** Hibernation, migration, grow thicker fur

Lesson plan

Reactivate knowledge

1 What do animals compete for?
2 What do plants compete for?
3 What is an adaptation?

Answers: 1 Food, water, space, mates **2** Light, water, space, minerals **3** Special features (that allow a cell to perform its function). Explain that the term 'adaptation' refers to any special characteristics a cell or organism may have

Lesson resources

Activity: *Climate change and polar bears* (student sheet, teacher and technician sheet, support sheet)

B2 Chapter 3: Ecosystems and adaptation

Trigger interest

Ask students to work in small groups to design the best-adapted predator or prey organism. This predator/prey can be real or imaginary, but a drawing of the organism must be accompanied by annotations of its adaptations. Students should then compare their organisms. Some adaptations are likely to be features of all organisms, such as good eyesight, being fast, and camouflage. This task will allow you to assess the level of knowledge students already have on adaptations from the work they covered in KS2.

If further explanation/examples are needed, discuss with students how the cactus and oryx are adapted using Figure 2, Figure 3, and information in the Student Book.

Exposition of main content

Introduce the concept that some plant species are adapted to changes in the seasons. Ask students to produce a timeline of the changes that take place in deciduous trees throughout the year, and how this is linked to seasonal changes.

Ask students to produce a list of ways animals are adapted to changing seasons using named examples of organisms. If needed, prompt students by giving them a list of organisms to discuss such as bears (hibernate), swallows (migrate), or squirrels (hide acorns). Then share students' ideas.

Main activity

Activity: Climate change and polar bears (20 mins)
Students read an article about environmental changes in the Arctic, and the effects of these changes on polar bears and their population. They then answer the questions that follow.

Review and reflect

Show students the two images of the snowshoe hare in Figure 4 from the Student Book. Ask them to explain how it is adapted to seasonal changes.

Homework

Students produce an ecosystems crossword to cover all the key terms in this chapter, such as competition, adaptation, interdependence, and population.

B2 Chapter 3: Ecosystems and adaptation

Introduction to checkpoint intervention

This checkpoint intervention provides suggestions for a lesson to follow up the B2 3 Ecosystems and adaptation checkpoint assessment. Depending on the outcomes of the assessment, these suggestions could move a class towards secure, to target specific learning outcomes, or to consolidate knowledge for students achieving secure outcomes. Use students' outcomes from the checkpoint assessment to address general misconceptions from the content covered. Be prepared to re-cover content as required; three key concepts from the chapter are covered in more detail below.

Checkpoint secure learning outcomes

- Describe the feeding relationships between organisms in a food chain.
- Describe what is meant by the interdependence of organisms.
- Suggest and justify how a population change of one organism affects the population of another within a food web.
- Describe how toxic materials can accumulate in a food chain.
- Give the definitions of habitat, community, and ecosystem.
- Explain the resources that plants and animals compete for.
- Describe how organisms are adapted to their environment.

Student Reflection

Encourage students to reflect on whether there were any checkpoint questions they found difficult or straightforward, as well as their preparation for the checkpoint assessment, including how they revised, the time spent on revision, and what areas they could improve on. For more strategies, see the Metacognition chapter or the Metacognition in Key Stage 3 Science guide on Kerboodle.

Intervention activity: Describe the feeding relationships between organisms in a food chain

There are lots of key terms associated with feeding relationships. This activity is designed to repeatedly practise using these terms to aid recall. It can also ensure students are drawing arrows in the food chain in the correct directions, thus avoiding a common error.

Describing the feeding relationships between organisms in a food chain

Provide students with cards on which they write the terms: producer, herbivore, carnivore (×2), consumer (×3), prey (×2), predator (×2). Discuss the terms and check students are clear on their meanings.

Write the names of a number of plants and animals on the board. Students use these to produce a range of food chains on a piece of paper. They then add to each organism in their food chain all the cards showing terms that can be associated with them. For example, a lamb, which feeds on grass, would have the cards herbivore and consumer linked to it. If a fox is then added to the food chain, the term prey can also be added to the lamb. Once complete, students should explain the feeding relationships in their chain to their partner.

B2 Chapter 3: Ecosystems and adaptation

Intervention activity: Explain the resources that plants and animals compete for

Most students can name resources that plants and animals compete for. However, they do not necessarily develop their answers to explain why this happens. This activity helps students master this skill.

Explain the resources organisms compete for

Provide students with the question: Explain **two** resources animals compete for. (4 marks)

Explain that the question is asking the student to:

- identify two resources that animals compete for (there are more than two resources, but naming more will gain no further marks)
- explain why the named resources animals compete for are essential for the survival of the population.

Model how the information should be included in their answer, using one resource. For example, space (1 mark) is essential for animals to hunt for food/for shelter for protection from the weather. (1 mark)

Ask students to then complete the same question for resources plants compete for. For support, students could refer to the information in the topic spreads for B2 3.4 Competition.

Intervention activity: Suggest and justify how a population change of one organism affects the population of another within a food web

When looking at the interactions between organisms in a food web, students often do not consider a range of outcomes. This activity is designed to look at all the possible outcomes that could arise from a change in the population of one organism.

Studying the effect of a change in one population on another

Provide students with a copy of the food web shown in the topic spreads for B2 3.1 Food chains and webs. Tell the students that the impala population has been killed off by a disease. They should put a cross through the impala. They should circle every organism that the impala feeds on in blue. The population of these organisms is likely to increase because they are being eaten less. Therefore, they will survive longer to grow and reproduce. Students should then circle every organism that directly feeds on the impala in red. The population of these organisms is likely to go down because they will have less food to eat. This means some organisms may starve and die. Depending on the ability of the class, students could then be asked what may happen to the lion population (now they know that the cheetah and leopard populations may go down).

Students should then repeat the task without help using a different food web.

B2 Chapter 4: Inheritance

Introduction to chapter

In this chapter, students will look at the variation in characteristics in organisms within a species and determine whether these are a result of inherited variation, environmental variation, or both. They will categorise characteristics as showing discontinuous or continuous variation and will plot this on appropriate graphs. Students will then study how characteristics are inherited through chromosomes. The final section in the chapter looks at evolution through the process of natural selection, why some organisms become extinct, and the role gene banks can play in trying to prevent extinction.

Core concepts in chapter

- Variation (genetic and environmental)
- Natural selection

Prerequisite knowledge

- Recognise that living things have changed over time and that fossils provide information about living things that inhabited the Earth millions of years ago (KS2)
- Recognise that living things produce offspring of the same kind, but normally offspring vary and are not identical to their parents (KS2)
- The functions of the cell wall, cell membrane, cytoplasm, nucleus, vacuole, mitochondria and chloroplasts
- Reproduction in humans including gametes and fertilisation
- Adaptations of organisms to their environment

GCSE links

- The genome, and how its interaction with the environment influences the development of the phenotype of an organism
- Single gene inheritance and single gene crosses with dominant and recessive phenotypes
- Sex determination in humans
- Genetic variation in populations of a species
- The process of natural selection leading to evolution
- The evidence for evolution
- The importance of selective breeding and modern biotechnology of plants and animals in agriculture

Key learning misconceptions

- Evolution happens in individuals rather than populations over time
- Characteristics are all caused by genetics
- When organisms are no longer found in one area of the world, they have become extinct
- Species are organisms that can reproduce, for example, a donkey and a horse are the same species
- The theory of evolution encompasses how life began
- 'Survival of the fittest' relates to strength and dominance between individual organisms
- Modern humans have stopped evolving
- Evolution and natural selection are the same thing

B2 Chapter 4: Inheritance

Misconception

Individual organisms evolve To help dispel this misconception, students could be shown the work of Lamarck. He thought giraffes stretched to reach leaves and therefore their necks evolved to get longer. These longer necks were then passed onto the next generation. We now know that changes to an organism's characteristics during their lifetime do not cause changes in their gametes and so cannot be passed on to the next generation.

Misconception

Evolution and natural selection are the same thing Ensure that students are clear on the distinction between evolution and natural selection. Evolution is a gradual change in the inherited traits of a population over many generations, whereas natural selection is the mechanism which drives evolution – members of a population best suited to their environment have the best chance of surviving to pass on their genes (survival of the fittest).

Working scientifically/maths skill

Differences between a histogram and a bar chart This is likely to be the first time that students have met histograms. You may wish to introduce this skill by showing a bar chart and a histogram next to each other, and then discuss how they differ. In a histogram, there are no gaps between the bars, the bars must be arranged on a continuous scale along the axis, bars are plotted against frequency density, and the bars represent a range of values (the bars may also be different widths if the selected class widths are not equal). Whereas in a bar chart, there are gaps between the bars, the bars can be in any order, the bars are plotted against frequency, the bars are always the same width, and the bars usually represent single values.

Working scientifically / maths skill

Plotting continuous variation This description uses height as an example, but you could use any continuous variable, for example, foot length (which could then be compared with shoe size, showing discontinuous variation).

Ask students to organise themselves from smallest to tallest. How do they think they could plot these data? Prompt them to think about organising people into groups of different heights. Measure the smallest and the tallest person, then use these as a guide to produce groups (as this is the first time students have met this skill it is best to keep class widths the same). If you have a large whiteboard, mark the top of each class boundary on the board from left to right so the width of the board represents the *x*-axis and the height of the board the *y*-axis. If the sample is large enough you should find more students standing in the middle groups. This can be compared with the graph in the SB.

Represent the class data using the following data table:

Height in cm	Tally	Frequency	Class width	Frequency density
$120 \leq h < 124$				
$125 \leq h < 129$				

Record the students' height as a tally, then a total frequency. Explain how to calculate class width (largest value – smallest value). Then introduce how to calculate frequency density using the formula:

$$\text{Frequency density} = \frac{\text{Frequency}}{\text{Class width}}$$

Finally, plot the class width against frequency density to produce a histogram.

4.1 Variation

Theme: Variation and evolution

Sub-themes: Classification systems, Variation

Biology NC link
- differences between species

Learning objective	Learning outcomes		
	Developing	Secure	Extending
Give the definition of variation	Give some ways that organisms of the same species are different from each other	**Give the definition of variation**	Suggest why identical twins look very similar, but not exactly the same
Use examples to describe the difference between inherited and environmental variation	Name some human characteristics that are inherited, and some that are affected by the environment	**Use examples to describe the difference between inherited and environmental variation**	Explain why many characteristics are affected both by the environment and through inheritance

Tier 2 vocabulary	Tier 3 vocabulary	SB in-text question answers
characteristic, difference, identical	environmental variation, inherited variation, organism, species, variation	**A** Any three relevant examples of variation, for example, height, colour of fur, straight or wavy hair **B** A group of organisms that can reproduce to produce fertile offspring **C** Eye colour, blood group, lobed or lobe-less ears **D** Piercings, scars, dyed hair

Lesson plan

Reactivate knowledge

1. What process produces new offspring?
2. What are the male sex cells?
3. What are the female sex cells?

Answers: **1** Reproduction **2** Sperm cells **3** Egg cells

Lesson resources

Activity: *Types of variation* (activity sheet, teacher and technician sheet, support sheet)

B2 Chapter 4: Inheritance

Trigger interest

Show students the photo of dogs from the Student Book. Allow two minutes for students to make a list of the differences between the dogs.

Introduce the fact that differences in characteristics between organisms are known as variation.

Exposition of main content

Variation within and between species Show students the image of the goldfish and the lizard. Ask: *How do they differ in characteristics?* Then show them the image of several goldfish. Ask: *How do these differ in characteristics?* Students should find it easy to identify variation between different species, but harder to identify variation within a species because they share many of the same characteristics. Introduce students to the definition of a species: organisms that can reproduce to produce fertile offspring. You may wish to use the example of a donkey being crossed with a horse to form an infertile mule to illustrate the misconception that different species are organisms that cannot mate.

Types of variation Use the diagram of students in Figure 2 of the Student Book to discuss some variations in human characteristics. Students should be aware that some characteristics are passed on from their parents, but may have thought less about the effect of the environment. Can they pick out examples from the diagram of characteristics that show inherited variation (eye colour, blood group)? They may select height. Explain that this is a characteristic that is affected by both the genetic material they inherit from their parents and their environment in terms of their diet. The example of environmental variation on the diagram is language spoken, but ask students to think of others. The image of dyed hair in Figure 4 of the Student Book could be used as a prompt. Students will then complete the Venn diagram and questions on the activity sheet.

Main activity

Activity: Types of variation (20 mins)
In pairs, students perform a card sort to identify whether a characteristic shows variation as a result of inheritance, the environment, or both. They then record their answers in a Venn diagram, before answering the questions that follow.

Review and reflect

Provide students with three colours of card (e.g., red for inherited, green for the environment, and blue for both). Read out a list of characteristics.

Students hold up the appropriate card to describe the type of variation the characteristic shows.

Homework

Provide students with a list of four pet animals. For example, two different dogs (e.g., a Labrador and a Yorkshire terrier), a rabbit, and a goldfish. Ask students to list as many variations between the animals as possible, classify the variations, and then suggest possible causes.

Extend the task by asking students to use their list to explain why the two dogs are from the same species, but rabbits, dogs, and goldfish are different species.

4.2 Continuous and discontinuous

Theme: Variation and evolution
Biology NC link
- the variation between individuals within a species being continuous or discontinuous, to include measurement and graphical representation of variation

Sub-theme: Variation
Working scientifically NC link
- present observations and data using appropriate methods, including tables and graphs

	Learning outcomes		
Learning objective	**Developing**	**Secure**	**Extending**
Use examples to describe the difference between continuous and discontinuous variation	State what is meant by continuous and discontinuous data	Use examples to describe the difference between continuous and discontinuous variation	Explain why some characteristics that are measured numerically (e.g., shoe size) show discontinuous variation
Choose and justify the most appropriate graph to display examples of variation data	Name the type of graph used to display continuous and discontinuous data	Choose and justify the most appropriate graph to display examples of variation data	Explain why variation in characteristics caused only as a result of inheritance is usually plotted on a bar chart

Tier 2 vocabulary	Tier 3 vocabulary	SB in-text question answers
characteristic, value	continuous variation, discontinuous variation, environmental variation, inherited variation, variation	**A** Sex, blood group, eye colour **B** Height, body mass, and arm span **C** Bar chart **D** Histogram, often with a line added

Lesson plan

Reactivate knowledge

1. What is variation?
2. What is inherited variation?
3. What is environmental variation?

Lesson resources

Activity: *Investigating arm span* (practical sheet, teacher and technician sheet, support sheet)

Answers: 1 Differences in characteristics within a species **2** Variation due to the characteristics/genetic material inherited from their parents **3** Variation caused by a person's surroundings and lifestyle

B2 Chapter 4: Inheritance

Trigger interest

Ask students to organise themselves into groups depending on different types of variation. For example: sex, whether they can roll their tongue, eye colour. Then ask students to organise themselves by height.

Discuss that some characteristics, such as sex, result in certain values. This is discontinuous variation. Other characteristics, such as height, can take any value within a range. This is continuous variation.

Exposition of main content

Plotting discontinuous variation Use the blood group bar chart in Figure 1 of the Student Book to explain that discontinuous data are always plotted on a bar chart, because the data always result in certain values. Parallels can be drawn to discrete data in maths if students are familiar with this. Discuss that 'inherited only' characteristics tend to show discontinuous variation.

Plotting continuous variation Use height as an example for how they can display continuous data. Ask: *How could you plot the heights in your class?* Prompt students to think about organising people into groups of different heights (this could be done practically if time allows). Show them the tally chart. Point out key features, such as organising heights into class widths and writing them in order from smallest to largest. Note that as this is the first time histograms have been met in science, the class widths are the same size in the Student Book and in the practical.

Show how the data are represented within the tally chart: a height h of any value between x (lowest value) and y (highest value) is written: $x \leq h < y$. The class width can then be calculated from $y - x$.

Pick some height values and ask students to decide in which category the data would fit. Work through the example of how to calculate frequency density. Ask students to calculate one or two examples on the remainder of the chart.

Show students the height histogram in Figure 2 of the Student Book. Point out the key ways a histogram differs from a bar chart (e.g., no gaps between the bars, bars need to be in a specific order). Point out the trends shown in the graph (e.g., few very tall/short people, most people being of 'average' height). Discuss that characteristics that occur as a result of inheritance and the environment tend to show continuous variation.

Main activity

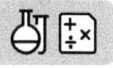

Practical: Investigating arm span (30 mins)
Students work in small groups to measure the arm spans of students within their own group. The class results are collated on a tally chart (using group sizes of fixed width). Students then plot a histogram to show the class results for arm span, and answer the questions that follow.

Review and reflect

Call out different types of continuous variation (e.g., hair length) and discontinuous variation (e.g., tongue-rolling) for students to decide on the correct type of variation using mini-whiteboards. Students should also identify the type of graph needed to display the results.

Homework

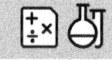

During the lesson, draw a tally chart on the board with a list for eye colour. Ask students to add their eye colour to the tally during the course of the lesson. At the end of the lesson, ask students to copy the tally, and then prepare a suitable graph to display the results for homework.

Students should state the type of variation this is, and describe any conclusions they can draw from the graph.

4.3 Inheritance

Theme: Genetics and inheritance

Biology NC links
- heredity as the process by which genetic information is transmitted from one generation to the next
- a simple model of chromosomes, genes, and DNA in heredity, including the part played by Watson, Crick, Wilkins, and Franklin in the development of the DNA model

Sub-theme: Inheritance and DNA structure

Working scientifically NC links
- use models and analogies as a way of understanding things
- evaluate the effectiveness of a model

Learning outcomes

Learning objective	Developing	Secure	Extending
Give the definitions of DNA, chromosome, and gene	State where genetic material is found within a cell	**Give the definitions of DNA, chromosome, and gene**	Describe the relationship between DNA, chromosomes, and genes (e.g., genes are sections of DNA on a chromosome)
Describe how characteristics are inherited	Describe the role of sperm and egg cells in fertilisation	**Describe how characteristics are inherited**	Explain why siblings appear similar, but not the same
Describe how scientists worked together to develop the DNA model	Identify some of the scientists involved in the development of the DNA model	**Describe how scientists worked together to develop the DNA model**	Explain the importance of collaborative working in scientific discoveries

Tier 2 vocabulary	Tier 3 vocabulary	SB in-text question answers
characteristic, helix, inherit, model	chromosome, DNA, egg cell, gene, nucleus, sperm cell	**A** Chemical that contains all the information needed to make an organism **B** A long strand of DNA **C** A section of DNA that contains the information to produce a characteristic **D** 46

Lesson plan

Reactivate knowledge

1. What cell component contains genetic material?
2. What happens during fertilisation?
3. What type of variation is shown in characteristics gained from your parents?

Answers: 1 Nucleus 2 Egg and sperm nuclei join together 3 Inherited variation

Lesson resources

Activity: *Building a model nucleus* (activity sheet, teacher and technician sheet, support sheet)

B2 Chapter 4: Inheritance

Trigger interest

Show students the image of the family in the Lesson presentation. Ask them to list what features each child inherited from which parent. What features do the children share?

Use this to explain that the children have inherited some characteristics from each of their parents. Brothers and sisters do not look completely the same because they each inherit a different mixture of characteristics.

Exposition of main content – Part 1

Show the Animation: *Inheritance*, which introduces students to how characteristics are passed on from parents to their offspring through chromosomes.

Use the diagrams in Figure 1 of the Student Book to recap what DNA, genes, and chromosomes are, and how genetic material is passed on from a parent to its offspring.

Main activity

Activity: Making a model nucleus (25 mins)
Students use the materials provided to create representations of a nucleus containing chromosomes and genes. Each structure in the model should be labelled using the cocktail sticks. Students then evaluate their finished models, before answering the questions that follow.

Exposition of main content – Part 2

Show the image of DNA from the Student Book. Ask students to suggest what it might be (DNA), and how the image may have been produced (using X-rays).

Use the information in the Student Book to introduce how Watson, Crick, Franklin, and Wilkins worked together to develop the model of DNA. Students should then complete the task in the Working scientifically box.

Review and reflect

Show students the statements on DNA. Ask students to identify whether the statements are true or false.

They should then correct the statements that are false.

Homework

Students write a multipart exam-style question, including the mark scheme, on inheritance or the development of the DNA model.

4.4 Natural selection

Theme: Variation and evolution

Biology NC links
- the variation between species and between individuals of the same species meaning some organisms compete more successfully, which can drive natural selection
- changes in the environment which may leave individuals within a species, and some entire species, less well adapted to compete successfully and reproduce, which in turn may lead to extinction

Sub-theme: Evolution, extinction, and the fossil record

Learning outcomes

Learning objective	Developing	Secure	Extending
Describe the role of the fossil record as evidence for evolution	State what is meant by the term evolution	**Describe the role of the fossil record as evidence for evolution**	Suggest why some species that once lived are not present in the fossil record
Describe the process of natural selection	Describe what is meant by an adaptation	**Describe the process of natural selection**	Use a named species to illustrate the process of natural selection (e.g., peppered moths)
Describe how new species evolve through the process of natural selection	Define what is meant by a species	**Describe how new species evolve through the process of natural selection**	Explain why environmental change can lead to the evolution of new species

Tier 2 vocabulary	Tier 3 vocabulary
bacteria, camouflage, characteristic, evolution, gradually, successful	adaptation, bacteria, evolution, fossil, gene, natural selection, species, unicellular

SB in-text question answers
A The process of species gradually developing/changing over time **B** The remains of plants or animals that lived a long time ago, which have changed to stone **C** Organisms with the characteristics that are most suited to the environment survive and reproduce; less well adapted organisms die

B2 Chapter 4: Inheritance

Lesson plan

Reactivate knowledge

1. How do we know that dinosaurs used to exist?
2. What are adaptations?
3. Why are many animals camouflaged?

Lesson resources

Activity: *Natural selection* (activity sheet, teacher and technician sheet, support sheet)

Answers: 1 Through fossils **2** Characteristics that enable an organism to survive **3** To blend in with their environment so they can't be seen

Trigger interest

Show images of how a mobile phone has changed over time. Ask students to discuss how and why it has changed. (To suit our lifestyle and demands.)

Use this analogy when you talk about the evolution of organisms – a gradual change in a named plant or animal species over time. Address the misconception that an individual organism itself adapts.

Exposition of main content

Fossils Show the class fossils or images of fossils from the Internet. Ideally, include images of gradual changes in fossil records. Ask students to state what is being shown, to explain what they are made from, and what scientists can deduce from the fossil record.

Natural selection Use the flow diagram in Figure 2 of the Student Book to introduce the process of natural selection. Then illustrate the process using the example of the peppered moth as described in the Student Book. (Note that a new species is not created, because the moths can still reproduce to produce fertile offspring. However, the frequency of the different forms of the moth in the species dramatically changes through natural selection.)

Main activity

Activity: Natural selection (20 mins)
In pairs, students play the Limpet Game, which represents the process of natural selection in action. They then answer the questions that follow.

Review and reflect

Students write a few sentences to explain what the image in the Lesson presentation shows. They should include the terms 'evolution' and 'natural selection'.

Homework

Students select an animal of their choice. They carry out research to write a description of how this animal has evolved over time.

4.5 Extinction

Themes: Biodiversity and human interactions with the environment, Variation and evolution

Sub-themes: Biodiversity, Evolution, extinction, and the fossil record, Variation

Biology NC links

- changes in the environment which may leave individuals within a species, and some entire species, less well adapted to compete successfully and reproduce, which in turn may lead to extinction
- the importance of maintaining biodiversity and the use of gene banks to preserve hereditary material

Working scientifically NC link

- understand that scientific methods and theories develop as earlier explanations are modified to take account of new evidence and ideas, together with the importance of publishing results and peer review

	Learning outcomes		
Learning objective	**Developing**	**Secure**	**Extending**
Describe some factors that may lead to extinction	State what is meant by the terms endangered and extinct	**Describe some factors that may lead to extinction**	Explain how changes to a species' environment can lead to extinction
Describe how gene banks can be used to prevent the extinction of a species	State what is meant by biodiversity	**Describe how gene banks can be used to prevent the extinction of a species**	Justify the importance of gene banks in maintaining biodiversity

Tier 2 vocabulary	Tier 3 vocabulary
biodiversity, endangered, extinct, research	fossil, gene bank, species

SB in-text question answers

A An extinct species is one that has completely died out; no new organism can be created
B Any three from: changes to the organism's environment, destruction of habitat, outbreak of a new disease, introduction of new predators and competitors **C** Dinosaur, dodo **D** Any three from: seeds, buds, pollen, embryo, sperm cells, egg cells

Lesson plan

Reactivate knowledge

1. What is a fossil?
2. What is the name of the process by which species evolve?
3. Name three things animals compete for.

Answers: 1 Remains, or traces, of plants or animals **2** Natural selection **3** Space/shelter/mates/food/water

Lesson resources

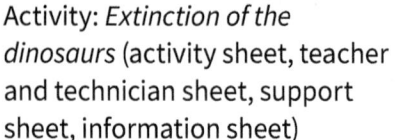

Activity: *Extinction of the dinosaurs* (activity sheet, teacher and technician sheet, support sheet, information sheet)

B2 Chapter 4: Inheritance

Trigger interest

Show students images on the board of extinct and endangered animals. For example: Siberian tigers, giant pandas, dinosaurs, and dodos. Ask students to suggest ways to separate these animals into two groups.

Then ask students to suggest definitions for the words 'endangered' and 'extinct'. Make sure students' definitions of extinct refer to organisms of the species being found nowhere in the world, because the term is often used incorrectly in everyday conversation.

Exposition of main content

Extinction Show the Video: *Extinction*. This introduces the difference between endangered and extinct organisms, some of the causes of extinction, and the role of gene banks. Ask students to make a list of some causes of extinction as they watch the video.

Discuss the factors that lead to extinction, and how the loss of a species leads to the reduction of biodiversity in an area. This is directly through the loss of the species itself, and indirectly through the loss of shelter/a food source for another species.

Gene banks Using the information gained from the video, ask students to explain what the term 'gene bank' means. Ask them to give examples of the gene banks available, using the information in the Student Book.

Main activity

Activity: Extinction of the dinosaurs (35 mins)
Students work in groups of three and use a 'home and expert' group format. They read three possible theories to explain the extinction of dinosaurs. They must teach each other about the different theories suggested, decide on the theory that seems most credible, and then answer the questions.

Review and reflect

Ask students to stand up. Read out a series of situations. For example, the arrival of a disease, an abundance of food. Students sit down each time a scenario that increases the risk of extinction is mentioned.

Homework

Students write a paragraph to explain in detail how scientists could have used gene banks to save the dinosaurs.

B2 Chapter 4: Inheritance

Introduction to checkpoint intervention

This checkpoint intervention provides suggestions for a lesson to follow up the B2 4 Inheritance checkpoint assessment. Depending on the outcomes of the assessment, these suggestions could move a class towards secure, to target specific learning outcomes, or to consolidate knowledge for students achieving secure outcomes. Use students' outcomes from the checkpoint assessment to address general misconceptions from the content covered. Be prepared to re-cover content as required; three key concepts from the chapter are covered in more detail below.

Checkpoint secure learning outcomes

- Give the definition of variation.
- Describe the difference between continuous and discontinuous variation using examples.
- Justify the choice of the most appropriate graph to display examples of variation data.
- Describe how characteristics are inherited.
- Describe the process of natural selection.
- Describe some factors that may lead to extinction.

Student reflection

Encourage students to reflect on whether there were any checkpoint questions they found difficult or straightforward, as well as their preparation for the checkpoint assessment, including how they revised, the time spent on revision, and what areas they could improve on. For more strategies, see the Metacognition chapter or the Metacognition in Key Stage 3 Science guide on Kerboodle.

Intervention activity: Describe how characteristics are inherited

Most students are able to state that inherited characteristics are a result of a combination of the genetic material inherited from an offspring's parents. However, their answers are not necessarily detailed enough for a longer answer question.

Modelling how characteristics are inherited

Show students a video clip of an egg cell being fertilised by a sperm and the first few divisions of the fertilised egg. Stop the video at appropriate points to describe each step. For example, comment on the number of chromosomes found in each structure.

Ask students to produce their own cartoonstyle flow diagram, or series of models using modelling clay, showing how characteristics are inherited as a result of fertilisation. They should include a sentence describing each stage on their diagram/model. Explain that each step should be included when answering the question, 'Describe how characteristics are inherited.' For support, students could refer to the diagram in Figure 2 from the topic spread of B2 4.3 Inheritance.

B2 Chapter 4: Inheritance

Intervention activity: Describe the difference between continuous and discontinuous variation using examples

Most students are able to categorise characteristics into those that show variation caused by inheritance, those that show variation caused by the environment, or a combination of both. However, they find it more difficult to categorise characteristics into those that show continuous and discontinuous variation.

Discontinuous and continuous variation

Draw a single line across the width of the board, representing lengths from 10 cm to 30 cm. Ask a number of students to measure their foot length and plot their result on the board. Discuss with students that any value – no matter to how many decimal places – could, in theory, be plotted on the line. Share that length is described as a continuous variable – any value within a range can exist.

Now repeat the activity, but divide the line up into shoe sizes (e.g., size 1 to size 10). Ask a number of students to plot their own shoe size on this line. This time, several students will have the same result – point out that only a specific group of sizes can be plotted. For example, 'size 3.6' does not exist. Discuss that shoe size is described as a discontinuous variable – only specific values within a range exist.

Then provide students with a list of examples of variation for them to classify as continuous or discontinuous variation.

Intervention activity: Describe the process of natural selection

Most students are able to describe the process of natural selection as survival of the fittest. However, they often link this only to survival and not the ability then to go on and reproduce. Weaker descriptions also fail to mention the passing on of genes from one generation to the next.

Main steps in natural selection

When describing the main steps in natural selection, encourage students to structure their answer using bullet points or a flow diagram. To aid this, provide students with the flow diagram from Figure 2 from the topic spread of B2 4.4 Natural selection (or similar) with the elements in the wrong order for them to cut up and rearrange. Then ask students to highlight the key terms they must include in each step. For example, variation and genes would be key terms in box 1.

Then, ask students to answer the examstyle question: Describe the process of natural selection.

(4 marks)

# 2 Chemistry

Introduction to unit

In order to be good global citizens, it is important to be aware of our place in the world and our interaction with it. We can do this by exploring what the Earth is made from, how we can extract useful substances from it, how we can change these substances into more useful ones, and our impact on the environment when we do this. Following on from our introduction to the particle model, this unit develops on the knowledge of how some materials and substances are used and behave. We discuss the differences between metal and non-metal elements and their reactions, we look at some different separation techniques, and we discuss how patterns in behaviours can be used to make useful predictions about substances. Students delve into the study of the Earth and rocks, they describe our impact and effect on the environment, and look at how we can best protect and look after our fascinating world.

Working scientifically links

Each lesson lists the relevant Working scientifically National Curriculum links at the top of the spread. For further details, please refer to the *Oxford Smart Curriculum for Science* document.

Chemistry NC links

- The particulate nature of matter
- Pure and impure substances
- Chemical reactions
- The Periodic Table
- Materials
- Earth and atmosphere

Learning journey

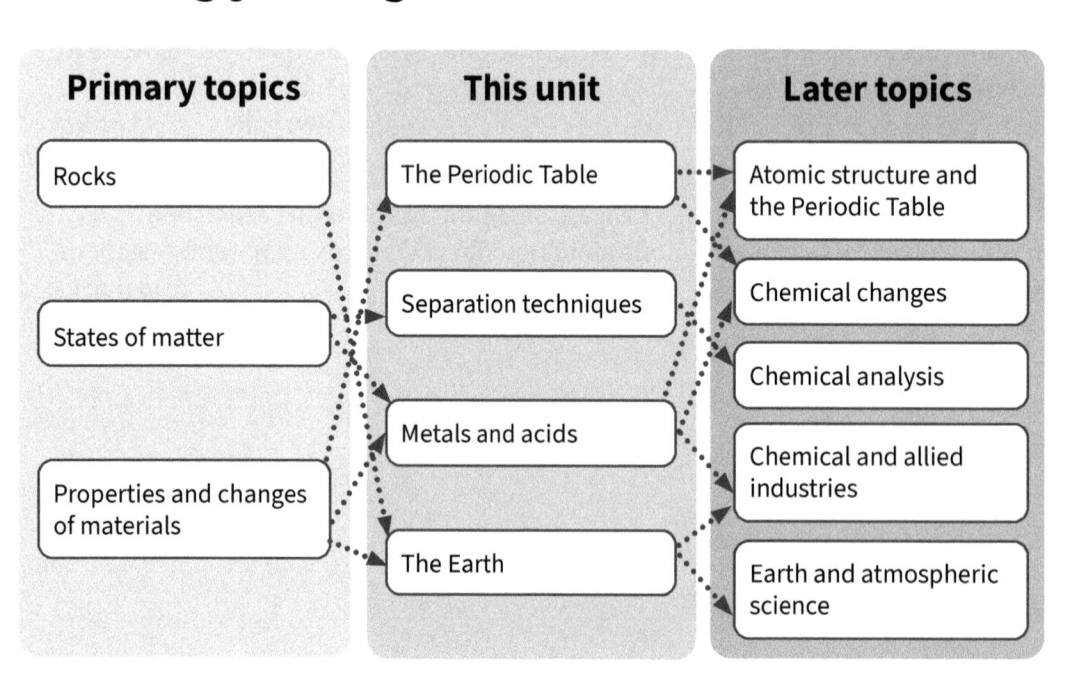

Primary topics
- Rocks
- States of matter
- Properties and changes of materials

This unit
- The Periodic Table
- Separation techniques
- Metals and acids
- The Earth

Later topics
- Atomic structure and the Periodic Table
- Chemical changes
- Chemical analysis
- Chemical and allied industries
- Earth and atmospheric science

2 Chemistry

Chemistry and you

Students often think that chemistry is only useful for people who want to become chemists or work in drug companies, but the skills and knowledge from studying chemistry provide a strong basis for many jobs.

Ask students to suggest why chemistry is useful, what skills they can gain from studying it, and which careers it might be useful for. Discuss that the skills and content learnt in chemistry, such as observation, analysis, evaluation, and problem solving, help to prepare us for many jobs. Discuss how everyone, including CEOs, charity workers, celebrities, parents, farmers, builders, and newsreaders, need these skills, plus a secure understanding of the environment we live in, how matter behaves, and how substances react, to make the most of our world.

Chemistry and the world

Ask students to explain what they know of vaccines, who uses toothpaste, and who has played with paints. Point out that these substances are all mixtures that were made using chemistry. Ask why water is important and whether we can just drink any water. Explain that we need to use chemistry to *make* some mixtures, ans we also use chemistry to separate mixtures, such as clean water, metals from rocks, salt from the sea, and life-saving gases from the air.

We also use chemistry to guide our decisions in everyday life. Students are probably used to seeing information on the internet and social media presented as facts. Discuss how they know whether something they read or are told is true or just made up. Discuss that chemistry skills help us to work this out and make educated, decisions to ensure we look after ourselves.

As global citizens, we need to understand our impact on, and look after, the Earth, in particular tackling the climate crisis. Explain that chemistry can help us understand climate change and global heating, and therefore how best to solve it and its challenges.

Big questions

How do we get the materials we need? Although many of us are used to going to the shops, or ordering online, to buy anything we want, the reality is that the new substances that we need and use have to come from somewhere. They need extracting from the ground, air, or oceans before we can use them.

Ask students where we get the metals used in their smart phones, the building materials for their houses, the fabric used in their clothes, or the rubber for their shoes. Discuss that chemists separate out these materials and often perform chemical reactions with them before they become useful. Explain that eventually we will run out of some materials, so chemists need to devise new ways to recycle substances into new materials.

Can you drink seawater? Students should vote – if they were stranded on a desert island with no drinking water, should they drink the sea water directly from the ocean? Hopefully most would say no or would point out you need to separate the salt from the sea water. Discuss that by using simple separating techniques, such as filtration and evaporation/distillation, you can separate and collect the drinking water.

How can we tackle the climate crisis? Students are probably well versed in the climate crisis but ask them if they know exactly what we need to do to combat it. They may suggest actions that people can take, such as using less energy, recycling, or car sharing, but why do these help to tackle climate change? Explain that we need to reduce the carbon dioxide in the atmosphere, so we need to add less carbon dioxide to the atmosphere, from burning fuels, cattle rearing, respiration, and decomposition, than plants and the oceans remove from it. This will reduce global heating and our climate crisis will end. You could discuss whether the climate crisis is the only environmental issue, and point out that we are also facing challenges with running out of resources including rare earth metals, potable water, and arable land.

C2 Chapter 1: The Periodic Table

Introduction to chapter

In this chapter, students develop their knowledge about elements, learning how to distinguish between metal and non-metal elements. Chemical and physical properties are introduced, and the chemical and physical properties and uses of some typical metals and non-metals, and elements in Group 1, 7, and 0 are explored.

Prerequisite knowledge

- Definitions of the terms atom, element, molecule and compound
- Names and chemical symbols of common elements
- How to name simple compounds such as oxides and sulfates
- How to write chemical formulae, showing the ratio of atoms of each element in a molecule or compound
- The definition of boiling and melting points

GCSE links

- Atomic structure and its link to the reactivity and trends in properties of groups and periods in the Periodic Table
- Further reactions of Groups 1, 7 and 0 in the Periodic Table
- The transition metals and comparing their reactions and properties with the reactions and properties of typical metals

Core concepts

- The meaning of the terms physical and chemical properties
- The uses and physical and chemical properties of typical metals and non-metals
- Groups and periods in the Periodic Table and trends in the properties of elements in Groups or Periods
- Group 1 elements, their physical properties including their melting and boiling points, and trends in the reactivity of Group 1 elements with water
- Group 7 elements, their states and colours at room temperature, their physical properties including trends in boiling and melting points, and trends in the reactivity of Group 7 elements with iron
- Group 0 elements, their physical properties including trends in boiling points, and how the properties of the Group 0 elements make them suitable for their uses

Key learning misconceptions

- You cannot have a molecule of an element
- All molecules are examples of compounds
- Compounds cannot be broken down into their elements
- Compounds display the properties of the elements they contain
- Compounds are mixtures of elements
- All elements exist as single atoms
- Mixtures are the same as compounds
- The numbers in chemical formulae are written as superscripts, for example H^2O
- Every compound has its own symbol
- The majority of chemical elements are non-metals
- The Periodic Table lists elements in order of their mass/weight/density/date of discovery
- All metals are magnetic
- Lithium is black and sodium is white
- There are no non-metallic elements that are conductors of electricity
- All metals behave the same
- All non-metals are gases

C2 Chapter 1: The Periodic Table

Teaching preparation

Broader context

The uses of substances rely heavily on their properties, so it is important that students get used to identifying how the properties of substances make them suitable for their uses. In order to do this, students need to understand the difference between the chemical and physical properties of a substance.

Lots of industries rely heavily on the use of trends in data to predict and make decisions about stocks, products, content, and other vital aspects of business, so it is important the students get used to identifying and using patterns in data.

Typical metals/non-metals

This chapter uses the concept of 'typical metals' and 'typical non-metals' by looking at the properties of Group 1 and Group 7/0 elements. These properties are considered to be the properties of the average/typical metal and non-metal elements, although there are some elements that do not follow these patterns of physical and chemical properties. It is important to use the term 'typical' to allow students to understand this is a model for most, but not all, metals and non-metals, and to help their awareness of the differing properties later on in the course.

1.1 Three elements

Theme: Atomic structure and the particle model

Chemistry NC links
- the varying physical and chemical properties of different elements
- the properties of metals and non-metals

Sub-theme: Elements

Working scientifically NC links
- ask questions and develop a line of enquiry based on observations of the real world, alongside prior knowledge and experience
- present reasoned explanations, including explaining data in relation to predictions and hypotheses

Learning objective	Learning outcomes		
	Developing	Secure	Extending
Describe the properties of three elements	Identify the properties of three elements	**Describe the properties of three elements**	Compare the properties of three elements
Explain how the uses of three elements are determined by their properties	Identify the uses of three elements	**Explain how the uses of three elements are determined by their properties**	Justify how the properties of an unfamiliar element make it suitable for its use

Tier 2 vocabulary	Tier 3 vocabulary
metal, non-metal	

SB in-text question answers

A It is a good conductor of electricity **B** Copper is shiny but sulfur is not; copper is a good conductor of electricity but sulfur does not conduct electricity; copper can be hammered into thin sheets but sulfur is brittle **C** Germanium is shiny but sulfur is not shiny

Lesson plan

Reactivate knowledge

1. What is an element?
2. How many elements are there: about 10, about 100, or about 1000?
3. Explain what the word *property* means in science.

Answers: 1 A substance that cannot be broken down into other substances – one type of atom 2 100 3 Quality of a substance or material that describes its appearance or how it behaves

Lesson resources *(k)*

Activity: *Uses of elements* (student sheet, support sheet, teacher and technician sheet)

Trigger interest

Show students images of useless objects, e.g., chocolate teapot and glass hammer. Ask why they are not suitable for their uses.

Examples to give could be: a chocolate tea pot, glass hammer, waterproof teabag, cement parachute, inflatable dartboard, or lead balloon.

Exposition of main content

Ask students to recall the definition of an element as a substance which cannot be broken down into other substances, and discuss that they are found on the Periodic Table. Recall the factors in the particle model that determine the properties of a material:

- what its particles are like, for example, their shape and size
- how its particles are arranged and separated
- how its particles move
- how strongly its particles hold together

Introduce copper, sulfur, and germanium and show samples of them to the students. Pass the samples around the class and ask students to suggest words they might use to describe the different elements. Write these on the board. Discuss what the term *property* means in science (properties describe what a substance looks like and how it behaves) and ask students to identify which terms on the board are properties of substances. Discuss the properties of copper, sulfur, and germanium, and their uses.

Main activity

Using the Student Book, create a knowledge organiser to summarise the information about the properties and uses of the three elements copper, sulfur, and germanium.

Activity: Uses of elements (20–25 mins) Answer questions on the elements copper, sulfur, and germanium, and explain why their properties make them suitable for these uses.

Review and reflect

Call out a property of copper, sulfur, or germanium and ask students to write on their whiteboard which element(s) it belongs to, and then ask students to explain why that property makes the element suitable for its use.

Homework

Students should find two different useful household objects and list as many properties of those objects as they can, and then explain why those properties make it suitable for their use. Students might need to be directed towards objects to describe, e.g., saucepan, cutlery.

1.2 Physical properties of metals and non-metals

Themes: Bonding and properties of materials, The Periodic Table

Sub-themes: Metals and non-metals, Properties of materials

Chemistry NC links

- the Periodic Table: periods and groups; metals and non-metals
- the properties of metals and non-metals
- the varying physical and chemical properties of different elements

Working scientifically NC links

- use appropriate techniques, apparatus, and materials during fieldwork and laboratory work, paying attention to health and safety
- make and record observations and measurements using a range of methods for different investigations; and evaluate the reliability of methods and suggest possible improvements
- interpret observations and data, including identifying patterns and using observations, measurements and data to draw conclusions

Learning objective	Learning outcomes		
	Developing	Secure	Extending
Use the Periodic Table to determine whether a given element is a metal or non-metal	Identify non-metals and metals on the Periodic Table	**Use the Periodic Table to determine whether a given element is a metal or non-metal**	Suggest why it is useful to be able to determine which elements are metals/non-metals using the Periodic Table
Give the definition of physical properties	Identify the definition of physical properties	**Give the definition of physical properties**	Write the meaning of physical properties, giving some examples
Describe the physical properties of typical metal and non-metal elements	From data presented in tables or bar charts, describe patterns in the properties of elements in groups or periods	**Describe the physical properties of typical metal and non-metal elements**	Compare the physical properties of typical metal and non-metal elements

Tier 2 vocabulary	Tier 3 vocabulary
metalloid, physical property	

SB in-text question answers

A No written answer required **B** Metal **C** Poor conductor of electricity, poor conductor of thermal energy, dull, low density, brittle, not sonorous

C2 Chapter 1: The Periodic Table

Lesson plan

Reactivate knowledge

1. List three metal elements and one non-metal element
2. Write the meaning of *melting point*.
3. The chemical symbol of copper is Cu. Explain what chemical symbols are.

Lesson resources

Activity: *Classifying metals and non-metals* (student sheet, support sheet, teacher and technician sheet)

Answers: 1 For example: metals – copper, silver, gold; non-metal – sulfur **2** Temperature at which a substance changes from the solid to the liquid state **3** The one or two letter code for an element

Trigger interest

Ask students how they know the horse sculpture in Figure 1 in the Student Book is made out of metal.

Discuss any observations they could make to show it is metal.

Exposition of main content

Grouping materials Show students some materials in the room, and on the board, and ask them to come up with as many ways as possible to group the materials. Examples could be by colour, state, metal/non-metal, use, etc.

Periodic Table Show the image of the Periodic Table, ask students to suggest names of elements that they know are metals and elements they know that are not metals. Highlight these on the board. Ask students to suggest if there is a pattern for which elements are metals and which are non-metals. Introduce the stepped line on the Periodic Table as a way of determining which is which.

Main activity

Practical: Classifying metals and non-metals (25–30 mins) Discuss the meaning of physical properties in chemistry (properties you can observe and measure without changing the material), and make a list of common physical properties used to classify materials, (e.g., electrical conductivity, density, ductility). Students then investigate the properties of metals and non-metals to determine typical properties of each, and answer the questions that follow. After the practical, discuss the typical properties of metals and non-metals the class have determined.

Review and reflect

Recalling properties Call out some physical properties of materials. Ask students to write on their white boards whether it is a property of a typical metal or a typical non-metal. Show the Periodic Table on the board again and call out the names of elements. Students should find the element on the Periodic Table and identify if it is a metal or non-metal.

Homework

Students should identify five materials in their house that they believe to be metals or non-metals, and for each write a sentence stating which they believe it to be and describing its physical properties.

1.3 Chemical properties of metals and non-metals

Themes: Bonding and properties of materials, Chemical reactions, The Periodic Table

Sub-themes: Metals and non-metals, Properties of materials, Reactions of metals

Chemistry NC links

- the varying physical and chemical properties of different elements
- the properties of metals and non-metals
- the chemical properties of metal and non-metal oxides with respect to acidity

Working scientifically NC links

- ask questions and develop a line of enquiry based on observations of the real world, alongside prior knowledge and experience
- make and record observations and measurements using a range of methods for different investigations; and evaluate the reliability of methods and suggest possible improvements
- interpret observations and data, including identifying patterns and using observations, measurements and data to draw conclusions

	Learning outcomes		
Learning objective	**Developing**	**Secure**	**Extending**
Give the definition of chemical properties	Identify the definition of chemical properties	**Give the definition of chemical properties**	Explain the difference between physical properties and chemical properties, giving examples
Describe the chemical properties of metals and non-metals	Identify the chemical properties of metals and non-metals	**Describe the chemical properties of metals and non-metals**	Compare the products of the chemical reaction between a metal and oxygen, and a non-metal and oxygen

Tier 2 vocabulary	Tier 3 vocabulary
acid rain, chemical property	

SB in-text question answers

A Less than 7, because nitrogen is a non-metal and most non-metal oxides are acidic **B** Non-metal **C** Chemical – metals react with oxygen to make basic oxides; Physical – e.g, shiny, malleable, ductile, sonorous

C2 Chapter 1: The Periodic Table

Lesson plan

Reactivate knowledge

1. Write the meaning of *compound*.
2. Name the two elements whose atoms are in sulfur dioxide.
3. Copy and complete: The pH of an acidic solution is less than _____.

Lesson resources

Activity: *Chemical properties of metals and non-metals* (student sheet, support sheet, teacher and technician sheet)

Answers: 1 A substance made up of atoms of two or more elements, chemically joined 2 Sulfur, oxygen 3 7

Trigger interest

Show image of coal burning in air – ask students what they can observe in the image that suggests a chemical reaction is occurring (light being given off, a smell being given off, new substances being made, hear crackling, feel heat being given off) and to suggest the reactants (carbon and oxygen) and products (carbon dioxide) of this reaction. This might be a good time to discuss some of the advantages and disadvantages of using coal as a fuel.

Exposition of main content

Introduction to the chemical properties of metals and non-metals: Ask students to suggest the meaning of the term 'chemical properties' in chemistry. The chemical properties of a substance describe its chemical reactions. Ask students to recall where to find metals (on the left) and non-metals (on the right) on the Periodic Table. Ask students to recall the colours that litmus/universal indicator paper will turn in acidic (red/pink) and alkaline (blue/purple) solutions.

Main activity

Practical: Chemical properties of metals and non-metals (30 mins) Demo burning magnesium in oxygen and write the word equation (magnesium + oxygen → magnesium oxide) for this reaction on the board. Demo or show a video of the reaction of sulfur with oxygen, write the equation (sulfur + oxygen → sulfur dioxide) for this reaction on the board, and discuss the reactions of metals and non-metals with oxygen.

Then students blow through a straw into a mixture of limewater and universal indicator (showing non-metal oxides and water make an acidic solution), collect magnesium oxide powder and dissolve in water then add universal indicator/litmus (showing many metal oxides in water make an alkaline solution), and make a note of observations.

Students then answer the questions that follow.

Review and reflect

Call out chemical properties of metal and non-metals and ask students to hold out their left or right hands to symbolise if that chemical property belongs to a typical metal or a typical non-metal.

Homework

Students should create a knowledge organiser that summarises the chemical properties of typical metals and non-metals, including examples and word equations where possible, and write the meaning of the term 'chemical properties'.

1.4 Groups and periods

Theme: The Periodic Table
Chemistry NC links
- the principles underpinning the Mendeleev Periodic Table
- the Periodic Table: periods and groups; metals and non-metals.
- how patterns in reactions can be predicted with reference to the Periodic Table.

Sub-theme: The Periodic Table
Working scientifically NC links
- interpret observations and data, including identifying patterns and using observations, measurements, and data to draw conclusions
- make predictions using scientific knowledge and understanding

Learning objective	Learning outcomes		
	Developing	Secure	Extending
Give the group and period number of an element in the Periodic Table	Give the name of the columns and rows in the Periodic Table	**Give the group number and period number of an element in the Periodic Table**	Compare two given elements' positions in the Periodic Table
From data presented in tables or bar charts, describe patterns in the properties of elements in groups or periods	Identify patterns in properties of elements in groups or periods	**From data presented in tables or bar charts, describe patterns in the properties of elements in groups or periods**	From data presented in tables or bar charts, compare patterns in the properties of elements in groups or periods
Using data, predict the properties of another element in a group or period	Using data, describe a pattern in the properties of elements in a group or period	**Using data, predict the properties of another element in a group or period**	Using data, justify errors in predictions of the properties of another element in a group or period

Tier 2 vocabulary	Tier 3 vocabulary
	group, period

SB in-text question answers
A 4 **B** Melting point increases from top to bottom of the group **C** 5

Lesson plan

Reactivate knowledge

1. Where in the Periodic Table are the non-metal elements?
2. Name two metal elements.
3. What does melting point mean?

Lesson resources

Activity: *Patterns, groups, and periods in the Periodic Table* (student sheet, support sheet, teacher and technician sheet)

Answers: 1 Left of the stepped line 2 For example, copper, gold 3 The temperature at which a substance changes state from the solid to liquid state

C2 Chapter 1: The Periodic Table

Trigger interest

Show Figure 1 in the Student Book of the metal palladium and ask students to predict its physical and chemical properties. Discuss how the position of palladium in the Periodic Table can give us more information about its properties.

Exposition of main content

Layout of the Periodic Table Show an image of the modern Periodic Table on the board and discuss the layout. Introduce the terms groups and periods on the table. Explain how a long time ago, scientists, including one called Mendeleev, built up a wealth of data on elements as they were discovered, and when Mendeleev arranged them in increasing atomic mass he noticed they had similar chemical properties. This grouping of elements with others with similar chemical and physical properties is what led to the layout of the modern Periodic Table.

Patterns in the Periodic Table Discuss how the elements in the groups in the Periodic Table have similar properties, e.g., Group 1 elements all have similar chemical properties while Group 7 elements all have similar properties (to be covered in more detail in later lessons). Show Figures 4 and 5 in the Student Book of the bar charts of melting points going across periods and discuss the trend in melting points across Period 2 and Period 3. Show they follow similar patterns.

Main activity

Activity: Patterns, groups, and periods in the Periodic Table (20–25 mins) Students carry out the task on the activity sheet to group together elements based on things they have in common. Highlight to students that they are practising finding similarities and patterns in groups of elements, not trying to reproduce or rewrite the Periodic Table. Students then identify groups and periods on the Periodic Table, describe the trends in the Periodic Table, and predict properties of elements using given data.

Review and reflect

Call out a group and a period and ask students to identify the element in that position, and vice versa. Then ask students to recall as much as they can about the patterns and trends in the Periodic Table.

Homework

Students write a short paragraph about the structure of the Periodic Table. You may wish to give students key words to include, such as patterns, Mendeleev, metals, non-metals, groups, and periods.

1.5 The elements of Group 1

Themes: Chemical reactions, The Periodic Table

Chemistry NC links

- the varying physical and chemical properties of different elements
- how patterns in reactions can be predicted with reference to the Periodic Table
- the properties of metals and non-metals

Sub-themes: Reactions of Group 1 elements, The Group 1 elements, Understanding chemical reactions

Working scientifically NC links

- make predictions using scientific knowledge and understanding
- make and record observations and measurements using a range of methods for different investigations; and evaluate the reliability of methods and suggest possible improvements
- interpret observations and data, including identifying patterns and using observations, measurements, and data to draw conclusions

	Learning outcomes		
Learning objective	**Developing**	**Secure**	**Extending**
Describe the physical properties of the Group 1 elements	Identify the physical properties of the Group 1 elements.	**Describe the physical properties of the Group 1 elements**	Compare the physical properties of Group 1 elements with those of a typical metal
Using data from tables or bar charts, describe patterns in the melting and boiling points of the Group 1 elements	Using data from a bar chart, identify the pattern in the melting and boiling points of the Group 1 elements	**Using data from tables or bar charts, describe patterns in the melting and boiling points of the Group 1 elements**	From data presented in tables, describe patterns in the melting and boiling points of the Group 1 elements
Use patterns to predict reactions of Group 1 elements with water	Describe the pattern in reactions of the Group 1 elements with water	**Use patterns to predict reactions of Group 1 elements with water**	Use the pattern in the reactions of the Group 1 elements with water to predict the reaction of another group 1 element with water, and justify the answer

Tier 2 vocabulary	Tier 3 vocabulary
reactive	Group 1

SB in-text question answers

A Group 1 elements have low densities, but most other metals have high densities; Group 1 elements have lower melting points than most other metals; Group 1 elements are softer than most other metals **B** From top to bottom of the group, boiling point decreases from 1330 °C (lithium) to 688 °C (rubidium) **C** Hydrogen

C2 Chapter 1: The Periodic Table

Lesson plan

Reactivate knowledge

1. State whether the elements on the left of the Periodic Table are metals or non-metals.
2. List three physical properties of a typical metal.
3. Give one chemical property of a typical metal.

Lesson resources

Activity: *How do Group 1 elements react?* (student sheet, support sheet, teacher and technician sheet)

Answers: 1 Metals **2** Three from: high melting and boiling points, good conductor of electricity/thermal energy, shiny, high density, malleable, ductile, sonorous **3** Reacts with oxygen to make a solid, basic oxide

Trigger interest

Ask students if they have used a smart phone or tablet. Discuss the fact that lithium, a Group 1 element, is found in the batteries of lots of smart phones and tablets, and is incredibly useful to the technology industry. Introduce the fact that the vast majority of the world's lithium can currently be found in the salt flats of South America. Ask students to recall where Group 1 is on the Periodic Table, and whether Group 1 elements are metals or non-metals.

Exposition of main content

Recalling pH values Ask students to recall the pH values for acids, alkalis, and neutral substances (< 7, > 7, and 7 respectively), and to describe the colours seen when universal indicator is added to each (red, blue, and green respectively).

Group 1 Ask students to recall the properties of typical metals and discuss how Group 1 metals are similar in their electricity and heat conduction, and shiny nature when freshly cut. Using Table 1 in the Student Book, discuss that Group 1 metals are also different to other metals in that they have lower melting points and are softer – they can be cut with a knife!

Main activity

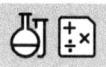

Practical: How do Group 1 elements react? (30 mins)
Discuss the reactivity of Group 1 metals with water, and then demonstrate the reactions of lithium, sodium, and potassium with water. Show the production of the alkaline solution which gives the group its name of the alkali metals. Students record their observations in their results table. Students should discuss and suggest what they would expect to observe from the reactions of rubidium, caesium, and francium, based on the reactivity trends they have observed already. Students then work through the questions that follow.

If time allows, you may want to show clips of water with rubidium and caesium. Note that the Periodic Videos from the University of Nottingham Youtube demonstrate genuine chemical reactions, whereas other videos of the same reactions are often inaccurate or staged.

Review and reflect

Students hold up whiteboards with 'True' and 'False' written on them in response to a statement on the board. Ask students to justify their answers.

Homework

Students write a paragraph detailing all the reasons why Group 1 metals would not be a good choice to make saucepans from. Encourage students to research other reactions of Group 1 metals to justify their answer too.

1.6 The elements of Group 7

Themes: Chemical reactions, The Periodic Table

Chemistry NC links
- the varying physical and chemical properties of different elements
- how patterns in reactions can be predicted with reference to the Periodic Table
- the properties of metals and non-metals

Sub-themes: Reactions of Group 7 elements, The Group 7 elements

Working scientifically NC links
- make and record observations and measurements using a range of methods for different investigations; and evaluate the reliability of methods and suggest possible improvements
- interpret observations and data, including identifying patterns and using observations, measurements, and data to draw conclusions

	Learning outcomes		
Learning objective	**Developing**	**Learning objective**	**Developing**
Describe the physical properties, including colour and states at room temperature, of the Group 7 elements	Identify the colours and states at room temperature of the Group 7 elements	**Describe the physical properties, including colours and states at room temperature, of the Group 7 elements**	Compare the physical properties of the Group 7 elements
Using data from bar charts, describe patterns in the melting and boiling points of the Group 7 elements	Using data from a bar chart, identify the pattern in the melting and boiling points of the Group 7 elements	**Using data from bar charts, describe patterns in the melting and boiling points of the Group 7 elements**	From data presented in tables, describe patterns in the melting and boiling points of the Group 7 elements
Use patterns to predict reactions of Group 7 elements with iron	Describe the pattern in reactions of the Group 7 elements with iron	**Use patterns to predict reactions of Group 7 elements with iron**	Compare the reactions of chlorine and iodine with iron

Tier 2 vocabulary	Tier 3 vocabulary
	Group 7, *halogen*

SB in-text question answers

A Chlorine is pale green, but iodine is grey; chlorine is in the gas state, iodine is a solid **B** Boiling point increases from fluorine (−188 °C) at the top of the group to iodine (184 °C) at the bottom of the group **C** Iron fluoride

C2 Chapter 1: The Periodic Table

Lesson plan

Reactivate knowledge

1. State whether the elements on the right of the Periodic Table are metals or non-metals.
2. List two physical properties of a typical non-metal.
3. Write the names of the elements with these chemical symbols – F, Cl, Br, I.

Answers: 1 Non-metals **2** Two from: low melting and boiling points, poor conductor of electricity/thermal energy; dull in solid state, low density in solid state, brittle, not sonorous **3** Fluorine, chlorine, bromine, iodine

Lesson resources

Activity: *The Group 7 elements* (student sheet, support sheet, teacher and technician sheet)

Trigger interest

Ask students what it is that causes the classic 'swimming pool smell'. Explain it is the addition of small amounts of chlorine and chlorine-containing compounds to the water which kills bacteria, and can make water clean and safe to swim in.

Exposition of main content

Introducing Group 7 Ask students to recall the typical properties of non-metals. Discuss where to find Group 7 on the Periodic Table, the elements in Group 7, and that the Group 7 elements are often called the halogens. Students can write this down in their books.

If possible, show students samples of chlorine, bromine, and iodine in a fume cupboard; otherwise show them on the board. Show how the colours of the Group 7 elements get darker from top to bottom of the group. Ask students to give the states of the three halogens at room temperature.

Main activity

Group 7 elements with iron If there is a fume cupboard available, demo the reaction of iron and chlorine, if not, use videos to compare the reactivity of Group 7 elements (also known as the halogens) down the group. Write the word equation for the reaction of iron and chlorine on the board and ask students to predict the word equation for the reaction of bromine and iodine.

Activity: The Group 7 elements (25–30 mins)
Students use the information on the activity sheet to complete the table describing the properties of the Group 7 elements, and then use this information to complete the questions that follow. Ask students to suggest the best ways to find the information from large blocks of text and how they might complete the information tables.

Review and reflect

Students should create a Plus, Minus, Interesting (PMI) grid for the lesson, detailing a plus, a minus and an interesting point. If time, discuss what went well/badly with their method of finding information from the text, and what they might do differently next time.

Homework

Students should create a knowledge organiser which summarises the physical properties of the Group 7 halogens including the colours, melting points, and states at room temperature, and the word equations for the reactions of the halogens with iron.

1.7 The elements of Group 0

Themes: Chemical reactions, The Periodic Table

Chemistry NC links
- the varying physical and chemical properties of different elements
- how patterns in reactions can be predicted with reference to the Periodic Table
- the properties of metals and non-metals

Sub-themes: The Group 7 elements, Understanding chemical reactions

Working scientifically NC links
- present observations and data using appropriate methods, including tables and graphs
- interpret observations and data, including identifying patterns and using observations, measurements, and data to draw conclusions

Learning outcomes

Learning objective	Developing	Secure	Extending
Describe the physical properties of the Group 0 elements	Identify the physical properties of the Group 0 elements	**Describe the physical properties of the Group 0 elements**	Compare the physical properties of the Group 0 elements with those of the Group 7 elements
From data presented in bar charts, describe patterns in the melting and boiling points of the Group 0 elements	From data presented in bar charts, identify patterns in the melting and boiling points of the Group 0 elements	**From data presented in bar charts, describe patterns in the melting and boiling points of the Group 0 elements**	From data presented in tables, describe patterns in the melting and boiling points of the Group 0 elements
Use patterns to predict properties of Group 0 elements	Describe the properties of the Group 0 elements	**Use patterns to predict properties of Group 0 elements**	Evaluate how the properties of Group 0 make them suitable for unfamiliar uses

Tier 2 vocabulary	Tier 3 vocabulary
unreactive	Group 0, noble gases

SB in-text question answers

A Increases from helium (−269 °C) at the top of the group to xenon (−108 °C) at the bottom of the group **B** A substance is unreactive if it takes part in very few chemical reactions **C** Argon is a better thermal insulator than air

Lesson plan

Reactivate knowledge

1. State whether metals or non-metals have higher boiling points, in general.
2. Write the chemical symbols of these elements – helium, neon, argon, krypton, xenon. Use the Periodic Table on page 240 to help you.

Answers: 1 Metals 2 He, Ne, Ar, Kr, Xe

Lesson resources

Activity: *Trends in the noble gases* (student sheet, support sheet, teacher and technician

Trigger interest

Show students Figures 1, 2 and 3 from the Student Book or the Lesson presentation on the board (double glazed windows, bar code scanner, balloons) and ask them what these things have in common. They all make use of elements from the same group, Group 0, in the Periodic Table. Ask students what they think makes the Group 0 elements suitable for these uses.

Exposition of main content

Introducing Group 0 Discuss where to find Group 0 on the Periodic Table and what the elements in Group 0 are called. Introduce the name 'noble gases' and ask students why they think these elements have that name. Discuss what the students understand noble to mean and how they think the noble gases might behave in reactions with other elements. Students could role play being 'noble people' around others. Introduce the Group 0 elements as inert and unreactive.

Main activity

Activity: Trends in the noble gases (25 mins)
Show students the melting point trends for Group 0 elements on the Lesson presentation and discuss the trends in physical properties and trends in chemical reactivity.

Students should then consider data on the boiling points of the Group 0 elements and use this data to plot a bar graph. Students should then complete the questions that follow on the activity sheet, describing the trends in melting and boiling points, and matching each element to its common use.

Review and reflect

Ask the students to define the terms 'reactive' and 'unreactive' with respect to the Group 1, Group 7, and Group 0 elements, and to recall as many trends in physical and chemical properties as they can from those three groups.

Give an example of a use for one of the Group 0 elements (helium – balloons; argon – in the gap between panes of glass in a double glazed window; neon – in advertising 'neon' signs) and ask students to justify why that element is suitable for that use.

Homework

Students should create a knowledge organiser which summarises the physical properties of the Group 0 elements, the trends in melting and boiling points, and their uses. They should also explain why each Group 0 elements is suitable for its use.

C2 Chapter 1: The Periodic Table

Introduction to checkpoint intervention

This checkpoint intervention provides suggestions for a lesson to follow up the C2 1 The Periodic Table checkpoint assessment. Depending on the outcomes of the assessment, these suggestions can move a class towards secure, to target specific learning outcomes, or to consolidate knowledge for students achieving secure outcomes. Use students' outcomes from the checkpoint assessment to address general misconceptions from the content covered. Be prepared to re-cover content as required; three key concepts from the chapter are covered in more detail below.

Checkpoint secure learning outcomes

- Describe the properties of three elements
- Use the Periodic Table to determine whether a given element is a metal or non-metal
- Describe the chemical properties of metals and non-metals
- Give the group and period number of an element in the Periodic Table
- From data presented in tables or bar charts, describe patterns in the properties of elements in groups or periods
- Use patterns to predict reactions of Group 7 elements with iron

Student reflection

Encourage students to reflect on whether there were any checkpoint questions they found difficult or straightforward, as well as their preparation for the checkpoint assessment, including how they revised, the time spent on revision, and what areas they could improve on. For more strategies, see the Metacognition chapter or the Metacognition in the Key Stage 3 Science guide on Kerboodle.

Intervention activity: Describe the chemical properties of metals and non-metals

Often the biggest challenge in describing the chemical properties of typical metals and non-metals is recalling which properties go with which metals or non-metals. As the majority of chemical elements are metals, and metallic elements are the ones students experience in the solid state most often in real life, students can sometimes assume that properties always belong to metals. This activity is designed to give students practice in determining the true chemical properties of typical metals and non-metals.

Chemical properties

Ask students to recall where to find metals and non-metals on the Periodic Table (metals are on the left of the stepped line, non-metals are on the right), then assign and label one side of the class as 'true' and the other as 'false'. Read out, or show on the board, true and false statements about the chemical properties of typical metals and non-metals (e.g., 'oxides of metals would typically have pH 8 or more' is true, but 'most non-metals react with oxygen to make a basic oxide' is false). Students should decide if they think the statement is true or false, and move to that side of the room. They can stay in the middle of the room if they are unsure, but if they move, they should be able to justify their decision or give an example to back up their choice. Repeat statements that students continue to get wrong and/or change the wording so some statements change from true to false and vice versa to ensure students are confident on which property belongs to which type of element.

C2 Chapter 1: The Periodic Table

Intervention activity: Give the group and period number of an element in the Periodic Table

Students can often get groups and periods the wrong way around (groups are columns, periods are rows), or just call them columns and rows. This activity is designed to give students practice with remembering these terms, as well as which is which.

Giant Periodic Tables

Ask students to recall which are the groups and which are the periods on the Periodic Table. Create the outline of a large Periodic Table (the bigger the better!) on the floor using tape or water-soluble pavement chalk, including the rows and columns. Number the periods (rows) and groups (columns) using the chalk or paper. Take it in turns to ask students to stand where they would find a particular element having given them the group and period numbers of that element. Students can work in teams of three, with one person identifying and standing by the correct group, the next by the correct period, and the third standing where they overlap to find the correct position of the element. Repeat this activity in reverse by placing a student in a box on the Periodic Table on the floor and asking them to identify which group and period they are in. The rest of the class can do this activity at the same time using a paper Periodic Table.

Intervention activity: From data presented in tables or bar charts, describe patterns in the properties of elements in groups or periods

Some students find extracting information from a bar chart harder than from a table, and others are the opposite, so it is useful to practise both. Often students can recognise a pattern in data, especially when it is represented visually, but lose marks in questions because of their phrasing or because their answer is missing the key word(s) necessary to get a mark. Here students can practise using relevant key words and phrases and can attempt to mark answers to help to highlight to them some phrases and key words that examiners are looking for.

Describing patterns in data

Provide students with information about the properties of elements in groups or periods, such as melting points of elements in a group, presented in a table or a bar chart. Ask an exam-style question to go with this data, such as:

Describe the pattern in the melting points of Group X. [2 marks]

Lead the students through how they would answer the exam question, identifying the command word, the pattern shown, and what they need to include to get each of the marks. Highlight key words they should use and phrases that are good to use to gain marks.

Then display three different example answers on the board (including the exemplar one just written) and discuss with the class how many marks the students think each would receive and why. Show a mark scheme and ask students to mark each answer. If needed, this activity can be repeated multiple times with different information displayed in a different way (either a bar chart or a table).

C2 Chapter 2: Separation techniques

In this chapter students learn about pure substances and mixtures, how to determine if a substance is pure, and the differences between the terms solute, solvent, solution, and solubility. They compare mixtures and compounds and learn about different ways to separate the substances in a mixture and when each is appropriate, including filtration, evaporation, distillation, and chromatography. Students develop their skills of representing and analysing data by plotting solubility data and using this to describe how solubility changes with temperature.

Core concepts

- Meaning of pure, mixture, solute, solvent, solution, dissolve, and solubility
- Use a temperature–time melting point graph to determine if a substance is pure
- Compare mixtures and compounds
- Explain dissolving and evaporation using the particle model
- Predict the mass of a solution made from given masses of solute and solvent
- Plot solubility data from data in a table
- Describe how solubility changes with temperature
- Name types of mixtures that can be separated by filtration
- Explain how filtration works
- Explain some uses of filtration
- Describe how to use distillation to separate a solvent from a solution
- Determine whether to use evaporation or distillation to separate a substance from a solution
- Describe how to use chromatography to separate the substances in a mixture
- Use evidence from chromatography to identify unknown substances in mixtures

Prerequisite knowledge

- Definitions of the terms atom, element, molecule, and compound
- The definition of melting and boiling points
- Understanding of three states of matter, and the changing states of matter
- The particle model for the three states of matter

GCSE links

- The bonding and structure of compounds and mixtures
- Determining properties of mixtures
- Separation of substances using filtration, distillation, evaporation, and chromatography

Common learning misconceptions

- All particles are the same
- Particles are all perfect squares
- The particles in a liquid are not touching their nearest neighbours
- Boiling and evaporation are the same thing
- Gases have no mass
- When particles dissolve, they disappear
- A pure substance contains more than one type of particle
- A mixture is just a substance containing more than one element
- Compounds are mixtures of elements
- Compounds display the properties of the elements they contain
- Mixtures are the same as compounds
- Compounds cannot be broken down into their elements

Teaching preparation

Broader context

The use of pure substances and mixtures relies heavily on their properties, so it is important to be able to determine the properties of mixtures, to ensure their correct use.

In lots of industries such as the petrochemical industry, agricultural industry, and food industry, substances are often produced or used in mixtures. So it is necessary to learn how to separate the different substances in a mixture, to ensure the right substance is made and used, and no waste or harmful substances continue down the production line.

Key vocabulary

It is important to use the terms 'substance', and 'sample' or 'mixture', correctly to ensure there are no misconceptions, as these terms are very useful when developing knowledge of bonding, structure, and separating substances. A pure substance has the same chemical make-up throughout, it has fixed proportions, and it cannot be easily separated into the elements that make it up. A mixture is made up of more than one substance – these could be elements or compounds – that are not chemically bonded. Mixtures can be separated relatively easily into their component parts and are not made with fixed proportions of their constituent elements, so the proportions of each substance in a mixture can be easily changed.

Modelling

To support students in their understanding of what happens when separating different substances, the particle model is used. This allows students to visualise an otherwise abstract concept, and makes it easier for students to apply their knowledge and understanding of these processes to new situations. The use of building bricks and/or food stuffs as real-life examples can help students to solidify this abstract concept. As with most models, there are limitations to each model, which can be discussed and highlighted if needed.

2.1 Pure substances

Theme: Chemical analysis
Chemistry NC links
- the concept of a pure substance
- the identification of pure substances

Sub-theme: Identifying substances
Working scientifically NC links
- present observations and data using appropriate methods, including tables and graphs
- interpret observations and data, including identifying patterns and using observations, measurements, and data to draw conclusions

Learning objective	Learning outcomes		
	Developing	Secure	Extending
Give the definition of pure in science	Identify the definition of pure in science	**Give the definition of pure in science**	Compare the meaning of pure in science and in everyday life
Use a temperature–time graph for a melting substance to determine whether it is pure	Identify the melting point of a substance on a temperature–time graph	**Use a temperature–time graph for a melting substance to determine whether it is pure**	Use temperature–time graphs to compare the purity of two different substances

Tier 2 vocabulary	Tier 3 vocabulary

SB in-text question answers

A It has other substances mixed with it **B** It contains more than one substance **C** The middle section of the line is sloped, showing that the sample does not have a fixed melting point

Lesson plan

Reactivate knowledge

1. What is a substance?
2. What is a molecule?
3. Name the apparatus used to measure temperature.

Lesson resources

Activity: *Temperature–time graphs* (student sheet, support sheet, teacher and technician sheet)

Answers: 1 A material that is not a mixture 2 A group of two or more atoms, strongly joined together 3 Thermometer

Chapter 2: Separation techniques

Trigger interest

Ask students if they have ever tasted tap water in other places and thought it tasted different to the tap water they have at home. Show Figure 1 in the Student Book of having a vaccine. Ask students if they have ever had a vaccine. Most students will have been vaccinated when they were younger. Discuss that vaccines contain pure water, but that this is not obtained from taps, as tap water is not pure and contains other substances mixed with it. The substances change depending on where in the country the tap water comes from due to the water processing methods, and hence tap water from different places tastes different.

Exposition of main content

Introducing pure substances Show Figure 3 in the Student Book of pure juice. Explain that the word 'pure' has different meanings in science and everyday life. Scientists do not call juice pure as it contains more than one substance, including water and fructose.

Ask students to recall the meanings of atom, (the smallest part of an element that can exist), element (a substance that cannot be broken down into other substances), compound (a substance made up of atoms of two or more elements with the atoms joined together strongly), and molecule (a group of two or more atoms strongly joined together).

Pure substances Show images of a chocolate bar and a gold bar. Discuss the differences between the chocolate and gold bars, and ask which item they think is pure. Explain that the gold bar is pure because it contains only gold atoms, but the chocolate bar is not pure since it contains multiple substances such as fats, glucose, and cocoa. Tell students that scientists say the chocolate is *impure*.

Temperature–time graphs Show the temperature–time graphs in Figures 5 and 6 in the Student Book for the pure and impure samples, X and Y, of stearic acid and explain they show the temperature of stearic acid taken every minute as it is heated. Discuss the differences between the graphs. Explain that pure stearic acid, sample X, has a fixed melting point, and the temperature stays at 70 °C until all of the solid stearic acid has melted. The impure stearic acid, sample Y, melts between 70 °C and 80 °C. It does not have a fixed melting point. The pure gold has a fixed melting point whereas the impure chocolate also does not – it goes gooey.

Main activity

Activity: Temperature–time graphs (15–20 mins) Students are provided with data for a sample that had been heated for 5 minutes, and the temperature taken every minute. They should plot temperature against time using the provided axes and then answer the questions that follow on the activity sheet.

Review and reflect

'Knowledge of' planning grids As a class, use a 'knowledge of' planning grid to plan the answer to the exam question, 'Explain how you can use melting point data to identify whether a substance is pure or impure, including giving the meaning of those terms'. Discuss what is expected of them in the task, the strategies they might use, and how they feel they would be able to successfully answer the question. Students should then attempt to answer the question in their books.

Homework

Students should create a PMI (Plus, Minus, Interesting) grid in their books detailing something that went well in the lesson, something they struggled with or found more complex, and something they found interesting, to reflect on their learning in this lesson.

2.2 Mixtures

Theme: Atomic structure and the particle model

Chemistry NC link
- mixtures, including dissolving

Sub-theme: Mixtures

Working scientifically NC links
- make and record observations and measurements using a range of methods for different investigations; and evaluate the reliability of methods and suggest possible improvements
- present observations and data using appropriate methods, including tables and graphs

	Learning outcomes		
Learning objective	**Developing**	**Secure**	**Extending**
Give the definition of a mixture	Identify the definition of a mixture	**Give the definition of a mixture**	Give examples of mixtures
Compare mixtures and compounds	Give the definition of a mixture and a compound	**Compare mixtures and compounds**	Compare unfamiliar mixtures and compounds

Tier 2 vocabulary	Tier 3 vocabulary

SB in-text question answers

A Contains two or more substances, which may be elements or compounds, that are not joined together **B** For example: mixture – its substances are not joined together, compound – the atoms of its elements are joined together strongly; mixture – usually easy to separate, compound – need to do chemical reactions to separate into its elements **C** To help stabilise the DNA in the vaccine

Lesson plan

Reactivate knowledge

1. What is a pure substance?
2. What is a compound?
3. What are properties?

Answers: 1 One substance only, with identical particles 2 A substance made up of atoms of two or more elements, with the atoms strongly joined together 3 A substance made up of atoms of two or more elements, with the atoms strongly joined together

Lesson resources

Activity: *Comparing mixtures and compounds* (student sheet, support sheet, teacher and technician sheet)

C2 Chapter 2: Separation techniques

Trigger interest

Show students Figure 1 in the Student Book of bath bombs. Ask students if they have ever used a bath bomb. Ask if they have had things in them, such as glitter, oils, or flower petals. Ask if they know what bath bombs are made of, or if they've ever made them at home.

Exposition of main content

Introducing mixtures Introduce a bath bomb as a mixture. Write the definition of a mixture, as something which contains two or more substances, on the board. Ask students to recall the definition of a compound as a substance made of atoms of two or more elements with the atoms joined strongly together.

Modelling mixtures Combine dried kidney beans and rice in a large beaker. Vary the amount of the beans in the mixture by adding more to the beaker. Explain that the mixture contains two types of particles which are not joined together and therefore can be separated out fairly easily, and that we can easily change the amount of the different particles in the mixture by adding more. Pour the mixture through a colander to separate out the rice and beans.

Main activity

Activity: Comparing mixtures and compounds (30 mins) Discuss the differences between mixtures and compounds. Fill in the table on the board during the demonstration that compares iron, sulfur, iron sulfide, and a mixture of iron and sulfur using a class discussion. Highlight that the compound iron sulfide does not have the same magnetic property as the element iron, but that the iron in the mixture still retains this magnetic property. Show it is relatively easy to separate the iron from the sulfur in the mixture, but not when it is in the compound.

More mixtures Introduce the idea that there are lots of mixtures that occur in nature, such as rocks, sea water, and air. Introduce the AstraZeneca vaccine, which is a mixture, and discuss the use of paint, which is also a mixture. Both mixtures are made up of substances that have different uses in the mixture.

Students should then copy the completed table from the board and complete the questions at the end of the activity sheet.

Review and reflect

Students should read the list of mixtures, compounds, and elements on the board, and then copy all of the elements onto a whiteboard. Discuss and check their answers. They should then write all of the mixtures onto their whiteboard, and finally all of the compounds.

Homework

Ask students to write a list of five mixtures from around the home and local environment. They should also explain how they decided the substances were mixtures.

2.3 Solutions

Theme: Atomic structure and the particle model

Chemistry NC links
- the properties of the different states of matter (solid, liquid and gas) in terms of the particle model, including gas pressure
- mixtures, including dissolving

Sub-theme: Solutions

Working scientifically NC links
- make and record observations and measurements using a range of methods for different investigations; and evaluate the reliability of methods and suggest possible improvements
- apply mathematical concepts and calculate results
- interpret observations and data, including identifying patterns and using observations, measurements, and data to draw conclusions

Learning objective	Learning outcomes		
	Developing	Secure	Extending
Give the definitions of solution, solute, solvent, and dissolve	Identify the definitions of solution, solute, solvent, and dissolve	**Give the definitions of solution, solute, solvent, and dissolve**	Explain the relationship between the terms solute, solvent, solution, and dissolve
Use the particle model to explain dissolving	Describe dissolving	**Use the particle model to explain dissolving**	Use the particle model to explain dissolving in an unfamiliar situation
Predict the mass of a solution made from given masses of solute and solvent	Determine the total mass of solvent and solute present	**Predict the mass of a solution made from given masses of solute and solvent**	Predict the missing mass of a solute or solvent, given the masses of a solution and either the solute or solvent

Tier 2 vocabulary	Tier 3 vocabulary	SB in-text question answers
dissolve, *solution*, solvent	solute	**A** Sugar **B** 90 g + 3 g = 93 g **C** Randomly mixed particles, moving around and sliding over each other

Lesson plan

Reactivate knowledge

1. What is a mixture?
2. How are the particles arranged in a solid?
3. How do the particles move in a liquid?

Answers: 1 Contains two or more substances, whose particles are not joined together **2** Regular pattern **3** Regular pattern

Lesson resources

Activity: *Conservation of mass* (student sheet, support sheet, teacher and technician sheet)

Chapter 2: Separation techniques

Trigger interest

Ask students what happens when a teaspoon of sugar is added to a cup of tea. Where does it go? Discuss that a solution is formed: the sugar dissolves in the tea.

Exposition of main content

Introducing solutions Discuss the meanings of the terms 'solution' (a mixture of a liquid with a solid or gas), 'solute' (the substance that dissolves), 'solvent' (the liquid it dissolves in), and 'dissolving' (the complete mixing of a solute with a solvent). Write these meanings on the board and highlight the differences and the spellings. Show a beaker of water, pour a spatula of sugar into it, and stir. Ask students to identify the solute, solvent, and solution in this example. Discuss that all parts of the solution are the same and the separate substances cannot be seen.

Does the solute disappear when it dissolves? Ask students if the sugar has disappeared when it dissolves in water. Correct the misconception that it does disappear by reminding students that the water would taste sugary, so the sugar particles must still be present, they just can't be seen.

Particle model Explain dissolving using the particle model: show Figures 2, 3, and 4 in the Student Book of sugar in the solid state and water in the liquid state, followed by the image of the sugar water solution. Explain that when sugar dissolves, its particles separate from each other and mix randomly with the water particles. The water particles surround the sugar particles and they all move around, sliding over each other.

Other models Show Figure 5 in the Student Book of the model of a sugar solution using rice and beans. Ask students to identify the solute, solvent, and solution in this model and which aspects of this model are represented by the rice, and which by the beans.

Other solvents Ask students if water is the only solvent. Discuss how nail varnish does not come off in the shower as it is not soluble in water. However, it does come off with nail varnish remover, which is made of propanone, another solvent.

Main activity

Activity: Conservation of mass (25 mins) Demonstrate the conservation of mass by dissolving a known mass of coffee powder in a known mass of water (mass of coffee solution = mass of coffee powder + mass of water). Ask students to identify the solute, solvent, and solution in this example.

Students complete the questions on the activity sheet, including predicting the mass of a solution made from given masses of solute and solvent.

Review and reflect

Write the meanings of the terms 'solute', 'solvent', 'solution', and 'dissolve' on the board. Students write the correct key word for each meaning on mini-whiteboards. Ask students to give examples of the key words from examples used in the lesson.

Homework

Students identify one example of dissolving that happens in the home and draw particle diagrams to illustrate this process. They should also write a description of their observations and identify the solute, solvent, and solution.

2.4 Solubility

Theme: Atomic structure and the particle model

Chemistry NC link
- mixtures, including dissolving

Sub-theme: Solutions

Working scientifically NC links
- make and record observations and measurements using a range of methods for different investigations; and evaluate the reliability of methods and suggest possible improvements
- present observations and data using appropriate methods, including tables and graphs
- interpret observations and data, including identifying patterns and using observations, measurements, and data to draw conclusions

Learning objective	Learning outcomes		
	Developing	**Secure**	**Extending**
Give the definition of solubility	Describe how to make a saturated solution	**Give the definition of *solubility***	Use data to compare the solubility of two different substances
Plot a solubility–temperature graph from data in a table	Describe what a solubility–temperature graph shows	**Plot a solubility–temperature graph from data in a table**	Using data given in a table, plot the solubility–temperature graphs for two different substances and compare them
Describe how solubility changes with temperature for a named substance, given data in a table or line graph	From data given in a table, identify the temperature at which a solute is most soluble	**Describe how solubility changes with temperature for a named substance, given data in a table or line graph**	Using data given in a table or line graph, compare how the solubility of two different substances change with temperature

Tier 2 vocabulary	Tier 3 vocabulary
insoluble, soluble	solubility

SB in-text question answers

A 36 g/100 g of water B Most soluble – lithium chloride; least soluble – sodium chloride
C Increases slightly from 36 g/100 g of water at 20 °C to 39 g/100 g of water at 20 °C

Lesson plan

Reactivate knowledge

1. What is a solution?
2. What is a solute?

Lesson resources

Activity: *How does temperature affect solubility?* (student sheet, support sheet, teacher and technician sheet)

3. What are the units of mass and temperature?

> **Answers: 1** A mixture of a liquid with a solid or gas, in which all parts of the mixture are the same **2** The substance that dissolves in a solution **3** The substance that dissolves in a solution

Trigger interest

Ask students which dissolves better in water, sugar or salt? Discuss ideas for working out which dissolves better.

Exposition of main content

What is solubility? Ask students to recall the meanings of the terms 'solute', 'solvent', 'solution', and 'dissolving'. Give the meaning of the term 'solubility' as the mass of solute that dissolves in 100 g of water to make a saturated solution. Discuss the meaning of saturated solution as a solution which contains the maximum mass of a solute that will dissolve. Discuss briefly how to make a saturated solution.

Comparing solubilities Compare the solubilities of four substances at 20 °C – copper chloride, lithium chloride, magnesium chloride, and sodium chloride – using Figure 3 in the Student Book. Ask students to use the graph to identify which substance is the most soluble.

Insoluble Ask students to give the meaning of the term 'insoluble' and give examples of substances they believe to be insoluble in water. A substance that cannot dissolve in water is insoluble in water, e.g., sand and chalk (calcium carbonate).

Main activity

Activity: How does temperature affect solubility? (25 mins) Ask students to predict if more sugar will dissolve in hot water or in cold water. Discuss the solubility of sugar at different temperatures using the data in the table.

Compare the solubilities of sugar and salt at 20 °C and 100 °C and ask which is more soluble at 20 °C. Discuss that different substances have different solubility patterns as temperature increases. The solubility of salt does not increase very much, but the solubility of sugar increases dramatically in comparison.

Students should plot a graph of the solubility of sugar with temperature and then answer the questions that follow.

Review and reflect

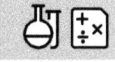

Discuss the solubility graph shown on the board. Call out a substance and ask students to use the graph in Figure 3 of the Student Book to describe the solubility pattern for that substance, using mini-whiteboards.

Homework

Students should create a knowledge organiser that summarises the meanings of the terms solute, solvent, solubility, dissolve, and saturated solution. It should also describe the solubility pattern of sugar in water as the temperature increases.

2.5 Filtration

Theme: Chemical analysis
Chemistry NC links
- mixtures, including dissolving
- simple techniques for separating mixtures: filtration, evaporation, distillation, and chromatography

Sub-theme: Separating mixtures
Working scientifically NC links
- interpret observations and data, including identifying patterns and using observations, measurements, and data to draw conclusions
- present reasoned explanations, including explaining data in relation to predictions and hypotheses

Learning objective	Learning outcomes		
	Developing	Secure	Extending
Name the types of mixtures that can be separated by filtration	Identify the types of mixtures that can be separated by filtration	**Name the types of mixtures that can be separated by filtration**	Give some examples of mixtures that can be separated by filtration
Explain how filtration works	Describe how to use filtration to separate a soluble substance from an insoluble one	**Explain how filtration works**	Suggest advantages and disadvantages of filtration as a separation technique
Explain some uses of filtration	Identify some uses of filtration	**Explain some uses of filtration**	Evaluate the use of filtration as a separation technique in given situations

Tier 2 vocabulary	Tier 3 vocabulary	SB in-text question answers
filter, filtration, residue	filtrate	**A** Two from: insoluble solid from liquid; small pieces of solid from gases; insoluble solid from a solution **B** Filtrate – water; residue – glitter **C** For example: face masks, coffee making, filtering oil, or making water safe to drink

Lesson plan

Reactivate knowledge

1. Name a useful mixture that scientists make.
2. What does *insoluble* mean?
3. What are the three states of matter?

Lesson resources

Practical: *Separating sand and salt* (student sheet, support sheet, teacher and technician sheet)

Answers: 1 For example: paint, vaccines 2 A substance that does not dissolve 3 Solid, liquid, gas

C2 Chapter 2: Separation techniques

Trigger interest

When is filtration used? Explain to students that in laboratories and industry, useful substances usually need to be separated from the substances they are made from or any by-products that are made at the same time. One method of separation used is filtration. Explain that filtration or filtering separates several types of mixtures: it can separate an insoluble solid from a liquid, it can separate an insoluble solid from a solution, and it can separate small pieces of solid from gases.

Exposition of main content

How does filtering work? Ask students to recall the meaning of the term 'mixture' in science as something that contains two or more substances that are not joined together. Show Figure 4 in the Student Book of filtration equipment and introduce it to the students. Explain that we have a mixture of dyed water and glitter and we want to separate them. Demonstrate the filtration of the mixture of glitter and dyed water. Ask students to identify each of the pieces of apparatus in the filtration experiment. Highlight to students that the liquid that passes through the filter is called the filtrate and the content left behind is the residue. Ask students to identify the filtrate and residue in this case: the dyed water is the filtrate and the glitter is the residue.

Filtration model Show students a mixture of dried kidney beans and rice; ask students to explain how they know this is a mixture. Pour the mixture through a colander to separate the rice and beans. Explain this is a model for using filter paper. Ask students to explain this model of filtration: colander = filter paper, kidney beans = residue, and rice = filtrate.

Main activity

Uses of filtration Ask students to recall uses of filtration. Introduce the filter in a car engine, which is made of cotton or wood fibre and traps solid bits of dirt, but allows the liquid oil to pass through, removing the dirt from the oil which would otherwise damage the car engine. Introduce the sand filters in water treatment, which trap bits of dirt but allow the water to flow through, removing the bits of dirt and making water safer to drink.

Practical: Separating sand and salt (25–30 mins)
Students separate salt from a mixture of sand and salt by dissolving the salt and then filtering the mixture. Students must identify the filtrate and residue.

Then answer the questions that follow about filtration.

Review and reflect

Call out the names of pieces of filtration apparatus. Students should draw this apparatus on their mini-whiteboards. Then call out examples of filtration and students identify the filtrate and the residue in each case.

Homework

Students should research four uses of filtration. They should include two examples where the residue is useful and two examples where the filtrate is useful. An explanation of how filtration works is required.

2.6 Evaporation and distillation

Theme: Chemical analysis
Chemistry NC links

- the properties of the different states of matter (solid, liquid and gas) in terms of the particle model, including gas pressure
- changes of state in terms of the particle model
- simple techniques for separating mixtures: filtration, evaporation, distillation, and chromatography

Sub-theme: Separating mixtures
Working scientifically NC links

- make and record observations and measurements using a range of methods for different investigations; and evaluate the reliability of methods and suggest possible improvements
- interpret observations and data, including identifying patterns and using observations, measurements, and data to draw conclusions

Learning objective	Learning outcomes		
	Developing	Secure	Extending
Use the particle model to explain how evaporation works	Describe how to use evaporation to separate the solute from a solution	**Use the particle model to explain how evaporation works**	Use the particle model to explain how evaporation works in unfamiliar situations
Describe how to use distillation to separate mixtures	Label the equipment and set up in a distillation experiment	**Describe how to use distillation to separate mixtures**	Use the particle model to explain how distillation works
Determine whether to use evaporation or distillation to separate a named substance from a solution	Describe the uses of evaporation and distillation	**Determine whether to use evaporation or distillation to separate a named substance from a solution**	Justify whether to use evaporation or distillation to separate a named unfamiliar substance from a solution

Tier 2 vocabulary	Tier 3 vocabulary
distillation	

SB in-text question answers

A Warm the solution. Water will evaporate, leaving salt behind **B** Make crystals from solutions, making glue dry, obtaining lithium from solutions of lithium compounds **C** Evaporating/boiling, condensing

Lesson plan

Reactivate knowledge

1. What is a solution?
2. Name the start and end states for evaporation.
3. Name the change of state when a gas becomes liquid.

Answers: 1 A mixture of a liquid with a solid or gas, in which all parts of the mixture are the same 2 Liquid, gas 3 Condensing

Lesson resources

Practical: *Distillation of salty water* (student sheet, teacher and technician sheet)

C2 Chapter 2: Separation techniques

Trigger interest

Ask students where they think salt is obtained from. Most will probably say the sea/seawater. Ask students to suggest methods for obtaining salt from seawater, and why this might be useful.

Exposition of main content

Evaporation: Show students the set up of the apparatus used for evaporation. Ask students what this is used for and ask them to identify the solute, solvent, and solution before demonstrating the evaporation of salty water. Students should be able to see the presence of small salt crystals. Ask students where the water particles have gone and how to get them back. Use the particle model to explain the process of evaporation: on heating, solvent particles evaporate and leave the surface of the solution. The solute particles remain in the container. Ask students to suggest when evaporation might be useful.

Main activity

Practical: Distillation of salty water (25 mins)
Demonstrate how pure water is extracted from salty water using distillation. Talk through the main steps in distillation: on heating, water in the salt solution boils, forming steam; salt does not boil, because its boiling point is much higher; steam leaves the solution; steam travels through the condenser and cools down; the steam condenses to liquid water; and liquid water drips into the flask. Ask students what the solute (salt), solvent (water), and solution (salty water) are here.

Comparing evaporation and distillation Call out mixtures or solutions and ask students to decide if they would be suitable for separation by evaporation, distillation, or both. Students display their answers using mini-whiteboards. Ask students to justify their answers by explaining the distillation and evaporation processes.

Students add labels to the diagram of the apparatus for distillation and should complete the questions that follow.

Review and reflect

Students should create a PMI (plus, minus, interesting) grid in their books to reflect their learning in this lesson.

Homework

Students write an article for a science magazine, either: describing how to get drinking water from seawater using distillation OR how to get salt from seawater using evaporation.

2.7 Chromatography

Theme: Chemical analysis
Chemistry NC links
- mixtures, including dissolving
- simple techniques for separating mixtures: filtration, evaporation, distillation, and chromatography
- the identification of pure substances

Sub-theme: Separating mixtures
Working scientifically NC links
- use appropriate techniques, apparatus, and materials during fieldwork and laboratory work, paying attention to health and safety
- make and record observations and measurements using a range of methods for different investigations; and evaluate the reliability of methods and suggest possible improvements
- interpret observations and data, including identifying patterns and using observations, measurements, and data to draw conclusions

Learning objective	Learning outcomes		
	Developing	Secure	Extending
Describe how to use chromatography to separate the substances in a mixture	Label the equipment in a chromatography experiment	Describe how to use chromatography to separate the substances in a mixture	Use the particle model to explain how chromatography separates mixtures
Analyse chromatograms to identify substances in mixtures	Use evidence from chromatography to determine how many different substances are contained in a mixture	Analyse chromatograms to identify substances in mixtures	Suggest advantages and disadvantages of using chromatography to identify unknown substances in mixtures

Tier 2 vocabulary	Tier 3 vocabulary	SB in-text question answers
	chromatogram, chromatography	**A** Separates substances in a mixture, if all the substances are soluble in the same solvent **B** Two **C** Orange

Lesson plan

Reactivate knowledge

1. What is a solvent?
2. What is dissolving?
3. What is a mixture?

Answers: 1 In a solution, the liquid that a substance dissolves in **2** The complete mixing of a solute with a solvent **3** Contains two or more substances, whose particles are not joined together

Lesson resources

Practical: *Who stole the money?* (student sheet, support sheet, teacher and technician sheet)

Chapter 2: Separation techniques

Trigger interest

Ask students if they enjoy coloured sugar-coated chocolates. Tell students the coatings of the sweets contain mixtures of dyes. Introduce chromatography as a method of separating mixtures that are soluble in the same solvent.

Exposition of main content

Colours Discuss with students that some coloured dyes are made of a mixture of other colours, usually different to what they may know about colours from art, e.g., black dyes and inks are often a mixture of blue, yellow, and red inks.

Colourful sweets Discuss what you intend to show with the demonstration: how we can separate soluble mixtures with just water. Demonstrate chromatography by placing a sugar-coated chocolate in the middle of a piece of filter paper. Place one drop of water on it very slowly using a pipette. Show students how the dyes in the sugar coating separate out. Discuss that the shell contains a mixture of colours. Some dissolve in the water more easily than others, and they dissolve in the water and travel outwards with the water. Discuss what this method of separation can be used for (separating mixtures of soluble substances) and discuss how chromatography can be useful: analysing different samples to find out what they are made from; comparing amounts of vitamins in different foods; and detecting or comparing identical samples.

Main activity

Practical: Who stole the money? (25 mins) Students carry out a chromatography experiment where they investigate a crime scene to identify a thief who used a forged cheque to steal money from a bank. Students prepare a chromatogram of three suspects' inks and compare their chromatograms to decide who the thief is. Students then complete the questions that follow.

Review and reflect

Students write a short news article or review of the lesson. They should describe how to carry out chromatography and explain how chromatography was used to catch the fraudster.

Homework

Students create a knowledge organiser summarising the different methods of separating mixtures: filtration, evaporation, distillation, and chromatography.

C2 Chapter 2: Separation techniques

Introduction to checkpoint intervention

This checkpoint intervention provides suggestions for a lesson to follow up the C2 2 Separation techniques checkpoint assessment. Depending on the outcomes of the assessment, these suggestions can move a class towards secure, to target specific learning outcomes, or to consolidate knowledge for students achieving secure outcomes. Use students' outcomes from the checkpoint assessment to address general misconceptions from the content covered. Be prepared to re-cover content as required; three key concepts from the chapter are covered in more detail below.

Checkpoint secure learning outcomes

- Use a temperature–time graph for a melting substance to determine whether it is pure
- Give the definitions of solution, solute, solvent, and dissolve
- Use the particle model to explain dissolving
- Predict the mass of a solution made from given masses of solute and solvent
- Explain how filtration works
- Describe how to use distillation to separate mixtures

Student reflection

Encourage students to reflect on whether there were any checkpoint questions they found difficult or straightforward, as well as their preparation for the checkpoint assessment, including how they revised, the time spent on revision, and what areas they could improve on. For more strategies, see the Metacognition chapter or the Metacognition in the Key Stage 3 Science guide on Kerboodle.

Intervention activity: Use the particle model to explain dissolving

A common misconception with dissolving is that particles disappear when they go into solution, and so no longer exist. This can lead to further misconceptions with mass changes and separating substances. Remind students that salt and sugar solutions, made from dissolving salt or sugar in water, still taste salty or sugary and therefore the salt or sugar must still be present in the solution. This activity aims to use a model to show students visually that the solute particles are still present in a solution.

Modelling dissolving

Recall the particle model for substances in the liquid and solid states and recall the arrangement, movement, and separation of particles in these states (particles in solids are arranged in a pattern touching each other and vibrating on the spot; particles in liquids also touch each other, but move randomly, sliding over each other). Divide the class into two: give one half of the students coloured bibs to identify them and ask them to model a substance in the solid state, such as a particle or crystal of sugar. Ask the other half of the students to model a substance in the liquid state next to them, such as water. Address any misconceptions or errors in the models, such as students not touching each other in the liquid state. Ask the students in the solid state to move into and 'dissolve' into the substance in the liquid state and start mixing. Highlight that although the students are dissolved, they are still present in the mixture, and that it would be possible to separate the mixture by removing the particles in the liquid state, leaving the particles in the solid state.

Chapter 2: Separation techniques

Intervention activity: Predict the mass of a solution made from given masses of solute and solvent

Often a big barrier to predicting a mass of a solution from a solute and a solvent, is recalling which substance is which, especially as the terms solute and solvent can easily be confused with each other. Students often believe that a substance no longer has mass when it has dissolved. This activity aims to ensure that students are secure in their knowledge of the dissolving process by demonstrating that the solute is still present in the solution, just not often visible.

Predicting the mass of a solution

Recall the definitions of the terms solute, solvent, and solution (a solute dissolves in a solvent to form a solution), along with the law of conservation of mass. Demonstrate measuring the mass of half a beaker of a solvent (such as water), making a note of the mass on the board, and the mass of a pile of a soluble substance on a weighing boat (such as sugar), also making a note of the mass of this on the board. Ask students to predict the mass of the solution formed when the solute is added to the solvent. Then add the solute to the solvent slowly, showing the mass increasing until all of the solute is added.

This activity can be repeated with varying amounts of different solutes if needed, such as sugar, salt, copper sulfate, etc.

Intervention activity: Describe how to use distillation to separate mixtures

Most students can recognise specific pieces of apparatus and could recognise the equipment set-up for a distillation experiment. However, often they will forget the order of steps needed, or forget the key words and phrases needed to describe distillation. This activity aims to support students in understanding distillation by recapping the types of mixtures that can be separated using this process.

Describing distillation

Provide the students with this exam-style question:

Describe how pure water can be obtained from sea water, using distillation. [4 marks]

Discuss why rain doesn't taste salty, and how it is only pure water that evaporates into the clouds as salt has very high melting and boiling points. Recap the names and functions of the equipment needed for a distillation experiment.

Show a diagram of the distillation apparatus needed on the board. At various points in the equipment, ask students to suggest which substances would be present and what state they would be in.

For example:

- in the round-bottomed flask – a mixture of aqueous salt and water in the liquid state, and steam (water in the gas state) above the mixture
- inside the condenser – water in the gas state and water in the liquid state dripping down into the collection vessel
- in the outside (jacket) of the condenser – water in the liquid state
- in the collection vessel – water in the liquid state
- there is no salt anywhere else in the apparatus, just in the round-bottomed flask.

Discuss how the substances move between states and highlight key words and phrases that students should be using by writing them on the board. Students can then write answers to the exam-style question.

If needed, ask students to repeat the task using the exam-style question:

Describe how pure water can be obtained from inky water, using distillation. [4 marks]

C2 Chapter 3: Metals and other materials

In this chapter students learn about the reactions of metals with acids, with oxygen, and with water, and write word equations for these reactions. They describe the reactivity series and use this to predict the reactivity of metals with acids, with oxygen, and with water. Displacement reactions are explored, including the displacement reaction between a metal compound and carbon as a method for extracting the metal from its ore. Students look at the properties of ceramics, some polymers, and some composites, and explain how the properties of these materials make them suitable for their uses.

Pre-requisite knowledge

- The position of metals on the Periodic Table
- Definitions of the terms atom, material, substance, element, and compound
- The meanings of the terms reactant and product
- Some changes cannot be reversed as new substances are made
- Materials are made of particles

GCSE links

- Writing chemical formulae
- Preparing salt from a metal carbonate or oxide
- How substances react
- Different types of chemical reactions
- Writing ionic equations
- Reactions of acids and reactions of metals
- REDOX reactions
- The bonding and structure of compounds and mixtures
- Determining properties of substances
- Extraction of metals
- Typical properties of transition metals vs Group 1 metals
- Group 7 displacement reactions

Core concepts

- Reactions of metals with acids, oxygen, and water
- Word equations for the reactions of metals with acids, oxygen, and water
- Comparing the pattern of reactivity of metals with acids, oxygen, and water
- Describing the reactivity series
- Using the reactivity series to predict reactivity of metals with acids, with oxygen, and with water
- Explaining displacement reactions and when they do/do not occur
- Extracting metals from their ores, including when carbon can be used
- Calculating the mass of metal in an ore
- Describing the properties of ceramics
- Explaining the properties of some polymers
- Explaining the properties of some composites
- Explaining how the properties of ceramics, polymers, and composites make them suitable for their uses

C2 Chapter 3: Metals and other materials

Key learning misconceptions

- Mixtures are the same as compounds
- A substance contains more than one type of material
- The majority of chemical elements are non-metals
- Rusting is not a chemical reaction
- All metals rust
- Air (oxygen) or water are required for iron to rust
- Displacement reactions only occur between metals and metal oxides (or between metals and metal salt solutions)
- Salts are all chlorides
- The reaction of a metal plus acid gives a salt plus water
- Metals 'fight' each other in displacement reactions
- Aluminium has many outdoor uses, so must be an unreactive metal
- Carbon is a metal as it is in the reactivity series
- Composite materials are compounds, so have different properties to their component materials
- All metals react the same

Teaching preparation

Broader context

Materials react all the time. Not only do chemists need to make new substances, but industries such as the food sector use chemical reactions every day. Understanding what occurs, why, and when can help students to understand these different industries. This chapter also looks at some common materials and their properties. Understanding how a material behaves or reacts allows us to use it safely and to its full capacity.

Modelling

Using 'general reactions' to model the reactions between substances can help students to learn reactions quicker. However, students do need to be confident about what the terms 'acid'/'metal'/'salt' etc. mean for this to be useful.

When explaining displacement reactions, it can be tempting to use analogies about 'fighting' or 'strong' vs 'weak' metals. However, this can introduce misconceptions that atoms fight or have inherent 'strengths' unrelated to the metal's physical properties. It is better to just use the reactivity of the metal, linked to the reactivity series, to explain displacement reactions.

Key learning misconception

It might be worth clarifying that rusting only refers to the formation of iron (III) oxide (the 'III' is an oxidation number; at KS3, students need only be familiar with 'iron oxide'), and that other metals corrode.

There is the possibility that students could get confused about composites being chemically bonded compounds, rather than mixtures. Mixtures, such as composite materials, retain the properties of the substances which make them up, whereas the properties of compounds are different to the properties of the elements whose atoms are in it.

3.1 Metals and acids

Theme: Chemical reactions

Chemistry NC links

- reactions of acids with metals to produce a salt plus hydrogen
- representing chemical reactions using formulae and using equations
- how patterns in reactions can be predicted with reference to the Periodic Table

Sub-themes: Reactions of acids, Reactions of metals

Working scientifically NC links

- use appropriate techniques, apparatus, and materials during fieldwork and laboratory work, paying attention to health and safety
- make and record observations and measurements using a range of methods for different investigations; and evaluate the reliability of methods and suggest possible improvements
- present observations and data using appropriate methods, including tables and graphs

	Learning outcomes		
Learning objective	**Developing**	**Secure**	**Extending**
Use a pattern to predict the products of the reaction of a metal with an acid	Identify the pattern in the products of the reaction of a metal with an acid	**Use a pattern to predict the products of the reaction of a metal with an acid**	Predict the products of the reaction of a metal with an acid
Write a word equation for the reaction of a metal with an acid, given the names of the reactants and products	Identify the word equation for the reaction of a metal with an acid, given the names of the reactants and products	**Write a word equation for the reaction of a metal with an acid, given the names of the reactants and products**	Write a word equation for the reaction of a metal with an acid

Tier 2 vocabulary	Tier 3 vocabulary
acid, alkali	

SB in-text question answers
A Iron chloride, hydrogen **B** 2
C Zinc + sulfuric acid → zinc sulfate + hydrogen

Lesson plan

Reactivate knowledge

1. Where are metals in the Periodic Table?
2. List three physical properties of a typical metal.
3. What is a salt?

Lesson resources

Practical: *Reacting metals with acids* (student sheet, support sheet, teacher and technician sheet)

Answers: 1 Left of the stepped line 2 For example, shiny when cut, good conductor of electricity, good conductor of thermal energy 3 A compound that forms when an acid reacts with a metal element or metal-containing compound

Chapter 3: Metals and other materials

Trigger interest

Show the image of the ill hyena from the Lesson presentation and explain that the zookeepers did an X-ray and found 20 zinc coins in its stomach. Explain that the zinc coins had reacted with the stomach acid (hydrochloric acid) to produce zinc chloride and hydrogen. Write the word equation for this reaction on the board:

zinc + hydrochloric acid → zinc chloride + hydrogen

Explain that zinc chloride dissolves in water and can travel around in the blood, causing zinc poisoning.

Ask students to recall signs that a chemical reaction is occurring, such as light, sound, smell, or heat being given off or new substances being made.

Exposition of main content

Introducing the reaction of metals with acids Show a strip of magnesium ribbon and a test tube containing dilute hydrochloric acid. Students predict if the two will react. Add the magnesium to the test tube, wait 10 seconds, then place an empty test tube over the mouth of the test tube containing the acid to fill the upturned test tube with hydrogen gas (this may take 1 minute). Ask students to make observations about the reaction. Discuss the observations and whether they think their prediction was correct. Explain that this reaction produces magnesium chloride and hydrogen gas. Show that it is hydrogen gas produced by performing the hydrogen pop test (With the gas-filled test tube still upside down, move it away from the reaction and – keeping fingers and faces away from the open end – place a lit splint near to its mouth. There should be a squeaky pop as the hydrogen combusts rapidly.) Write the word equation for the reaction on the board:

magnesium + hydrochloric acid → magnesium chloride + hydrogen

Ask students to determine the products (magnesium chloride + hydrogen) and the reactants (magnesium + hydrochloric acid) in this equation.

What happens with other acids? Introduce the idea that the reactions of metals with an acid produce a salt (e.g., magnesium chloride) and hydrogen. Explain that some metals react more vigorously with acids than others, and some don't react at all, such as gold.

Which salt? Remind students that hydrochloric acid makes chloride salts, sulfuric acid makes sulfate salts, and nitric acid makes nitrate salts. Highlight that the spelling of these salts changes from the name of the acid, for example, sulfuric to sulfate.

Main activity

Practical: Reacting metals with acids (20–25 mins)
Students carry out four reactions of metals with hydrochloric acid, and practise testing for hydrogen.

They note down their observations and answer the questions that follow.

Review and reflect

Give the names of the reactants and products in reactions between metals and acids to form metal salts and hydrogen. Ask students to write word equations for these reactions on mini-whiteboards.

Give students the names of a metal and an acid from the lesson and ask them to predict the products of the reaction and write these on their mini-whiteboards.

Homework

Students should create a PMI (plus, minus, interesting) grid in their books detailing something that went well in the lesson, something they struggled with or found more complex, and something they found interesting, to reflect their learning in this lesson.

3.2 Metals and oxygen

Theme: Chemical reactions
Sub-theme: Reactions of metals

Chemistry NC links
- representing chemical reactions using formulae and using equations
- combustion, thermal decomposition, oxidation, and displacement reactions
- reactions of acids with metals to produce a salt plus hydrogen

Working scientifically NC links
- interpret observations and data, including identifying patterns and using observations, measurements, and data to draw conclusions
- use appropriate techniques, apparatus, and materials during fieldwork and laboratory work, paying attention to health and safety
- make and record observations and measurements using a range of methods for different investigations; and evaluate the reliability of methods and suggest possible improvements

Learning objective	Learning outcomes		
	Developing	Secure	Extending
Use a pattern to predict the products of the reaction of a metal with oxygen	Identify the pattern in the products of the reaction of a metal with oxygen	**Use a pattern to predict the products of the reaction of a metal with oxygen**	Predict the products of the reaction of a metal with oxygen
Write a word equation for the reaction of a metal with oxygen, given the names of the reactants and products	Identify the word equation for the reaction of a metal with an acid, given the names of the reactants and products	**Write a word equation for the reaction of a metal with oxygen, given the names of the reactants and products**	Write a word equation for the reaction of a metal with oxygen
Compare the patterns in the reactivity of metals with acids and with oxygen	Describe how gold and magnesium react with acids and oxygen	**Compare the patterns in the reactivity of metals with acids and with oxygen**	Predict how a metal will react with oxygen, given information about how it reacts with acids

Tier 2 vocabulary	Tier 3 vocabulary
unreactive	

SB in-text question answers
A Magnesium oxide B Iron + oxygen → iron oxide
C Reacts vigorously with oxygen

Lesson plan

Reactivate knowledge

1. What are chemical properties?
2. What does *reactive* mean?
3. Which metal reacts more vigorously with acids – magnesium or iron?

Answers: 1 Properties that describe the chemical reactions of a substance 2 Easily take part in chemical reactions 3 Magnesium

Lesson resources

Practical: *How do metals react with oxygen?* (student sheet, support sheet, teacher and technician sheet)

Chapter 3: Metals and other materials

Trigger interest

Ask students if they have ever seen magnesium burning in oxygen. Ask them what they observed. Explain that magnesium burns vigorously – it reacts with oxygen from the air. The product is magnesium oxide. Show a piece of magnesium ribbon and explain that the duller/grey bits are where the surface atoms of magnesium have reacted with oxygen from the air, forming a thin layer of magnesium oxide.

Exposition of main content

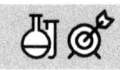

What is happening to these metals? Show students a shiny new iron nail and a rusty iron nail. Show how the shiny iron nail does not instantly become dull. Cut a piece of lithium on a white tile and show the shiny cut surface rapidly becoming dull. Explain that the iron nail reacts more slowly than the lithium, but both metals have reacted with oxygen to form metal oxides. Clarify that rusting requires moisture and only refers to the formation of iron oxide (specifically iron(III) oxide, but referred to as 'iron oxide' at KS3) – other metals corrode. Explain that most metals react with oxygen (without needing moisture) to form metal oxides, but there are differences. Ask students to predict if gold reacts with oxygen in the same way as lithium. Explain that gold does not react easily with oxygen, which is why it stays shiny.

Writing word equations Recall that air is a mixture of oxygen and other gases, and discuss that burning metals react with the oxygen in the air. Demonstrate the reaction of iron filings burning in oxygen by sprinkling them over a tilted Bunsen flame. Ask students to identify the reactants (iron and oxygen) and product (iron oxide) in this reaction. Recall the use of the word ending '-ide' when naming compounds containing only two elements. Write the word equation for this reaction on the board:

$$\text{iron} + \text{oxygen} \rightarrow \text{iron oxide}$$

Main activity

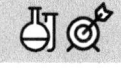

Practical: How do metals react with oxygen? (25–30 mins) Demonstrate the reactions of magnesium and calcium burning in oxygen to produce magnesium and calcium oxides respectively. Do not look directly at burning magnesium or burning calcium. Students should then carry out the reactions of iron wool and copper with oxygen using a Bunsen flame and record their observations.

Comparing patterns of reactivity Recall the vigorous reactions of magnesium with a dilute acid and oxygen. Discuss that gold is unreactive: it does not react with dilute acids, oxygen, or other substances. Discuss the relative reactivities of some metals with oxygen and dilute acids using the table. Show the relationship between the reactivities: metals that react vigorously with dilute acids also react vigorously with oxygen.

Students then answer the questions that follow on the practical sheet.

Review and reflect

Give the names of the reactants and products in reactions between metals and oxygen to form metal oxides, and ask students to write word equations for these reactions on mini-whiteboards. Give students the name of a metal from the lesson and ask them to predict the product of the reaction with oxygen and write these on their mini-whiteboards.

Ask students to compare the reactivities of elements with either oxygen or acids.

Homework

Students write a paragraph to explain why some metals lose their shine over time, but why gold does not. Students should include some examples of metals that lose their shine.

3.3 The reactivity series

Theme: Chemical reactions

Chemistry NC links

- combustion, thermal decomposition, oxidation, and displacement reactions
- the order of metals and carbon in the reactivity series
- how patterns in reactions can be predicted with reference to the Periodic Table

Sub-themes: Reactions of metals, Reactivity series

Working scientifically NC links

- ask questions and develop a line of enquiry based on observations of the real world, alongside prior knowledge and experience
- make and record observations and measurements using a range of methods for different investigations; and evaluate the reliability of methods and suggest possible improvements
- interpret observations and data, including identifying patterns and using observations, measurements, and data to draw conclusions

	Learning outcomes		
Learning objective	**Developing**	**Secure**	**Extending**
Use a pattern to predict the products of the reaction of a metal with water	Identify the pattern in the reactions of metals with water	Use a pattern to predict the products of the reaction of a metal with water	Predict the products of the reaction of a metal with water
Write a word equation for the reaction of a metal with water, given the names of the reactants and products	Identify the word equation for the reaction of a metal with water, given the names of the reactants and products	Write a word equation for the reaction of a metal with water, given the names of the reactants and products	Write the word equation for the reaction of a metal with water
Use the reactivity series to predict how vigorously metals react with acids, oxygen, and water	Write the meaning of the reactivity series	Use the reactivity series to predict reactions	Using reactivity data given, predict where a metal sits in the reactivity series

Tier 2 vocabulary	Tier 3 vocabulary
	reactivity series

SB in-text question answers

A Calcium hydroxide and hydrogen
B Lithium + water → lithium hydroxide + hydrogen **C** Calcium

Lesson plan

Reactivate knowledge

1 Name a reactive metal and an unreactive metal.
2 What is the product of the reaction of zinc and oxygen?
3 Name three metals in Group 1 of the Periodic Table.

Lesson resources

Activity: *The reactivity series* (student sheet, support sheet, teacher and technician sheet)

Answers: 1 Reactive metal – for example: potassium, sodium, lithium, calcium, magnesium; unreactive metal – for example: gold, copper 2 Zinc oxide 3 Three from: lithium, sodium, potassium, rubidium, caesium

C2 Chapter 3: Metals and other materials

Trigger interest

Ask students to look at the metals around them and decide if they react with water: stainless steel taps do not, nor stainless steel cutlery, gold jewellery, or copper pipes. Recall the reactions of lithium, sodium, and potassium with water. Discuss that some metals do react with water, and others do not.

Exposition of main content

How do different metals react with water?
Demonstrate (or show a video of) the (vigorous) reaction of calcium with water and the (too slow to be visible) reaction of magnesium with water. Discuss the differences between the reactions observed. Show that the reaction of calcium and water produces calcium hydroxide (a white substance) and hydrogen (the bubbles that are formed), and write the word equation for this reaction on the board.

The reactivity series Tell students that the patterns of metal reactions with acids, oxygen, and water are similar. Discuss that the reactivity series lists the metals by how vigorously they react with other substances. The metals at the top have vigorous reactions and the metals get less reactive going down the list.

Main activity

Reaction with steam Show students the Royal Society of Chemistry video on Youtube, which shows the reaction of magnesium with water is slow – no visible reaction occurs. However, when magnesium is reacted with steam, there is a reaction that produces magnesium oxide and hydrogen. Write its word equation on the board:

magnesium + water → magnesium oxide + hydrogen

Discuss that copper is not reactive enough to react with water, even if the water is heated to form steam. Discuss that zinc and iron also react with steam to form hydrogen and a metal oxide.

Activity: The reactivity series (25 mins)
Demonstrate (or show videos of) the reactions of the Group 1 metals lithium, sodium, and potassium with water. Write word equations for these reactions on the board, showing that the products are a metal hydroxide and hydrogen. Ask students to make observations about the reactivity of the three Group 1 metals. Compare these reactions with those of steam with iron, zinc, and magnesium. Show that magnesium, iron, and zinc are all less reactive than the Group 1 metals as the water must be heated for them to react.

Students then complete the activity, ordering metals by reactivity based on the descriptions given and their observations from class. Students should use this reactivity series to predict how vigorously metals react with oxygen, dilute acids, and water.

Review and reflect

Give students the name of a metal from the lesson and ask them to predict the products of the reaction with water and write these on their mini-whiteboards.

Ask students to compare the reactivity of elements with either oxygen, acids, or water, and to explain their answer using the reactivity series.

Homework

Students should create a knowledge organiser summarising their learning from the last few lessons, including the reactions of metals with dilute acids, oxygen, and water, and give examples of word equations for these reactions. They should include a unique mnemonic, written by them, to remember the order of metals in the reactivity series.

3.4 Metal displacement reactions

Themes: Applied chemistry, Chemical reactions

Sub-themes: Extraction of metals, Reactions of metals

Chemistry NC links
- the order of metals and carbon in the reactivity series
- how patterns in reactions can be predicted with reference to the Periodic Table
- chemical reactions as the rearrangement of atoms

Working scientifically NC links
- make predictions using scientific knowledge and understanding
- make and record observations and measurements using a range of methods for different investigations; and evaluate the reliability of methods and suggest possible improvements
- interpret observations and data, including identifying patterns and using observations, measurements, and data to draw conclusions
- present reasoned explanations, including explaining data in relation to predictions and hypotheses

Learning objective	Learning outcomes		
	Developing	Secure	Extending
Write the meaning of displacement reaction	Identify the meaning of displacement reaction	**Write the meaning of displacement reaction**	Give examples of displacement reactions
Identify pairs of substances that do, and do not, react in displacement reactions	Use the reactivity series to identify more and less reactive metals	**Identify pairs of substances that do, and do not, react in displacement reactions**	Explain why a pair of substances can, or cannot, react in a displacement reaction
Predict the products of displacement reactions	Identify the products of a metal displacement reaction	**Predict the products of displacement reactions**	Write a word equation for a displacement reaction

Tier 2 vocabulary	Tier 3 vocabulary
displace, displacement	

SB in-text question answers

A A reaction in which a more reactive metal displaces, or pushes out, a less reactive element from its compound
B The metal on its own (copper) is less reactive than the metal in the compound (magnesium)

Lesson plan

Reactivate knowledge

1. What is the reactivity series?
2. Calcium is reactive. Is it near the top or bottom of the reactivity series?
3. In a word equation, what does the arrow mean?

Lesson resources

Practical: *Will a displacement reaction occur?* (student sheet, support sheet, teacher and technician sheet)

Answers: 1 A list of metals in order of how vigorously they react with other substances 2 Top 3 Reacts to make

Chapter 3: Metals and other materials

Trigger interest

Ask students to recall the meanings of the terms element, compound, and mixture. Recall where to find copper in the reactivity series. Ask students where we find copper, a very useful metal, in nature, and how we get it ready to use. Discuss that scientists use chemical reactions to remove copper from its compounds. They add sulfuric acid to the rock, which produces copper sulfate solution, and then add some waste iron to the solution. There is a chemical reaction and copper is produced.

Exposition of main content

Introduction to displacement reactions Set up a boiling tube containing silver nitrate solution and a coil of copper wire. Ask students to make observations about the colours of the metal and the solution. Dangle the copper wire into the silver nitrate solution. Ask students to identify the positions of silver and copper in the reactivity series and compare their reactivities. Explain that in a displacement reaction a more reactive element displaces, or pushes out, a less reactive element from its compound. But if the more reactive metal is already the one in the compound, no reaction takes place. Ask students to predict what they might observe with the more reactive copper as an element, and the less reactive silver as a solution. The more reactive copper will displace – push out – the less reactive silver from its compound, silver nitrate. So the copper will go into solution, as copper nitrate, and the silver will come out of solution, as elemental silver. Write the word equation on the board:

copper + silver nitrate → copper nitrate + silver

Highlight to students that the nitrate bit stays the same and does not take part in the chemical reaction, but the silver and copper swap. The displacement reaction may not occur quickly but will be returned to at the end of the lesson.

Products of a displacement reaction Discuss the thermite reaction, which is the displacement reaction between aluminium and iron oxide. Ask students to identify which is the more reactive metal and to predict if a displacement reaction will occur. Ask students to predict the products of the reaction. Write the equation on the board and show the metals swapping places. The aluminium (the more reactive metal) displaces iron (the less reactive metal) from the compound:

aluminium + iron oxide → aluminium oxide + iron

Thermite is used in welding for railway repairs (videos can be found online) and provide a real life example of displacement reactions.

Main activity

Practical: Will a displacement reaction occur? (25–30 mins) Students use the reactivity series to predict whether displacement reactions will occur between different combinations of four metals (Mg, Zn, Cu, Fe) and their sulfates. Students then carry out a practical combining metals with their sulfates on a spotting tile, record their observations, and answer the questions that follow.

Review and reflect

Look back at the demonstration of the copper wire in the silver nitrate solution. Ask students to describe what they can now see (they should see silver in the solid state on the coiled wire. Ask students to explain in their own words what has happened to the particles and why. Students should use the reactivity series, the word displacement, and a word equation in their explanation.

Homework

Ask the students to draw a cartoon to show and explain what happens during a displacement reaction.

3.5 Extracting metals

Themes: Applied chemistry, Chemical reactions

Sub-themes: Extraction of metals, Reactivity series

Chemistry NC links
- the order of metals and carbon in the reactivity series
- the use of carbon in obtaining metals from metal oxides

Working scientifically NC links
- interpret observations and data, including identifying patterns and using observations, measurements, and data to draw conclusions
- present reasoned explanations, including explaining data in relation to predictions and hypotheses
- use and derive simple equations and carry out appropriate calculations

	Learning outcomes		
Learning objective	**Developing**	**Secure**	**Extending**
Describe the two steps needed to extract a metal from its ore	Identify the two steps needed to extract a metal from its ore	**Describe the two steps needed to extract a metal from its ore**	Describe the two steps needed to extract a metal from its ore, and explain why this is necessary
State which metals in the reactivity series can be extracted by heating their oxides with carbon	Identify which metals in the reactivity series can be extracted by heating their oxides with carbon	**State which metals in the reactivity series can be extracted by heating their oxides with carbon**	Use the reactivity series to predict and justify whether a given metal can be extracted from its oxide by heating with carbon
Calculate the mass of metal in an ore	Identify the mass of metal in an ore	**Calculate the mass of metal in an ore**	Calculate the percentage of metal in an ore

Tier 2 vocabulary	Tier 3 vocabulary	SB in-text question answers
ore		**A** 25% × 20 kg = 5 kg **B** Step 1 **C** Zinc, iron, lead, copper

Lesson plan

Reactivate knowledge

1 What is a displacement reaction?
2 Which is more reactive, iron or zinc? (You may need a reactivity series to answer this.)
3 List three physical properties of metals.

Ask students to recall the meanings of the terms element, compound, and mixture.

Lesson resources

Activity: *Methods of extracting metals* (student sheet, support sheet, teacher and technician sheet)

Answers: 1 A chemical reaction in which a more reactive element displaces, or pushes out, a less reactive element from its compound 2 Zinc 3 For example – good conductor of electricity, good conductor of thermal energy, malleable, ductile

C2 **Chapter 3:** Metals and other materials

Trigger interest

Ask students to give any uses of iron they know. An example is that iron is the main part of steel, which is used in making vehicles, as well as other things. Discuss that iron comes from rocks in the Earth's crust that contain iron compounds, but that other substances, such as gold, can be found as an element. Metals that are found naturally as compounds need to be extracted before they can be used.

Exposition of main content

What is an ore? Ask students if it is worth extracting every atom of metal from rocks – is it energy and cost efficient? Discuss that some rocks that contain metal compounds have very little metal in them and the metal is not worth extracting. Rocks that you can extract metals from, and that contain enough of the metal to make it worth extracting, are called ores.

Introduction to metal extraction Show students a reactivity series with carbon slotted in between aluminium and zinc. Ask students to spot what is wrong with this reactivity series of metals – they should be able to spot that carbon is not a metal. Explain the presence of carbon in this series by introducing the displacement of metals using carbon.

Which metals can be extracted using carbon? Remind students what a displacement reaction is, and discuss that not all metals can be extracted with carbon. As the extraction of a metal with carbon is a displacement reaction, the metal needs to be less reactive than carbon, so carbon can displace (push out) the less reactive metal from its compound. Ask students to predict if aluminium, which is more reactive than carbon, can be extracted from its ore using carbon. Students should decide that it cannot, as aluminium is more reactive than carbon, so will stay in the compound.

Main activity

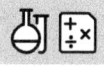

How much metal is in an ore? Recall that different ores contain different amounts of metal. Companies need to calculate the mass of metal in a sample of an ore to decide if the metal is worth extracting. Explain that you need to know the mass of the ore and the percentage of metal in the ore.

$$\text{mass of metal in the ore} = \text{percentage of metal in the ore} \times \text{mass of the ore}$$

Using the example on the Lesson presentation, work through the calculation process with students, calculating the mass of iron in the iron ore.

Activity: Methods of extracting metals (25 mins) Show a demonstration of iron(III) oxide reacting with carbon to produce iron, by rolling a damp non-safety match in sodium carbonate, and then iron(III) oxide, and heating it in a blue Bunsen flame. The resulting crushed product can be shown to be magnetic – iron was produced. Discuss the steps involved in separating a metal from its ore.

Students will then consider an early method for extracting iron by reading an old 'recipe' and applying their understanding of scientific concepts to answer the questions that follow, explaining the steps in iron extraction and calculating the mass of metal in an ore.

Review and reflect

Students should create a PMI (plus, minus, interesting) grid in their books, detailing something that went well in the lesson, something they struggled with or found more complex, and something they found interesting, to reflect on their learning in this lesson.

Homework

Students should create a knowledge organiser summarising their learning from the last few lessons, including which metals can be extracted from their ore using carbon, and why.

3.6 Ceramics

Theme: Bonding and properties of materials

Chemistry NC link
- properties of ceramics, polymers, and composites (qualitative)

Sub-theme: Ceramics

Working scientifically NC links
- make and record observations and measurements using a range of methods for different investigations; and evaluate the reliability of methods and suggest possible improvements
- interpret observations and data, including identifying patterns and using observations, measurements, and data to draw conclusions
- present reasoned explanations, including explaining data in relation to predictions and hypotheses

	Learning outcomes		
Learning objective	**Developing**	**Secure**	**Extending**
Describe the properties of ceramics	Identify the properties of ceramics	**Describe the properties of ceramics**	Explain the properties of ceramics
Explain how the properties of ceramics make them suitable for their uses	State some properties of ceramics	**Explain how the properties of ceramics make them suitable for their uses**	Evaluate the properties of ceramics for an unfamiliar use

Tier 2 vocabulary	Tier 3 vocabulary	SB in-text question answers
ceramic		**A** A hard, brittle material that is made by firing a material, such as clay, at a high temperature **B** Physical: four from – hard, brittle, stiff, solid at room temperature/high melting point, strong when forces press on them, easy to break when pulled, electrical insulator; chemical – do not react with water, acids, or alkalis **C** For example: building, because ceramics are strong when forces press on them; jet engine turbine blades, because ceramics have high melting points

Lesson plan

Reactivate knowledge

1 What are materials?
2 A substance has a melting point of 3000 °C. What is its state at 20 °C?

Lesson resources

Activity: *Explaining uses of ceramics* (student sheet, support sheet, teacher and technician sheet)

3 Give the meaning of *physical properties*.

> **Answers: 1** The different types of stuff that things are made from **2** Solid **3** Properties that you can observe or measure without changing the material

Trigger interest

Ask students what toilets are made from. Toilets are made of pottery. Discuss what the students know about the properties of pottery.

Exposition of main content

Introduction to ceramics Introduce students to ceramics. A ceramic is a hard, brittle material that is made by firing a substance, such as clay, at a high temperature. Discuss that pottery is an example of a ceramic material. Show examples of other ceramic materials: brick, china, and earthenware. Ask students to suggest properties of these materials – they should all be similar.

Properties of ceramics Show an example or two of a real ceramic item, such as a plate. Use the example to discuss that ceramics are hard, brittle, stiff, solid at room temperature (with high melting points), strong, easy to break when pulled, and electrical insulators. Write a list of the properties of ceramics on the board. Discuss that ceramics also have similar chemical properties to each other, and do not react with water, acids, or alkalis.

Main activity

What gives ceramic materials their properties? Ask students to suggest explanations for some of the properties (hardness and high melting points) of ceramics. Explain that in ceramic materials, millions and millions of atoms join together in one big structure. There are strong forces between the atoms. A large amount of energy is needed to break the forces between the atoms – this explains the high melting points. The bonds between the atoms are very strong – this explains why ceramic materials are hard.

Activity: Explaining uses of ceramics (20-25 mins) In groups students look at and discuss the images of four uses of ceramics. Together they describe the properties of ceramics, identify the uses, and determine which of those properties make them suitable for their uses. Students then individually answer the questions on the sheet.

Review and reflect

Ceramic properties and uses Students use a list of the properties of ceramics and suggest one use of ceramics that utilises each property.

Homework

Students should create a PMI (plus, minus, interesting) grid in their books detailing something that went well in the lesson, something they struggled with or found more complex, and something they found interesting, to reflect on their learning in this lesson.

3.7 Polymers

Theme: Bonding and properties of materials

Chemistry NC link
- properties of ceramics, polymers, and composites (qualitative)

Sub-theme: Polymers

Working scientifically NC links
- interpret observations and data, including identifying patterns and using observations, measurements, and data to draw conclusions
- present reasoned explanations, including explaining data in relation to predictions and hypotheses

Learning outcomes

Learning objective	Developing	Secure	Extending
Explain why the properties of polymers make them suitable for their uses	Describe the properties of some polymers	**Explain why the properties of polymers make them suitable for their uses**	Compare the uses of two polymers

Tier 2 vocabulary	Tier 3 vocabulary	SB in-text question answers
polymer	natural polymer, synthetic polymer	**A** A substance with very long molecules, in which identical groups of atoms are repeated many times **B** Flexible, waterproof, durable **C** Its properties make it suitable for this use – it is strong, and can have smooth surfaces, and it does not decay in the body

Lesson plan

Reactivate knowledge

1. What is a molecule?
2. What is density?
3. Why do different materials have different uses?

Lesson resources

Activity: *Choosing suitable polymers* (student sheet, teacher and technician sheet)

Answers: 1 A group of two or more atoms, strongly bonded together 2 Density of a substance is its mass in a certain volume 3 Different materials have different properties, making them suitable for different uses

C2 Chapter 3: Metals and other materials

Trigger interest

Ask students what jumpers and tyres have in common. Explain that jumpers and tyres are made from polymers. Discuss that polymers have many uses and ask students to suggest materials they think might also be polymers.

Exposition of main content

Modelling polymers Show students an array of polymers, both natural and synthetic (e.g., plastic bottles, carrier bags, wool, nylon, rubber). Describe polymers as long chains, made up of a huge number of repeating groups of atoms. Highlight 'poly' meaning many. Ask students to link arms in pairs, and then in one long chain. Explain that the properties of polymers can depend on the repeating units, and this makes them extremely useful for many different products.

Main activity

Different polymer properties Discuss some different polymers that are readily available and their uses: natural polymers (wool and rubber) and synthetic polymers (low density and high density poly(ethene)). Ask students to deduce and compare differences in common properties (such as flexibility, strength, conduction of thermal energy, conduction of electricity, water resistance, and opaqueness).

Activity: Choosing suitable polymers (25 mins) Students interpret information on different polymers from a table in order to choose suitable polymers for different functions. Students explain their choices and answer the questions that follow.

Review and reflect

Properties and uses Students make a list of polymers they have learnt about in the lesson. They categorise these polymers according to whether they are natural or synthetic, then explain the properties they possess that make them suitable for their uses.

Homework

Students write a newspaper article about a polymer of their choice. In their articles they must state what a polymer is, describe its properties, give some of its uses, and explain how its properties make it suitable for its uses.

3.8 Composites

Theme: Bonding and properties of materials

Chemistry NC link
- properties of ceramics, polymers, and composites (qualitative)

Sub-theme: Composites

Working scientifically NC links
- interpret observations and data, including identifying patterns and using observations, measurements, and data to draw conclusions
- present reasoned explanations, including explaining data in relation to predictions and hypotheses

Learning objective	Learning outcomes		
	Developing	**Secure**	**Extending**
Explain the properties of some composites	Describe the properties of some composites	**Explain the properties of some composites**	Use information given to suggest advantages and disadvantages to the properties of composites
Explain why the properties of composites make them suitable for their uses	Identify the properties of components of composite materials	**Explain why the properties of composites make them suitable for their uses**	Evaluate the properties of composites for an unfamiliar use

Tier 2 vocabulary	Tier 3 vocabulary	SB in-text question answers
carbon fibre, composite		**A** Concrete and steel **B** A mixture of materials, each with different properties. The composite has properties that are a combination of the properties of the materials that are in it **C** Low density, does not rust, can be moulded to any shape

Lesson plan

Reactivate knowledge

1. What are properties?
2. What are ceramic materials?
3. What is a polymer?

Lesson resources

Activity: *Explaining the properties of some composites* (student sheet, support sheet, teacher and technician sheet)

Answers: 1 Properties describe what a substance looks like and how it behaves 2 Hard, brittle materials that are made by firing materials like clay at high temperatures 3 A substance with very long molecules, in which identical groups of atoms are repeated many times

Ask students to recall the common properties of ceramics and some polymers (such as LDPE). Discuss how we might improve on the properties of those materials.

Trigger interest

Show the image of the Burj Khalifa in Dubai, the world's tallest building. Ask students what it is made from. Ask why this material is so strong.

Inform students the Burj Khalifa is made from a composite material, reinforced concrete.

Exposition of main content

Introducing composite materials Discuss composite materials as a mixture of materials. Each material has different properties, and the composite material has properties that are a combination of the properties of the materials that are in it. Explain that composite materials can be incredibly useful, as we can design and tailor their properties to suit our needs.

Mud bricks Show an image of mud bricks from the Lesson player and explain that they are a composite material used in the developing world. They consist of mud (strong under compression) mixed with straw or grass (strong under tension) and allowed to dry. This is a less expensive and more available version of reinforced concrete.

Main activity

Describing the properties of composite materials Introduce reinforced concrete as a composite material, made of steel bars with concrete around them. Ask students to describe the properties of steel (it is strong when stretching forces are applied) and the properties of concrete (it is not damaged by squashing forces). Ask students to suggest the properties of reinforced concrete (it can withstand both high squashing forces and high stretching forces).

Introduce carbon-fibre-reinforced plastic (CFRP) as a composite material made of carbon fibres and a glue-like polymer. Discuss the properties of the carbon fibres (tubes of carbon which have a low density and do not react with water) and the glue-like polymer (easily moulded into different shapes when soft). Ask students to suggest the properties of CFRP (it makes lighter bicycles, does not rust, and can be moulded into any shape). CFRP does have some disadvantages though. Ask students to suggest what these may be (expensive, easy to break if crashed).

Activity: Explaining the properties of some composites (25–30 mins) Students should pick an example of a composite material and write a newspaper article imagining they were around when the material was invented, introducing the material to the world. They should include a description of the composite material, and the materials it is made from. Students should give an explanation of the properties of the materials it is made from, and the composite material itself, and give a use of the composite, explaining why it is suitable for that use.

Review and reflect

Ask students to describe one of the composite examples discussed in the lesson, describing its properties of its starting materials to the properties of the final composite material. They should then give a use of that composite material and explain why its properties make it suitable for its use.

Homework

Students should create a knowledge organiser summarising their learning from the last few lessons, including describing the properties of ceramics, some polymers, and some composites. They should describe the use of one ceramic, one polymer, and one composite, and explain how each of their properties make it suitable for their uses.

C2 Chapter 3: Metals and other materials

Introduction to checkpoint intervention

This checkpoint intervention provides suggestions for a lesson to follow up the C2 3 Metals and other materials checkpoint assessment. Depending on the outcomes of the assessment, these suggestions can move a class towards secure, to target specific learning outcomes, or to consolidate knowledge for students achieving secure outcomes. Use students' outcomes from the checkpoint assessment to address general misconceptions from the content covered. Be prepared to re-cover content as required; three key concepts from the chapter are covered in more detail below.

Checkpoint secure learning outcomes

- Write a word equation for the reaction of a metal with an acid, given the names of the reactants and products
- Use a pattern to predict the products of the reaction of a metal with water
- Name the metals in the reactivity series that can be extracted by heating their oxides with carbon
- Explain why the properties of ceramics make them suitable for their uses
- Explain why the properties of polymers make them suitable for their uses
- Explain why the properties of composites make them suitable for their uses

Student reflection

Encourage students to reflect on whether there were any checkpoint questions they found difficult or straightforward, as well as their preparation for the checkpoint assessment, including how they revised, the time spent on revision, and what areas they could improve on. For more strategies, see the Metacognition chapter or the Metacognition in the Key Stage 3 Science guide on Kerboodle.

Intervention activity: Write a word equation for the reaction of a metal with an acid, given the names of the reactants and products

Writing word equations can be hard for students. Often the biggest challenge is understanding the question and determining the reactants and products from the substances given. This activity recaps the terms reactant and product, and how to write a word equation.

Writing word equations

Show students this exam-style question on the board:

Calcium reacts with nitric acid to make calcium nitrate and hydrogen. Write the word equation for this reaction. [2 marks]

Write 'reactants → products' on the board underneath the question, and underline 'reactants' in one colour and 'products' in another. Ask students to identify the reactants and products, and underline these in their different colours. Write the reactants (calcium + nitric acid) on the left side under the word 'reactants' using the reactants' colour. Add an arrow then write the products (calcium nitrate + hydrogen) on the right side under 'products', using the products' colour. Highlight the use of '+' to signify that there is more than one reactant or product.

Repeat this process with other acids (hydrochloric acid, sulfuric acid) and/or metals (magnesium, zinc, lead, iron, calcium). Mark the answer with two ticks, one by the correct reactants and one by the correct products.

Repeat this process but change the wording of each question (for example: *Magnesium sulfate and hydrogen can be formed from the reaction between magnesium and sulfuric acid. Write the word equation for this reaction*). When appropriate, students could be given questions to work through on their own or in pairs and then mark them together.

C2 Chapter 3: Metals and other materials

Intervention activity: Name the metals in the reactivity series that can be extracted by heating their oxides with carbon

The biggest challenge when using the reactivity series is forgetting the elements' order. This activity helps students visualise the reactivity series and reminds them of the order of elements within it. To determine which metals can be extracted from their ores using carbon, students must remember that carbon displaces any element less reactive than it from its compound. A recap of this and the definitions of metal, displacement, and compound would be useful here (a metal is an element left of the stepped line in the Periodic Table; a compound is a substance containing more than one element; and 'displace' means 'push out').

Forehead detectives

Label one side of the classroom 'most reactive' and the other 'least reactive'. Divide the class into teams of 14 or less. Give each student in each team the name of a metal (or hydrogen or carbon) in the reactivity series (potassium, sodium, lithium, calcium, magnesium, carbon, zinc, iron, lead, hydrogen, copper, silver, gold) and a description of its reactivity on a piece of paper. Each student should stick/hold the paper on their forehead without looking at it.

The students need to arrange themselves into the reactivity series in their groups, from most reactive to least reactive. Students can describe the reactivity of another person's element, any reactions they think the element undertakes or its relative position in the reactivity series. However, they should never say the name of any element, or reveal anyone's element. Once the teams think they have the correct order, check for mistakes.

Then ask students to all name the elements that can be extracted from ores by heating their oxides with carbon (zinc, iron, lead, copper), emphasising that these are the metals below carbon in the reactivity series. Discuss why it is not necessary to extract gold using carbon (it is so unreactive it does not form compounds, so just needs separating from the substances it is mixed with).

Intervention activity: Explain why the properties of polymers make them suitable for their uses

It is helpful for students to practise linking properties of substances with their uses. This activity helps students to link properties of polymers to specific uses, using polymers that students have experience of in everyday life.

Explaining properties of polymers

Pass an example of a polymer (e.g., LDPE – cling film) around the class. Ask the students to describe its properties (flexible, low density, strong, doesn't absorb water) and list these on the board on the left side. Then ask students to describe the polymer's uses (packaging, wrapping food) and write these on the right side of the board. Draw links between the properties and the uses they make the polymer suitable for. Students should then pick a use and write a sentence on a whiteboard describing why the linked properties of the polymer make it suitable for this use. Share answers and address misconceptions, highlighting good uses of phrases in their answers. This activity should then be repeated with a different polymer (e.g., natural polymers such as wool and rubber; synthetic polymers such as HDPE and poly(styrene)).

C2 Chapter 4: The Earth

In this chapter students learn about the composition of the Earth and the atmosphere. They are reintroduced to three different types of rocks, sedimentary, igneous, and metamorphic rocks, and describe how they are made, their properties and uses, and how their properties make them suitable for their uses. The rock cycle and the carbon cycle are explored, allowing students to consider how materials are recycled naturally. Students also study the greenhouse effect, global heating, and climate change, and explore how to look after and protect the Earth by preventing climate change and preserving our natural resources by recycling.

Prerequisite knowledge

- Definitions of the terms atom, material, substance, element, and compound
- Some changes cannot be reversed as new substances are made
- Materials are made of particles
- The differences between chemical and physical changes
- States of matter and changes of state
- Rocks are made of grains or crystals

GCSE links

- Evidence for composition and evolution of the Earth's atmosphere since its formation
- Evidence, and uncertainties in evidence, for additional anthropogenic causes of climate change
- Common atmospheric pollutants: sulphur dioxide, oxides of nitrogen, particulates and their sources
- Using fuels
- Natural resources and their uses
- The viability of recycling of certain materials
- Life cycle assessment and recycling to assess environmental impacts associated with all stages of a product's life
- Atom economy and yields

Core concepts

- The composition of the Earth and atmosphere
- The process of making sedimentary, igneous, and metamorphic rocks
- Uses of sedimentary, igneous, and metamorphic rocks
- Explaining the properties of sedimentary, igneous, and metamorphic rocks
- Explaining how the properties of sedimentary, igneous, and metamorphic rocks make them suitable for their uses
- Using the rock cycle to describe how materials in rocks are recycled
- Explaining how uplift provides evidence for the rock cycle
- Describing how carbon moves between carbon stores in the carbon cycle
- Explaining why the concentration of carbon dioxide in the atmosphere did not change for many years
- Describing the greenhouse effect, global heating, and climate change
- Explaining why global heating occurs
- Describing some impacts of global heating and how to prevent climate change
- Describing how aluminium is recycled
- Describing advantages and disadvantages of recycling

Key learning misconceptions

- Carbon dioxide is always harmful
- Rocks with layers are always sedimentary rocks
- Weathering is the same process as erosion
- Lava can only flow on land
- Rocks always take a long time to form
- Rocks cannot change their structure
- Volcanoes are all active
- Igneous rocks are only found on volcanoes
- The greenhouse effect just involves the Sun's rays being trapped in the atmosphere
- The greenhouse effect is always bad
- Energy from the sun is immediately trapped when it enters the Earth's atmosphere
- Climate change means the temperature of the whole surface of the Earth increases
- All rocks were formed when the Earth was formed
- Rocks cannot move away from where they were formed
- Recycling is the only way of preserving the Earth's resources
- All types of plastic can be recycled

Teaching preparation

Broader context

It is important for us to be aware of the world we are living in, and this chapter helps students to understand the Earth and its atmosphere and consider their impact on it. By looking at how rocks form we can better understand how our Earth developed and how we can look after it. By highlighting the scarcity of some resources, students can be encouraged to reduce, reuse, and recycle.

Climate change and global heating are prominent and important issues in society. Because of this, they are topics that can feel scary to some students and so can evoke strong emotions and cause stress. It is important to help students to understand the science behind what is happening to alleviate any fears and empower them to take positive actions. The role of governments and big businesses in tackling and preventing climate change should also be highlighted and discussed, to reassure students that it is not just up to the individual.

Modelling

Students will have seen rocks in nature but are unlikely to have experienced rock formation in person. We use models to visualise the processes involved in rock formation, allowing students to picture processes that often occur on large scales or over long periods of time. These models, as with most, come with their own limitations. Although the practicals and demonstrations can be exciting and fun, it is important to highlight the processes and ensure the students recall the key words associated with each, and not just how fun the 'chocolate rock cycle experiment' is. We can do this by allowing students time to reflect on how the models relate to the natural world and the larger scale processes the model is representing.

4.1 The Earth and its atmosphere

Theme: Chemistry of the Earth

Chemistry NC links
- the composition of the Earth
- the structure of the Earth
- the composition of the atmosphere

Sub-theme: Earth and its atmosphere

Working scientifically NC links
- present observations and data using appropriate methods, including tables and graphs
- interpret observations and data, including identifying patterns and using observations, measurements, and data to draw conclusions

Learning objective	Learning outcomes		
	Developing	Secure	Extending
Compare the layers of the Earth	Name the layers of the Earth	**Compare the layers of the Earth**	Compare the physical properties of the layers of the Earth
Describe the composition of the Earth's atmosphere	Identify the four main gases that comprise the Earth's atmosphere	**Describe the composition of the Earth's atmosphere**	Compare the quantities of the four main gases in the Earth's atmosphere

Tier 2 vocabulary	Tier 3 vocabulary
atmosphere, crust, mantle, ore	inner core, outer core, troposphere

SB in-text question answers

A Inner core, outer core, mantle, crust
B Oxygen, silicon, aluminium, iron, calcium, sodium **C** Elements – nitrogen, oxygen, argon; compound – carbon dioxide

Lesson plan

Reactivate knowledge

1. Describe two properties of a substance in the solid state.
2. Describe two properties of a substance in the gas state.
3. What is an element?

Lesson resources

Activity: *The structure of the Earth* (activity sheet, support sheet, teacher and technician sheet)

Answers: 1. Two from: cannot compress/squash; does not flow; fixed shape, unless you apply a force **2.** Two from: cannot compress/squash; flows; takes the shape of the bottom of its container **3.** An element is made up of one type of atom

C2 Chapter 4: The Earth

Trigger interest

Ask students about the components of a packet of crisps, and to suggest where we get the components from. Discuss where they come from (potatoes – plants, which use water, carbon dioxide from the air, and nutrients from the soil; salt – from the sea or mines in the Earth; aluminium (for the bags) – from bauxite rocks; nitrogen (the crisps are packed in nitrogen) – from the air) and highlight that it is necessary to use lots of different parts of the Earth, oceans, and the air in order to make a seemingly 'simple' everyday packet of crisps.

Exposition of main content

Why is the Earth like a Scotch egg? Show students a large Scotch egg. Ask them to give ideas about how this is similar to the Earth. Then cut the Scotch egg in half and ask the students if they can see any similarities now, and if there are any key words they can use to do with the composition of the Earth. Explain to students that the Scotch egg can be used as a scientific model (a simplified version of the real thing). Ask students to state the three layers of the Earth and which layers this corresponds to in the Scotch egg.

Introduction to the composition of the Earth Ask students what they think they would find if they dug a very deep hole through to the centre of the Earth. Explain that scientists have not dug down to the centre of the Earth, but we can still determine the structure of the Earth by studying shock waves from earthquakes and examining different rocks. Show an image of the structure of the Earth and name each layer, giving a description of that layer.

Main activity

What's in the crust? Ask students which layer of the Earth they think we know most about. Discuss the elements that make up some of the compounds found in the crust using the pie chart on the board.

The Earth's atmosphere Discuss the atmosphere as an envelope made from a mixture of gases that surrounds the Earth. Name the layer of the atmosphere closest to the Earth as the troposphere, explaining that it extends up approximately 10 km above the surface of the Earth. Ask students to suggest the names of the elements that make up the majority of the troposphere (nitrogen, 78%, and oxygen, 21%) and any other substances present. Show and discuss a pie chart that represents the composition of the atmosphere. Emphasise that this is the compsition of dry air, as the amount of water vapour varies significantly, but the composition of other gases is constant.

Activity: The structure of the Earth (20 mins) Students label the structure of the Earth, before describing each layer, including, where possible, the size of the layer, the state of most matter in the layer, and what substances the layer is made up of. They then answer the questions that follow.

Review and reflect

Describing the Earth Provide students with mini-whiteboards, dry wipe pens, and erasers and call out a layer of the Earth, including the atmosphere. Students should write down as many facts as they can about that layer. Discuss answers given. Repeat in reverse, calling out facts about a layer, asking students to determine which layer you are describing and to write it on their whiteboards.

Homework

Students make labelled models/collages showing the structure of the Earth. They do not need to worry about using substances in the liquid state, but must include descriptions of each layer to go with their model.

4.2 Sedimentary rocks

Theme: Chemistry of the Earth

Chemistry NC link

- the rock cycle and the formation of igneous, sedimentary, and metamorphic rocks

Sub-theme: Earth and its atmosphere

Working scientifically NC links

- ask questions and develop a line of enquiry based on observations of the real world, alongside prior knowledge and experience
- make and record observations and measurements using a range of methods for different investigations; and evaluate the reliability of methods and suggest possible improvements
- present reasoned explanations, including explaining data in relation to predictions and hypotheses

Learning objective	Learning outcomes		
	Developing	Secure	Extending
Explain two properties of sedimentary rocks	State two properties of typical sedimentary rocks	**Explain two properties of sedimentary rocks**	Suggest and justify the properties of unfamiliar sedimentary rocks
Describe the four stages in the formation of sedimentary rock	Give the four stages in the formation of sedimentary rock	**Describe the four stages in the formation of sedimentary rock**	Compare the processes of weathering and transport
Explain how the properties of sedimentary rocks make them suitable for their uses	State a use of sedimentary rocks	**Explain how the properties of sedimentary rocks make them suitable for their uses**	Suggest disadvantages of using sedimentary rocks for making statues; justify your answer

Tier 2 vocabulary	Tier 3 vocabulary
compaction, deposition, erosion, porous, sediment, weathering	cementation, sedimentary

SB in-text question answers

A Porous (air or water can get into the gaps between the grains); soft (easy to scratch) **B** Weathering, erosion and transport, deposition, compaction or cementation **C** It can withstand strong pushing forces; it is attractive

Lesson plan

Reactivate knowledge

1. What is the name of the Earth's outer layer?
2. Which layer is at the centre of the Earth?
3. If a material is soft, what can you easily do to it?

Lesson resources

Practical: *Modelling the formation of sedimentary rocks* (practical sheet, teacher and technician sheet)

Answers: **1.** Crust **2.** Inner core **3.** Scratch it

Trigger interest

Show the image of the sphinx in Egypt and ask students if they know what type of rock it is made from. Explain that it is made from limestone and was carved by stonemasons more than 4000 years ago.

Exposition of main content

Show images of sedimentary rock formations. Highlight the layers visible in the formations, and explain that limestone, from which the sphinx is made, and the formations being shown, belong to a group of rocks called sedimentary rocks.

What are the properties of sedimentary rocks? Hand around small samples of sedimentary rocks. You may wish to give out hand lenses and mounted needles for students to make closer visual observations and complete scratch tests. In pairs, ask students to describe the rocks and state any properties of the rocks. Discuss findings as a class. Explain that sedimentary rocks are porous (there are gaps between the separate grains that allow air or water into them) and soft (the forces between the grains are weak so they are easy to scratch). You may wish to extend students by asking them to use a top pan balance and take the mass of their sample of sedimentary rock. Put their sample in water, then remove and remeasure the mass. They should find the mass increases as some of the water has been absorbed into the holes or pores in the rock.

How are sedimentary rocks useful? Ask students to suggest uses of sedimentary rocks. Discuss their use as beautiful building materials, and how they can withstand strong pushing forces.

Main activity

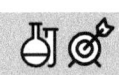

Practical: Modelling the formation of sedimentary rocks (25 mins) Students watch a demonstration of the formation of sedimentary rocks using chocolate, filling in the table to show descriptions in each step of the process: weathering, erosion and transport, deposition, and compaction or cementation.

Discuss the origins of the names of the processes to help students differentiate between them. Explain the different types of weathering (freeze–thaw, chemical, and biological), giving examples of each on the board. Students then answer questions on the formation, properties, and uses of sedimentary rocks.

Review and reflect

Name the process To check students' knowledge, name a stage in the formation of sedimentary rocks, and ask students to describe it on their whiteboards. Address any misconceptions. Then ask students to write two properties of sedimentary rocks on their whiteboards and discuss why these properties mean some limestones are used as building materials.

Homework

Students should draw a story board or comic strip showing the formation of a sedimentary rock, including the four different stages necessary for making sedimentary rock.

4.3 Igneous and metamorphic rocks

Theme: Chemistry of the Earth
Chemistry NC link
- the rock cycle and the formation of igneous, sedimentary, and metamorphic rocks

Sub-theme: Earth and its atmosphere
Working scientifically NC links
- make and record observations and measurements using a range of methods for different investigations; and evaluate the reliability of methods and suggest possible improvements
- interpret observations and data, including identifying patterns and using observations, measurements, and data to draw conclusions.
- present reasoned explanations, including explaining data in relation to predictions and hypotheses

Learning objective	Learning outcomes		
	Developing	Secure	Extending
Describe how igneous and metamorphic rocks form	Identify how igneous and metamorphic rocks form	**Describe how igneous and metamorphic rocks form**	Compare how igneous and metamorphic rocks are made
Explain the properties of igneous and metamorphic rocks	Describe two properties of typical igneous and metamorphic rocks	**Explain the properties of igneous and metamorphic rocks**	Suggest and justify the properties of unfamiliar igneous and metamorphic rocks
Explain how the properties of igneous and metamorphic rocks make them suitable for their uses	State some uses of igneous and metamorphic rocks	**Explain how the properties of igneous and metamorphic rocks make them suitable for their uses**	Compare the advantages and disadvantages of using igneous rocks and metamorphic rocks for roof tiles

Tier 2 vocabulary	Tier 3 vocabulary
lava, magma	igneous, metamorphic

SB in-text question answers

A Not porous, hard, durable **B** High pressure underground squashes the mudstone, which squeezes out water and makes layers of new crystals **C** Not porous, made up of layers that can be split into sheets

Lesson plan

Reactivate knowledge

1 Name two sedimentary rocks.
2 What does porous mean?
3 Name the before and after states for freezing.

Lesson resources

Activity: *What affects crystal size?* (activity sheet, support sheet, teacher and technician sheet)

C2 Chapter 4: The Earth

Answers: **1.** For example: sandstone, limestone **2.** For example, a rock that has gaps that air or water can get into **3.** Before – liquid; after – solid

Trigger interest

Show the image of Giant's Causeway in Northern Ireland on the Lesson presentation. Ask students to consider this natural landmark and to suggest what the columns are made from. Discuss that it is made from basalt, and it formed around 50 million years ago. Ask students to discuss ideas as to why it forms the very regular crystalline structure, and to suggest properties of the rock.

Exposition of main content

Observing rocks Provide students with samples of igneous and metamorphic rocks, and hand lenses. Ask students to observe the rocks under the hand lenses: what colours can they see? Can they see the grains and crystals? Are the crystals big or small? Are they hard or soft? Discuss the samples of rock and describe any properties the students have observed.

Igneous and metamorphic rocks Introduce the different types of rocks in the samples as igneous and metamorphic rocks, showing examples of each on the board. Discuss how each type is formed and what that means for the properties of each type. Non-porous, hard, and durable igneous rocks are formed when liquid rock cools down. This can happen slowly within the Earth's crust, or rapidly outside the crusts (including under water). Metamorphic rocks are formed when other types of rocks are under high pressure and/or temperature but do not melt. They are also non-porous, and are made of thin sheets.

Main activity

Uses of igneous and metamorphic rocks
Ask students to suggest uses for both igneous and metamorphic rocks, and discuss why the properties of slate (a metamorphic rock) make it useful for roofing tiles, why the properties of marble (a metamorphic rock) make it useful for worktops, and why the properties of granite (an igneous rock) make it useful for a path.

Activity: What affects crystal size? (25 mins)
Provide students with a selection of building bricks each; give them 15 seconds to connect together as many bricks as possible into one block. Compare the sizes the students managed. Then ask students to break their blocks apart and repeat, but this time only give them 5 seconds. Compare the sizes as a class and ask students why they didn't manage to make their brick blocks as big. Discuss that this is similar to the formation of crystals in igneous and metamorphic rocks. If they cool quickly, only small crystals can form, but if they cool slowly over a longer period of time, much bigger crystals can form. Students then complete the questions that follow.

Review and reflect

Show the image of Giant's Causeway in the Lesson presentation on the board again. On whiteboards, ask students to give a use for this rock and explain why the properties make it suitable for this use. Encourage students to think about how they might approach this question, and what hints they can take from this lesson to help. They should discuss what type of rock it is, how it formed, and the properties of the rock.

Homework

Students should create a knowledge organiser summarising their learning from the last three lessons, including the structure of the Earth and the atmosphere, the three different types of rock covered (sedimentary, igneous, and metamorphic), how they form, their properties, and some uses.

4.4 The rock cycle

Theme: Chemistry of the Earth
Sub-theme: Earth and its atmosphere

Chemistry NC links
- chemical reactions as the rearrangement of atoms
- the rock cycle and the formation of igneous, sedimentary, and metamorphic rocks

Working scientifically NC links
- make and record observations and measurements using a range of methods for different investigations; and evaluate the reliability of methods and suggest possible improvements
- interpret observations and data, including identifying patterns and using observations, measurements, and data to draw conclusions
- present reasoned explanations, including explaining data in relation to predictions and hypotheses

Learning objective	Learning outcomes		
	Developing	Secure	Extending
Use the rock cycle to describe how the materials in rocks are recycled	Label the types of rock and the processes in the rock cycle	Use the rock cycle to describe how the materials in rocks are recycled	Use the rock cycle to explain in detail how the materials in rocks are recycled
Explain how uplift provides evidence for the rock cycle	Describe the process of uplift	Explain how uplift provides evidence for the rock cycle	Apply understanding of uplift to explain unfamiliar rock formations

Tier 2 vocabulary	Tier 3 vocabulary
uplift	rock cycle

SB in-text question answers

A For example, by weathering, by the action of high pressure, as a result of heating or thermal energy
B As a result of heating/as a result of the action of high pressure **C** The movement of rock upwards when continents collide

Lesson plan

Reactivate knowledge

1. What is weathering?
2. What is deposition?
3. What are metamorphic rocks?

Lesson resources

Practical: *Modelling the rock cycle* (practical sheet, support sheet, teacher and technician sheet)

Answers: 1. The breaking up of rock of all types into sediments **2.** The settling of sediments in one place **3.** Rocks formed when thermal energy/heat or high pressure, or both, change existing rock

C2 Chapter 4: The Earth

Trigger interest

Ask students to imagine they could visit the Earth a million years from now. How would the rocks be different? How might the rocks have changed?

Ask students to describe how rocks change nowadays. Have they seen volcanoes? Landslides? Waterfalls or canyons? What are the rocks like at the beach?

Exposition of main content

Introducing the rock cycle Ask students to describe all they know about the rock cycle. Then display the rock cycle diagram on the board and discuss the key components of the formation of sedimentary, igneous, and metamorphic rocks. Keeping the formations separate, ask students to remind the class what some of the processes are in the rock cycle (weathering, erosion and transport, deposition, compaction or cementation, heating and pressure, melting, cooling and freezing), and highlight the key words they have already met.

Rock cycle recycling Discuss the rock cycle, explaining that there are many routes around the cycle. Pick one and discuss the route around it, explaining how the materials in the different types of rock change into other types of rock, and how their materials are recycled over millions of years.

Main activity

What is uplift? Describe the process of uplift and explain how it has meant we can find fossils from the sea floor at the top of Everest. Discuss how the process of uplift can therefore provide evidence for the rock cycle.

Practical: Modelling the rock cycle (25 mins)
Students carry out a short practical where they use wax to model the processes in the formation of sedimentary, metamorphic, and igneous rocks as part of the rock cycle. They will then answer the questions that follow. Note that water should NOT be poured onto very hot wax to cool it down – this will start a chip pan fire that will need to be extinguished using a fire blanket.

Review and reflect

As a class, discuss and name the different processes the students modelled in the practical. Ask students to think about and discuss how their models represented those different processes. Discuss the strengths and limitations of the model.

Homework

Students produce a story of a route around the rock cycle. They should include key words, and names and descriptions of the processes involved.

4.5 The carbon cycle

Theme: Chemistry of the Earth

Chemistry NC links
- chemical reactions as the rearrangement of atoms
- the composition of the atmosphere
- the production of carbon dioxide by human activity and the impact on climate

Sub-themes: Climate change, Materials cycling

Working scientifically NC links
- interpret observations and data, including identifying patterns and using observations, measurements, and data to draw conclusions
- present reasoned explanations, including explaining data in relation to predictions and hypotheses

	Learning outcomes		
Learning objective	**Developing**	**Secure**	**Developing**
Explain the relative stability in the concentration of carbon dioxide in the atmosphere over part of the Earth's history	Name two process that add carbon dioxide to the atmosphere, and two that remove it from the atmosphere	Explain the relative stability in the concentration of carbon dioxide in the atmosphere over part of the Earth's history	Compare two processes causing the relative stability in the concentration of carbon dioxide in the atmosphere over part of Earth's history
Describe the processes by which carbon atoms move from one store to another	Name some carbon stores	Describe the processes by which carbon atoms move from one store to another	Compare the processes by which carbon moves from one store to another

Tier 2 vocabulary	Tier 3 vocabulary	SB in-text question answers
combustion, photosynthesis, respiration	carbon cycle, carbon store	**A** Combustion or respiration **B** Photosynthesis **C** Dissolving

Lesson plan

Reactivate knowledge

1 What is the atmosphere?
2 What is the percentage of carbon dioxide in the atmosphere?
3 What are fossil fuels?

Lesson resources

Activity: *Completing the carbon cycle* (activity sheet, teacher and technician sheet)

Answers: 1. The mixture of gases that surrounds the Earth **2.** 0.04% **3.** Fuels from under the ground or sea, such as coal and oil. They cannot be replaced once they have been used, so they will run out

C2 Chapter 4: The Earth

Trigger interest

Ask students if they know how much of the atmosphere is made up of carbon dioxide molecules, and whether they think carbon dioxide is a useful gas or a harmful gas. A common misconception is that carbon dioxide is harmful, but most plants and algae need carbon dioxide daily to function, and the greenhouse effect keeps our planet warm enough to sustain life. Therefore, carbon dioxide can be useful.

Exposition of main content

Carbon and its compounds Ask students to suggest substances they believe contain the element carbon, and places or objects they think contain carbon and its compounds. Discuss why carbon is important to all of us, developing on earlier discussions about carbon dioxide. Highlight that there are places called carbon stores, where carbon and its compounds may remain for long periods of time. These can be the atmosphere, the oceans (dissolved carbon dioxide), some sedimentary rocks (such as calcium carbonate), fossil fuels (such as coal, oil, and natural gas), plants and animals, and the soil.

Carbon dioxide: Into and out of the atmosphere Discuss ways carbon dioxide enters and leaves the atmosphere, such as respiration and combustion as processes that add carbon dioxide into the atmosphere, and photosynthesis and dissolving as processes that remove carbon dioxide from the atmosphere.

Discuss that during the 1700s, the total amount of carbon dioxide in the atmosphere did not change. Ask students to suggest why this was, and clarify that this is because during this period of time, carbon dioxide was added to and removed from the atmosphere at the same rate.

Main activity

Introducing the carbon cycle Using the image of the carbon cycle, describe how carbon atoms move between carbon dioxide in the atmosphere and carbon compounds on Earth. Describe how carbon dioxide can move rapidly within the carbon cycle, for example, during the combustion of fossil fuels; or extremely slowly, for example, being stored in sedimentary rocks at the bottom of oceans for long periods of time. Highlight the carbon stores discussed earlier.

Activity: Completing the carbon cycle (20–25 mins) Students complete a diagram of the carbon cycle, before using this to draw a story board/cartoon strip showing a possible journey of one particular carbon atom. Students should then answer the questions that follow.

Review and reflect

Using mini-whiteboards, students decide if a process adds carbon dioxide to the atmosphere or removes it from the atmosphere. Students should then make a rough sketch of the carbon cycle on a mini-whiteboard, including labelling as many carbon stores as they can remember and the processes that move carbon and its compounds between the atmosphere and the Earth. Students can check their diagrams against the complete one and add in anything they missed.

Homework

Students should create a knowledge organiser summarising their learning from the last two lessons, creating diagrams of the rock cycle and the carbon cycle, including descriptions of the processes and carbon stores in the carbon cycle.

4.6 Global heating

Theme: Chemistry of the Earth
Chemistry NC links

- the composition of the atmosphere
- the production of carbon dioxide by human activity and the impact on climate

Sub-theme: Climate change
Working scientifically NC links

- understand that scientific methods and theories developed as earlier explanations are modified to take account of new evidence and ideas, together with the importance of publishing results and peer review
- interpret observations and data, including identifying patterns and using observations, measurements, and data to draw conclusions
- present reasoned explanations, including explaining data in relation to predictions and hypotheses

Learning objective	Learning outcomes		
	Developing	Secure	Extending
Describe what the greenhouse effect is	Label a diagram to show the greenhouse effect	**Describe what the greenhouse effect is**	Evaluate the advantages and disadvantages of having carbon dioxide in the atmosphere
Give the definition of global heating	Identify the definition of global heating	**Give the definition of global heating**	Interpret a graph showing how average air temperature has changed over time
Describe how the concentration of carbon dioxide in the atmosphere has changed	Name two greenhouse gases	**Describe how the concentration of carbon dioxide in the atmosphere has changed**	Suggest why the concentration of greenhouse gases in the atmosphere has changed

Tier 2 vocabulary	Tier 3 vocabulary
global warming, greenhouse effect	global heating

SB in-text question answers
A The overall transfer of energy from the Sun to the thermal store of gases in the Earth's atmosphere **B** The increase in air temperature at the surface of the Earth **C** About 416 ppm

Lesson plan

Reactivate knowledge

1. Name the two most common gases in the Earth's atmosphere.
2. Name two processes that add carbon dioxide to the atmosphere.
3. Name five carbon stores.

Lesson resources

Activity: *Modelling the greenhouse effect* (activity sheet, support sheet, teacher and technician sheet)

Answers: 1. Nitrogen and oxygen **2.** Combustion and respiration **3.** Five from: atmosphere, oceans, some sedimentary rocks, fossil fuels, plants and animals, soil

Trigger interest

Ask students to imagine what would be different if our Earth had no atmosphere. Discuss how, without the atmosphere, the surface of the Earth would be much colder, with the average air temperature being around −18 °C. Ask students to suggest what might be affected by this, and highlight that there would be no liquid water, and therefore no life as we know it.

Exposition of main content

Introducing the greenhouse effect Ask students to discuss what they know about the greenhouse effect, and then share their ideas as a class. Address any misconceptions and then discuss the greenhouse effect using the diagram on the board, emphasising that the greenhouse effect is a natural phenomenon. Highlight the misconception of the energy from the Sun being trapped immediately in the atmosphere, and use Figure 1 in the Student Book to show the transfer of energy from the Sun to the Earth, and then from the Earth to the gases in the atmosphere or out into space. Explain that the greenhouse effect is the overall transfer of energy from the Sun to the thermal store of gases in the Earth's atmosphere. Ask students to recall some of the gases in the atmosphere and explain how they all store energy. However, carbon dioxide and methane store much more energy than others and this is why they (along with water vapour) are called greenhouse gases.

Global heating Show the graph of the average global air temperatures and ask students to describe the trend shown. Ask students to explain what the term 'average' means. Explain that the increase in the average global air temperature at the surface of the Earth is called global heating, or global warming. Emphasise that it is likely human activity that is causing global heating by accelerating the natural greenhouse effect.

Main activity

What causes global heating? Describe how scientists set up a laboratory on a mountain in Hawaii to measure the concentration of carbon dioxide in the atmosphere. Using the graph of data collected, ask students to describe the trend shown.

Activity: Modelling the greenhouse effect (20–25 mins) Students design a model to illustrate the greenhouse effect and global heating that can be used to explain these concepts to primary school children. They will then complete the table to show how their model represents the greenhouse effect and global heating. (Models could include: people wearing coats, a thermos flask, a hot car, a greenhouse, wrapping food in tin foil, putting on a sleeping bag, etc.) Students then complete the questions that follow.

Review and reflect

Using teacher-led questioning, ask students to describe what the greenhouse effect is, describe how the concentration of carbon dioxide in the atmosphere has changed, and give the meaning of global heating, addressing any misconceptions and asking students to improve on previous answers.

Homework

Students write a newspaper article to explain to members of the public what the greenhouse effect is, and which describes global heating. Students could be encouraged to write it as a tabloid-style disaster report or a scientific journal article.

4.7 Climate change

Theme: Chemistry of the Earth
Chemistry NC links

- the production of carbon dioxide by human activity and the impact on climate
- Earth as a source of limited resources and the efficacy of recycling

Sub-theme: Climate change
Working scientifically NC links

- understand that scientific methods and theories developed as earlier explanations are modified to take account of new evidence and ideas, together with the importance of publishing results and peer review
- present reasoned explanations, including explaining data in relation to predictions and hypotheses

Learning objective	Learning outcomes		
	Developing	Secure	Extending
Explain why global heating happens	Describe how people add extra carbon dioxide to the atmosphere	**Explain why global heating happens**	Analyse evidence to identify natural sources of greenhouse gases
Describe some impacts of global heating	Identify some impacts of global heating	**Describe some impacts of global heating**	Explain some impacts of global heating
Describe how to prevent climate change	Identify the meaning of climate change	**Describe how to prevent climate change**	Suggest how some methods of preventing climate change might work

Tier 2 vocabulary	Tier 3 vocabulary
climate change, deforestation	

SB in-text question answers
A For example, burning fossil fuels for heating or transport; deforestation **B** Laboratory experiments show that carbon dioxide molecules trap thermal energy **C** Long-term changes to weather patterns

Lesson plan

Reactivate knowledge

1. What is the greenhouse effect?
2. What is global heating?
3. Name two gases involved in global heating.

Lesson resources

Activity: *Preventing climate change* (activity sheet, support sheet, teacher and technician sheet)

Answers: 1. The overall transfer of energy to the thermal store of gases in the atmosphere 2. The increase in air temperature at the surface of the Earth 3. Carbon dioxide and methane

C2 Chapter 4: The Earth

Trigger interest

Ask students what links Figures 1 and 2 in the Student Book (a forest fire and an aeroplane) and discuss their answers, then explain that these images depict two human activities (burning forests to make space for crops or cattle, and burning fossil fuels to generate electricity to power aeroplanes) that add extra carbon dioxide to the atmosphere.

Exposition of main content

What causes global heating? Ask students if they know of any other human activities that increase the amount of carbon dioxide in the atmosphere, and discuss them (burning fossil fuels to generate electricity to heat homes and fuel cars/other vehicles, cutting down forests (deforestation) to make space for crops or cattle, farming animals, etc.). Ask students to recall how the concentration of carbon dioxide in the atmosphere has changed over time, and how the average global air temperature has changed over time, and how this, together with other data from experiments in laboratories, shows scientists that the increase in the concentration of greenhouse gases in the atmosphere from human activity definitely causes global heating.

The impacts of global warming Ask students to give any impacts of global warming they have heard about in the news. Discuss reasons (glaciers and polar ice melt, making sea levels rise, causing flooding on low-lying coasts; local weather patterns change, leading to flooding, or drought and heat waves), and address any misconceptions (a common misconception is that it is only the melting of icebergs that is causing sea levels to rise, rather than the combined effect of melting icebergs, ice caps, etc.). Describe climate change as long-term changes to weather patterns, which can lead to the extinction of plant and animal species and make it harder to grow sufficient food.

Main activity

How can we stop climate change? Discuss the climate change conference COP26 in November 2021, and describe how world leaders came together to discuss how to prevent climate change. Ask students to suggest what they might have discussed, and any actions we, as individuals, schools, companies, or countries, can take to stop climate change.

Activity: Preventing climate change (20–25 mins) Students should create a poster explaining why global heating happens, describing some of the damaging impacts of global heating, and giving suggestions as to what countries, governments, and/or individuals can do to stop climate change.

Review and reflect

Show students definitions of global heating and climate change. Ask students to identify which is which. Students then list some impacts of global heating on mini-whiteboards; then as a class describe and discuss ideas about how to prevent climate change.

Homework

Students should make a list of five things that they and their family can do at home to prevent or combat climate change (e.g., use energy-efficient light bulbs, have a solar panel on the roof, share lifts to school/ take the bus, switch to a renewable energy supplier, plant trees in their garden, turn off lights when leaving a room, use the local recycling centre weekly).

4.8 Recycling

Theme: Using resources
Sub-theme: Recycling

Chemistry NC links
- the composition of the Earth
- Earth as a source of limited resources and the efficacy of recycling
- the production of carbon dioxide by human activity and the impact on climate

Working scientifically NC links
- ask questions and develop a line of enquiry based on observations of the real world, alongside prior knowledge and experience
- make and record observations and measurements using a range of methods for different investigations; and evaluate the reliability of methods and suggest possible improvements
- present reasoned explanations, including explaining data in relation to predictions and hypotheses

Learning objective	Learning outcomes		
	Developing	Secure	Extending
Give the definition of recycling	Identify the definition of the term recycling	**Give the definition of recycling**	Give some examples of recycling
Describe how aluminium is recycled	Identify the stages in recycling aluminium	**Describe how aluminium is recycled**	Use data to compare the process of recycling aluminium with the process of recycling another metal
Describe some advantages and disadvantages of recycling	Identify some advantages and disadvantages of recycling	**Describe some advantages and disadvantages of recycling**	Evaluate the advantages and disadvantages of recycling

Tier 2 vocabulary	Tier 3 vocabulary

SB in-text question answers
A 2035 **B** Collecting and processing used objects so that their materials can be used again **C** Natural resources will last longer; needs less energy than using new materials; reduces waste and pollution

Lesson plan

Reactivate knowledge

1. Where do all the materials that we use come from originally?
2. What is an ore?
3. Name the before and after states for freezing.

Lesson resources

Activity: *Should we recycle?* (activity sheet, support sheet, teacher and technician sheet)

C2 Chapter 4: The Earth

Answers: **1.** The Earth's crust, oceans, and the atmosphere **2.** A rock that you can extract a metal from, and that contains enough of the metal to make it worth extracting **3.** Before – liquid; after – solid

Trigger interest

Ask students to name as many substances as they can that they think they recycle at home. Add to that list any other substances they can think of that can be recycled outside of the home. State that many types of material, including paper, metals, and plastic, can be recycled.

Exposition of main content

Where do resources come from? Discuss with students that the materials we use to make everything have to come from somewhere – the Earth's crust, atmosphere, or oceans – and that these stocks of new materials will eventually run out. Show Table 1 in the Student Book, which lists some elements and when the ores that we get the metal from may run out. Highlight that two of these are well within the students' lifetimes. Ask students to discuss what we can do about this. Discuss the phrase 'reduce, reuse, and recycle', specifically discussing the terms 'reduce', as cutting down on the amount of waste you produce, and 'reuse', as when you or someone else uses an object again, either for its original purpose, or for another purpose. Discuss examples of reducing (e.g., putting kitchen waste into a compost bin to use as compost, mending clothes instead of buying new ones), and reusing (e.g., using old milk cartons as bird feeders).

What is recycling? Ask students what recycling means (collecting and processing objects that have been used so that their materials can be used again), and to recall which materials can be recycled. Discuss examples of recycling, such as recycling paper to make new paper, recycling plastic bottles to make clothing and stationery, and recycling aluminium cans to make aluminium sheets to make more cans.

Main activity

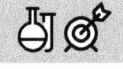

Recycling aluminium Using the steps shown on the board and the images of squashed aluminium cans and an aluminium ingot in the Lesson presentation, discuss the process of recycling aluminium as: taking the aluminium cans to a factory; shredding and then melting the cans; cooling and freezing the liquid metal into an ingot; and finally softening and rolling the ingot into thin sheets to make new cans. Discuss some advantages (such as ensuring natural resources can last longer, it uses less energy than extracting new materials, reducing waste and pollution) and disadvantages (such as it is costly, it takes a lot of time and effort, some people do not like sorting their waste, recycling lorries use fuel and make pollution, not everything can be recycled).

Activity: Should we recycle? (20–25 mins) Students write an informative newspaper article or detailed letter to a friend about recycling. They should explain how aluminium is recycled, and describe some advantages and disadvantages of recycling.

Review and reflect

Students should create a PMI (plus, minus, interesting) grid in their books detailing something that went well in the lesson, something they struggled with or found more complex, and something they found interesting, to reflect their learning in this lesson.

Homework

Students should write a short paragraph to explain why it is better for the environment to compost kitchen waste in their own garden than it is to send it to landfill, even though it would rot in both locations.

C2 Chapter 4: The Earth

Introduction to checkpoint intervention

This checkpoint intervention provides suggestions for a lesson to follow up the C2 4 The Earth checkpoint assessment. Depending on the outcomes of the assessment, these suggestions can move a class towards secure, to target specific learning outcomes, or to consolidate knowledge for students achieving secure outcomes. Use students' outcomes from the checkpoint assessment to address general misconceptions from the content covered. Be prepared to re-cover content as required; three key concepts from the chapter are covered in more detail below.

Checkpoint secure learning outcomes

- Compare the layers of the Earth
- Describe the four stages in the formation of sedimentary rock
- Use the rock cycle to describe how the materials in rocks are recycled
- Describe the processes by which carbon moves from one store to another
- Explain why global heating happens
- Give the definition of recyclin

Student reflection

Encourage students to reflect on whether there were any checkpoint questions they found difficult or straightforward, as well as their preparation for the checkpoint assessment, including how they revised, the time spent on revision, and what areas they could improve on. For more strategies, see the Metacognition chapter or the Metacognition in the Key Stage 3 Science guide on Kerboodle.

Intervention activity: Use the rock cycle to describe how the materials in rocks are recycled

If students are not confident with how the different aspects of the rock cycle link, they will find it difficult to describe how materials are recycled within the rock cycle. This activity allows students to create a giant rock cycle and practise finding routes around it.

A giant rock cycle

Recap how the three main types of rocks (sedimentary, metamorphic, and igneous) are formed, highlighting key words and described each process named (weathering, erosion, transport, deposition, compaction or cementation, heating and/or pressure, melting, cooling and freezing, and uplift). The rock cycle can be on the board as support. Then set up a giant 'classroom' rock cycle. Give individuals or pairs of students a label/paper with a different rock type or a process with an arrow (weathering, erosion, transport, deposition, compaction or cementation, heating and/or pressure × 2, melting × 2, cooling and freezing × 2, uplift × 3) written on it. Arrange students around the room to create a classroom-sized rock cycle, with students labelled as processes ensuring their arrow is pointing in the correct direction. This activity could be completed in a playground/outside using a chalk/tape outline on the floor, or students could be provided with string to 'link' the sections of the rock cycle.

Pick points to start and end on the rock cycle. Students take it in turns to hold up/shout out their type of rock, or process, showing the next step/process the material in the rock cycle would take. Write these on the board to describe how the materials in rocks are recycled from your start point to your end point. Discuss any alternative routes and address misconceptions. Repeat with different start and end points if needed.

C2 Chapter 4: The Earth

Intervention activity: Describe the processes by which carbon moves from one store to another

This activity gives students practice naming carbon stores and processes in the carbon cycle, and describing processes that move carbon between stores. Students can mistake carbon stores for processes that move carbon between stores, so time should be taken to recap the differences. Examples and details can be given to allow students to link the processes to their real life experiences and to aid with understanding how carbon is stored.

Describing processes

Show students the carbon cycle on the board and ask them to recall information about it. The carbon cycle can then be removed from the board, depending on the quality of responses.

Ask students to name the carbon stores from the carbon cycle (the atmosphere, oceans, sedimentary rocks, fossil fuels, plants, animals, and soil) and write these on the left side of the board. Then ask students to name the processes that move carbon between these stores (burning fossil fuels, photosynthesis, respiration, decay in absence of oxygen, dissolving and photosynthesis, respiration and coming out of solution, and deposition) and write these on the right side. Encourage the recall by asking students to name/describe the process that moves carbon between two specified stores.

Finally, remove the processes from the board and give each group a mini-whiteboard and pen. Name two (linked) carbon stores; students should describe the process that moves the carbon between those stores on their mini-whiteboards and hold them up. Address misconceptions and discuss key words in their descriptions. Repeat the activity with two more stores.

Intervention activity: Explain why global heating happens

There is a lot of theory needed to explain why global heating happens. Students need an understanding of key terms and the greenhouse effect. This activity provides a model so students experience the greenhouse effect and link the increase in carbon dioxide in the atmosphere to global heating.

Modelling global heating

Ask students to write meanings of 'greenhouse effect' (the absorbing of energy by gases in the atmosphere) and 'global heating' (the gradual increase in the Earth's mean air temperature) on whiteboards. Address misconceptions and identify good key word use. Write these definitions on the board and show a diagram of the greenhouse effect.

Model global heating using a sink (or container with a drain) with water running into it.

Explain the model: the sink is the Earth, and the water is the heat energy entering or leaving the Earth. Show the water entering the sink but draining away quickly – explain this is what Earth would be like without an atmosphere/greenhouse effect. Highlight the importance of the greenhouse effect for keeping the Earth's temperature up and sustaining life on Earth.

Block up the drain a little – explain that the drain blockers are greenhouse gases stopping the heat energy from escaping – and run the water so the amount in the sink remains constant. Explain that this is how the atmosphere keeps the Earth's temperature constant. The heat energy entering the Earth's atmosphere is roughly equal to the amount leaving it.

Block up the drain further and ask students to identify what is happening: less heat energy is leaving the sink than is entering it – the temperature of the Earth is increasing.

Explain that this is a model for global heating. Too much carbon dioxide (a greenhouse gas) in the atmosphere stops heat energy from leaving the Earth and so increases the global temperature.

Ask students to name and explain human activities that increase the carbon dioxide in the atmosphere.

In groups, students should then write an explanation for why global warming happens, including the key terms: heat energy, increase, greenhouse effect, greenhouse gas, and carbon dioxide.

2 Physics

Introduction to unit

In Chapter 1, students are introduced to the abstract idea of electricity, and gain an understanding of how objects can be charged. They meet the (fundamental) concept of a 'field' as a region where objects experience forces. They build circuits and take measurements when learning about current, potential difference, and resistance. They investigate the shape of the magnetic field around a bar magnet and explore how electricity and magnetism are linked.

In Chapter 2, students are introduced to the difficult concept of energy. They compare energy values in foods and fuels, and look at different energy resources. They learn about different energy stores and how energy is transferred between stores. They use their knowledge of energy and power equations to calculate the cost of using domestic appliances.

In Chapter 3, students learn to calculate the speed of an object and look at how distance–time graphs can be used to describe motion. They extend their Year 7 knowledge of forces with the concept of pressure and apply it to situations where a force can produce a turning effect.

Working scientifically

Each lesson lists the relevant Working scientifically National Curriculum links at the top of the spread. For further details, please refer to the *Oxford Smart Curriculum for Science* document.

Physics NC links

- Energy
- Motion and forces
- Electricity and magnetism

Learning journey

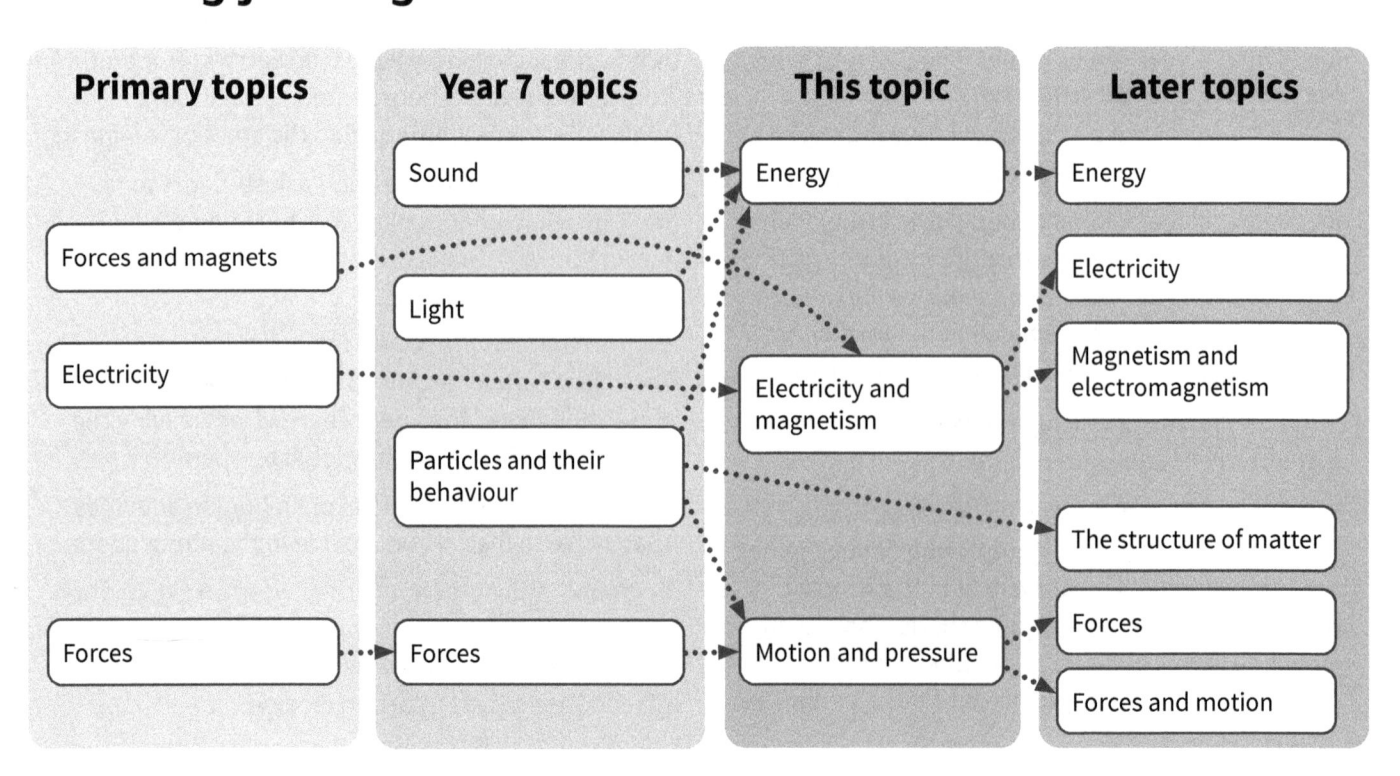

Primary topics	Year 7 topics	This topic	Later topics
	Sound	Energy	Energy
Forces and magnets			Electricity
	Light		Magnetism and electromagnetism
Electricity		Electricity and magnetism	
	Particles and their behaviour		The structure of matter
			Forces
Forces	Forces	Motion and pressure	Forces and motion

2 Physics

Physics and you

Everyday physics A knowledge of physics helps to explain observations that students make of the world around them. Physics also enables students to understand key ideas such as forces, pressure, energy, electricity, and magnetism. Every day, students experience and interact with physics either personally or through the use of machines.

Physics careers Explain that there are many careers in which physics plays a key role – even if the application of 'school' physics is not obvious. Here are three examples:

Opticians need to understand how lenses work, how light travels, and how white light can be split into different colours.

Architects need to understand forces so that buildings are safe in varying conditions, such as weather extremes.

Airline pilots must understand how the forces acting on an aircraft can affect its behaviour. They need to understand weight distribution, wind speed and varying atmospheric pressure.

Physics and the world

From cars to computers, physics impacts our everyday lives; a life without electricity would be very different. However, we have to reverse those activities that are warming the planet and produce toxic waste. This provides exciting challenges for physicists, other scientists, and engineers. How do we ensure that our electricity generation is not harming the planet or that our energy transfers are efficient? How do we make the necessary changes while retaining convenience and luxury? The future of our planet is dependent on this work.

Big questions

How will we keep the lights on? There are limited supplies of fossil fuels on Earth and their use has adverse impacts on the environment. Scientists and engineers are working hard to find alternative, sustainable forms of power generation. Nuclear power was considered to be a solution but concerns over safety and managing nuclear waste mean that this is falling out of favour. The use of renewable sources is a more attractive way of generating electricity; physicists play a key role in developing these methods.

What can we do to reduce climate change? Replacing fossil fuels with renewable sources will reduce the emission of harmful greenhouse gases. However, using renewables to meet our demand for electricity is a challenge, so we need to reduce our use of fossil fuels quickly. Another challenge is to make our energy use more efficient. This includes insulating homes and businesses, and developing effective, convenient forms of transport. These – and other areas of development – require understanding of energy transfers, electricity, and many other basic ideas covered in school physics.

Why is electromagnetism so important? A current flowing through a wire in a magnetic field makes an electric motor work. Many houses have at least 50 electric motors in them and, as technology develops, this number will increase. It is essential to understand electromagnetism to ensure motors are energy efficient, and we can use common appliances such as electric toothbrushes or vacuum cleaners. In the future, motorised transport will rely on powerful, reliable, and efficient electric motors.

In this book, we look at the basic ideas of electricity and magnetism which are fundamental to understanding how electricity is generated and how electric motors work.

P2 Chapter 1: Electricity and magnetism

Introduction to chapter

This chapter introduces students to electric fields, current, and magnetism. Students will look at how to build simple circuits and take measurements of current and potential difference.

Students will study electromagnets and plan how to investigate the shape of magnetic fields. Throughout the chapter, students will develop their mathematical skills as they learn how to change the subject in an equation.

Core concepts
- Static electricity
- Building circuits and taking measurements
- Effects of magnetic fields and uses of electromagnets

Prerequisite knowledge
- Notice that some forces need contact between two objects, but magnetic forces can act at a distance (KS2)
- Observe how magnets attract or repel each other and attract some materials and not others (KS2)
- Compare and group together a variety of everyday materials on the basis of whether they are attracted to a magnet, and identify some magnetic materials (KS2)
- Describe magnets as having two poles (KS2)
- Predict whether two magnets will attract or repel each other, depending on which poles are facing (KS2)
- Identify common appliances that run on electricity (KS2)
- Construct a simple series electrical circuit, identifying and naming its basic parts, including cells, wires, bulbs, switches and buzzers (KS2)
- Identify whether or not a lamp will light in a simple series circuit, based on whether or not the lamp is part of a complete loop with a battery (KS2)
- Recognise that a switch opens and closes a circuit and associate this with whether or not a lamp lights in a simple series circuit (KS2)
- Recognise some common conductors and insulators, and associate metals with being good conductors (KS2)
- Associate the brightness of a lamp or the volume of a buzzer with the number and voltage of cells used in the circuit (KS2)
- Compare and give reasons for variations in how components function, including the brightness of bulbs, the loudness of buzzers and the on/off position of switches (KS2)
- Use recognised symbols when representing a simple circuit in a diagram (KS2)

GCSE links
- Measuring resistance using p.d. and current measurements
- Exploring current, resistance and voltage relationships for different circuit elements; including their graphical representations
- Quantity of charge flowing as the product of current and time
- Drawing circuit diagrams; exploring equivalent resistance for resistors in series
- The domestic a.c. supply; live, neutral, and earth mains wires, safety measures
- Power transfer related to p.d. and current, or current and resistance
- Exploring the magnetic fields of permanent and induced magnets, and the Earth's magnetic field, using a compass
- Magnetic effects of currents, how solenoids enhance the effect
- How transformers are used in the national grid and the reasons for their use

Chapter 1: Electricity and magnetism

Common learning misconceptions

- All metals are attracted to a magnet
- Larger magnets are always stronger than smaller magnets
- Magnetic poles are always at the end of the magnet
- Only metals conduct electricity
- Objects become positively charged because they have gained protons/electrons have been destroyed
- All the electrons in an electrical circuit are initially contained in the battery or other source of the electricity
- Potential difference is the same as current
- Potential difference flows through components
- A larger battery will always make a motor run faster or a bulb glow brighter
- Current flows from a battery to a light bulb, but not from the light bulb to the battery
- A battery gives out a certain current, but if the circuit has lots of resistance that current will get smaller as it flows round the circuit
- Electrons which are lost by an object disappear
- Current flows out of both terminals of a battery or power-pack (the 'clashing' current model)
- Current is used up in a circuit
- The magnetic pole of the Earth in the northern hemisphere is a north pole, and the pole in the southern hemisphere is a south pole
- Magnetic poles are charged
- Voltmeters are connected in series

Teaching preparation

Key maths skill

Substituting values into an equation to calculate resistance when potential difference and current are known Students apply their Year 7 knowledge of equations to help calculate the resistance of a component. You may need to remind them of the best way to set out questions involving equations; that is, write the equation out in full, substitute the values in, then calculate the final answer.

Key maths skill

Changing the subject of an equation All students will learn how to change the subject of an equation and apply this to the resistance equation in order to calculate current and potential difference. Developing students could also use the 'magic triangle' method if they are struggling.

Key vocabulary

Scientific terms This chapter has many key terms that students will not have come across before. Students need to know the definitions of terms such as 'potential difference' and 'electric field'.

Encourage students to make their own glossary of key terms which they can add to throughout the topic and refer to when answering questions.

Key working scientifically skills

Using ammeters and voltmeters Students will use ammeters and voltmeters, probably for the first time. Demonstrate how to use the meters and revisit the idea of zero error.

Students will practise different working scientifically skills, such as evaluating risks, making predictions, planning how to test their predictions, recording measurements in a table, and identifying trends and patterns in their results. They should also evaluate their data, identifying possible sources of errors and suggesting improvements to their experimental technique.

1.1 Charging up

Theme: Electricity and magnetism
Physics NC links

- separation of positive or negative charges when objects are rubbed together: transfer of electrons, forces between charged objects
- the idea of electric field, forces acting across the space between objects not in contact

Sub-theme: Charge
Working scientifically NC link

- ask questions and develop a line of enquiry based on observations of the real world, alongside prior knowledge and experience

	Learning outcomes		
Learning objective	**Developing**	**Secure**	**Extending**
Describe how charged objects interact	Describe how charged particles interact	**Describe how charged objects interact**	Explain how charged objects can be useful
Describe how objects can become charged	Identify positive and negative charges	**Describe how objects can become charged**	Explain how objects become charged in unfamiliar scenarios
Give the definition of an electric field	Identify objects that have been and are affected by an electric field	**Give the definition of an electric field**	Compare and contrast electrostatic and gravitational fields

Tier 2 vocabulary	Tier 3 vocabulary
atom, electric charge, *neutral*	electric field, electron, neutron, proton

SB in-text question answers

A They will attract **B** There are equal numbers of protons and electrons **C** They will repel/move away

Lesson plan

Reactivate knowledge

1. Define 'non-contact force'.
2. State when two magnets will attract.
3. State when two magnets repel.

Lesson resources

Activity: *Electrostatics* (student sheet, support sheet, teacher and technician sheet)

Answers: 1 A force that can act when objects are not touching 2 When the poles are different 3 When the poles are the same

P2 Chapter 1: Electricity and magnetism

Trigger interest

Show students the images on the Lesson presentation. Ask: *What is happening in these images? What do they have in common? How is this similar to what happens with magnets?* Share some responses. Revisit the concept of an electric field as a non-contact force (as per Student Book 1, Chapter 1).

Exposition of main content

Types of charge and electric fields Ask students to '*think pair share*' examples of static electricity. Explain that there are two types of charge: positive and negative. Show students the image of an unlabelled atom on the Lesson presentation. Ask: *What are the particles called? What charge do the particles have?* Use the labelled image to state the charge of each particle.

Explain that an electric field exists around a charged particle or object. Use the images on the Lesson presentation to show that charged particles in an electric field experience a repulsive or attractive force.

Discuss misconceptions: for example, there is nothing smaller than an atom, or that static electricity and electric fields only occur around metal objects.

Demonstration: Charging an object Demonstrate how to charge an object by rubbing it with a cloth.

Show the image on the Lesson presentation. Ask: *What happens to the charges when the polyethene is rubbed with the cloth? What charge does the polyethene rod gain? What charge does the cloth gain?* Then show the image with the Perspex rod to explain how it becomes positively charged. Students often think an object becomes positively charged because it gains protons – make sure they understand that *only the negative charges can move*. Balance two rods on an upside-down watch glass to demonstrate that two charged rods of the same type will repel and two oppositely charged rods will attract.

Show students the electrostatic paint-spraying image. Discuss how charging objects can be useful.

Main activity

Activity: Electrostatics (20 mins) Ask students to complete Activity: *Electrostatics*, and answer the questions. Students self- or peer-mark their answers.

Encourage students to use different coloured pens to suggest improvements.

Review and reflect

Show students the image of a plastic ruler being charged. Ask students to decide which of the six statements are correct and improve any incorrect statements.

Homework

Ask students to research one use or danger of static electricity and write a short paragraph or draw a labelled diagram to describe it to other students.

1.2 Circuits and current

Theme: Electricity and magnetism

Physics NC link
- electric current, measured in amperes, in circuits, and current as flow of charge

Sub-themes: Charge, Currents, resistance, and potential difference

Working scientifically NC links
- evaluate risks
- use appropriate techniques and apparatus during laboratory work, paying attention to health and safety

Learning objective	Learning outcomes		
	Developing	Secure	Extending
Give the definition of current	Identify the unit of current	**Give the definition of current**	Give examples of electric currents in everyday life
Describe how to measure current in a simple circuit	Name the component used to measure current	**Describe how to use an ammeter to measure current in a simple circuit**	Describe how to use an ammeter to measure current in an unfamiliar circuit
Draw circuit diagrams	Identify a range of circuit symbols	**Draw circuit diagrams**	Identify errors in unfamiliar circuits

Tier 2 vocabulary	Tier 3 vocabulary	SB in-text question answers
battery, *current*, motor, *switch*	ammeter, amps, *cell*, circuit symbol	**A** The charges are in an electric field **B** There is far more charge flowing per second in lightning than in a bulb **C** The torch would not work

Lesson plan

Reactivate knowledge

1. Name the charged particle used to explain electrostatic phenomena.
2. Define 'electric field'.
3. Name three circuit components used to make a torch.

Answers: 1 Electron 2 A region where a charged particle experiences a force 3 Cell/battery, lamp, switch

Lesson resources *(k)*

Activity: *Investigating current* (student sheet, support sheet, teacher and technician sheet)

Chapter 1: Electricity and magnetism

Trigger interest

Show students the images on the Lesson presentation. Explain that an electric current can be dangerous and/or useful. Ask: *Can you think of other examples where electricity is dangerous or useful?* Share some responses.

Exposition of main content

Current Set up a simple circuit with a cell, switch, and lamp. Ask students to *'think pair share'*: *Why does the lamp light up when the switch is closed but not when the switch is open?* Share ideas until somebody mentions 'current'.

Show the images of free electrons and atoms inside the wire. Ask: *What is different inside the wire when it is connected to the battery?* Explain that the battery 'pushes' the electrons around the circuit. Discuss any misconceptions, such as current flows from a battery to a light bulb, but not from the light bulb to the battery, or that the battery produces the electrons in the wire.

Circuit symbols Working in pairs, ask students to draw the symbols for a cell, lamp, buzzer, switch, and connecting wire. Ask them to draw a circuit diagram containing each of these components. Students can comment on each other's circuits and help correct errors. Ask a volunteer to draw the correct circuit diagram on the board.

Main activity

Demonstration: Using an ammeter (5 mins) Show students the image of the circuit on the Lesson presentation. Ask for two volunteers to each set up the circuit. Ask other students to compare the similarities and differences between the two circuits and suggest changes. Discuss risks, such as: turn off the circuit when changing components, keep the circuit away from water, or that wires may become hot.

Practical: Investigating current (15 mins) Ask students to complete Practical: *Investigating current* and answer the questions. It is important to check the circuits and correct any errors during the lesson. Students can then self- or peer-mark their answers.

Review and reflect

The rope model helps to visualise what happens in an electric circuit. Ask for volunteers to stand in a circle holding a rope. One student passes the loop around the circle; the other student(s) allow it to pass lightly over their fingers.

Use the model to address misconceptions: for example, the student doesn't 'produce' the rope (cells/batteries do not produce electrons); all of the rope moves at the same time (as do electrons; the rope does not get 'used up' as it moves (neither do electrons).

Homework

Ask students to make flash cards for circuit components.

1.3 Potential difference

Theme: Electricity and magnetism
Physics NC link
- potential difference, measured in volts, battery and bulb ratings

Sub-theme: Circuits, Current, resistance, and potential difference
Working scientifically NC links
- evaluate risks
- use appropriate techniques and apparatus during laboratory work, paying attention to health and safety
- make predictions using scientific knowledge and understanding

Learning outcomes

Learning objective	Developing	Secure	Extending
Give the definition of potential difference in terms of energy and force	Identify the units of potential difference	**Give the definition of potential difference in terms of energy and force**	Describe examples of potential difference in unfamiliar scenarios
Describe how to measure potential difference in a simple circuit	Name the component used to measure potential difference	**Describe how to measure potential difference in a simple circuit**	Explain why a voltmeter is placed in parallel to a component
Describe what the rating of a circuit component means	Identify components with different ratings	**Describe what the rating of a circuit component means**	Select appropriate cells and components based on their ratings

Tier 2 vocabulary	Tier 3 vocabulary
voltage	potential difference, *terminal*, voltmeter, volts

SB in-text question answers

A An ammeter is connected in a circuit, but a voltmeter is connected either side of a component/across a component **B** The higher the rating of a battery, the more energy is transferred to charges **C** It cannot measure the change in energy transferred between two points

Lesson plan

Reactivate knowledge

Students should have prior knowledge from Key Stage 2 of how the voltage of a cell affects the brightness of a lamp.

1. Name a circuit component you need for a current to flow.
2. Name the circuit component used to measure current.
3. Write down what happens to a bulb when you add more cells to the circuit.

Answers: **1** Cell or battery **2** Ammeter **3** It gets brighter

Lesson resources

Activity: *Investigating potential difference* (student sheet, support sheet, teacher and technician sheet)

P2 Chapter 1: Electricity and magnetism

Trigger interest

Show students the defibrillator on the Lesson presentation. Ask students to 'think pair share': *What piece of equipment is being used? Why is it being used? How does it work?* Share some responses. Explain what defibrillators do – try to use the term 'potential difference' (p.d.) and not 'voltage' from now on, so that students are less confused!

Exposition of main content

Potential difference (p.d.) Show students the images of appliances. Ask: *What are the similarities and differences between these objects?* Discuss misconceptions, such as 'the bigger the battery, the larger the p.d.', and 'all the electrons in an electrical circuit are initially contained in the battery or other source of the electricity'. Explain that chemical reactions take place in a cell to produce a p.d. between the positive and negative terminals.

Demonstration: Using a voltmeter Set up a simple circuit with a cell, switch, and lamp. Discuss where the ammeter should be positioned so it measures the current through the lamp. Show students a voltmeter and explain that it measures p.d. across a component. Ask them to suggest how to connect the voltmeter in the circuit to measure the p.d. across the lamp. Note: you could introduce the terms 'series' and 'parallel' at this stage (the ammeter is in series with the lamp, but the voltmeter is in parallel). Ask a volunteer to draw the correct circuit diagram on the board.

Main activity

Practical: Investigating potential difference (20 mins) Ask students to complete Practical: *Investigating potential difference* and answer the questions. It is important to check the circuits and correct any errors during the lesson. Students can self- or peer-mark their answers.

Review and reflect

Use the rope model, as per the previous lesson. Discuss how a battery with a bigger p.d. would be represented using the model. Ask: *Why would it be difficult to represent a voltmeter?*

Homework

Ask students to make a Venn diagram to show the similarities and differences between current and p.d.

1.4 Resistance

Theme: Electricity and magnetism

Physics NC links
- resistance, measured in ohms, as the ratio of potential difference (p.d.) to current
- differences in resistance between conducting and insulating components (quantitative)

Sub-theme: Current, resistance, and potential difference

Working scientifically NC links
- pay attention to concern for precision and repeatability
- make predictions using scientific knowledge and understanding
- plan the most appropriate types of scientific enquiries to test predictions, including identifying independent, dependent, and control variables

Learning objective	Learning outcomes		
	Developing	Secure	Extending
Give the definition of resistance	Give the units of resistance	**Give the definition of resistance**	Use a model to explain why a wire gets hotter when there is a current in it
Calculate resistance using simple values of potential difference and current	Give the equation for resistance	**Calculate resistance using simple values of potential difference and current**	Change the subject of the resistance equation to calculate potential difference or current
Describe the difference between conductors and insulators in terms of resistance	Give the definitions of a conductor and an insulator	**Describe the difference between conductors and insulators in terms of resistance**	Explain why conductors and insulators have different values of resistance

Tier 2 vocabulary	Tier 3 vocabulary
conductor, insulator *resistance*	ohms

SB in-text question answers

A The television **B** The lamp **C** More posts, posts closer together, bigger posts

Lesson plan

Reactivate knowledge

1. State the unit of current.
2. State the unit of potential difference.
3. Which of these objects conduct well: carbon or wood?

Answers: 1 Amperes, amps **2** Volts **3** Carbon

Lesson resources

Activity: *Investigating the resistance of a wire* (student sheet, support sheet, teacher and technician sheet)

P2 Chapter 1: Electricity and magnetism

Trigger interest

Show students the images on the Lesson presentation. Ask them to 'think pair share' similarities and differences between the appliances. Share some responses before explaining that all of the appliances have a current passing through them, but the size of the current differs due to resistance. Discuss misconceptions, such as that all appliances have the same current as the current comes from the same socket/power station.

Exposition of main content

What is resistance? Show students the images on of the Lesson presentation. Discuss what the term 'electrical resistance' means.

Set up a circuit with a cell, ammeter, and lamp; leave a gap. Ask students to use the word 'resistance' to explain why the lamp lights up if a conductor is connected in the gap, but not when an insulator is connected.

Calculating resistance Ask students to suggest which two things in the circuit affect the size of the current. Explain that the current depends on the resistance of the circuit and the potential difference provided by the cell. Resistance, current, and p.d. are related by the equation:

$$\text{resistance} = \frac{\text{potential difference}}{\text{current}}$$

Work through the example on the Lesson presentation.

Main activity

Demonstration: Investigating the resistance of a wire (5 mins) Show students the circuit used to investigate the resistance of different lengths of wire. Ask them to identify what each of the variables are in this experiment. Discuss how many lengths of wire should be tested and how many repeats taken. Ask students to suggest the column headings for the results table and the axis labels on the graph.

Demonstrate how to take measurements. A complete set of example measurements is on Activity: *Investigating the resistance of a wire*.

Activity: Investigating the resistance of a wire (15 mins) Ask students to answer the questions on the activity sheet. Note that the wire can get hot, so make sure that the potential difference used is not high.

Review and reflect

Ask students to self- or peer-mark their answers using the success criteria on the Lesson presentation. Encourage students to use different coloured pens to make comments about what they did well and suggest improvements.

Homework

Ask students to draw a cartoon diagram to describe why there is resistance in a wire. For example, a person running through an obstacle course.

1.5 Changing the subject

Theme: Electricity and magnetism

Physics NC link
- potential difference, current and resistance

Sub-theme: Current, resistance, and potential difference

Working scientifically NC link
- apply mathematical concepts and calculate results

Learning objective	Learning outcomes		
	Developing	**Secure**	**Extending**
Change the subject of an equation	Substitute values into a given equation	Change the subject of an equation	Change the subject of an unfamiliar equation
Change the subject of the resistance equation to calculate values for current and potential difference	Substitute values into equations for current and potential difference	Change the subject of the resistance equation to calculate values for current and potential difference	Use the resistance equation to explain the effect of changing one variable on another

Tier 2 vocabulary	Tier 3 vocabulary
triangle	

SB in-text question answers

A The chair is the thing that I am sitting on; Sitting is what I am doing on the chair **B** Correct division and cancelling **C** 0.1 = 2/20, 20 = 2/0.1

Lesson plan

Reactivate knowledge

1. State the equation for calculating resistance.
2. State the equation for calculating weight.
3. State Hooke's Law.

Lesson resources

Activity: *Changing the subject* (student sheet, support sheet, teacher and technician sheet)

Answers: 1 Resistance = $\dfrac{\text{potential difference}}{\text{current}}$ 2 Weight = mass × gravitational field strength
3 The extension of a spring is proportional to the force up to the elastic limit

Trigger interest

Show students the image of the cat on the Lesson presentation. Ask students to 'think pair share': *Make up a sentence about the image where the cat is the subject. Now change the sentence so the mat is the subject.*

Show students the image of the rope model on the Lesson presentation. Ask: *What is the relationship between the three quantities?*

Discuss that the relationship can be shown in the resistance equation that they learnt last lesson. If the p.d. and resistance are known, the current can be calculated, but the equation has to be rearranged.

Exposition of main content

Changing the subject Use the Lesson presentation to demonstrate how the equation can be rearranged to make p.d. the subject. In general, 'rearrange' is used in science and 'change the subject' is used in maths, but these refer to the same transferable skill.

Ask students to work in pairs to make current the subject, showing all the stages of their workings. Discuss some answers so that students can comment on their peers' work.

Work through another example, such as rearranging force = mass × acceleration to make mass, and then acceleration, the subject.

Ask students to make notes. Show them the method in the Student Book, 'How can I check that I have done it correctly?', as some students may find it easier to substitute the values into the equation before changing the subject.

Main activity

Activity: Gallery walk (20 mins) Ask students to work through the 'gallery walk' questions set out around the room. At the front of the room, have 'hints' and a mark scheme available for each question: students can use these if they are struggling, and when they have finished each question and need to mark their work. Encourage students to use a different coloured pen to make any improvements to their method of changing the subject.

Review and reflect

Show students examples of incorrectly rearranged questions on the Lesson presentation. Ask students to identify the mistake and write the correct answer on mini-whiteboards.

Homework

Ask students to make a flow chart to describe each step they make when rearranging the weight equation to make mass the subject.

1.6 Series and parallel

Theme: Electricity and magnetism

Physics NC link
- electric current in series and parallel circuits, currents add where branches meet

Sub-theme: Circuits

Working scientifically NC link
- interpret observations and data, including identifying patterns and using observations, measurements, and data to draw conclusions

Learning objective	Learning outcomes		
	Developing	Secure	Extending
Describe the difference between series and parallel circuits	Identify series and parallel circuits	Describe the difference between series and parallel circuits	Evaluate why some circuits are better suited to be parallel or series
Describe how current varies in series and parallel circuits	Identify where to place ammeters in a series circuit	Describe how current varies in series and parallel circuits	Calculate current values in unfamiliar circuits
Describe how potential difference varies in series and parallel circuits	Identify where to place voltmeters in a series circuit	Describe how potential difference varies in series and parallel circuits	Calculate potential difference values in unfamiliar circuits

Tier 2 vocabulary	Tier 3 vocabulary
parallel, series	

SB in-text question answers
A Two from: in a parallel circuit, if one bulb breaks the others stay on; components can be turned on and off independently; parallel circuits have more than one loop or branch **B** 4 A **C** The rope goes at the same speed everywhere

Lesson plan

Reactivate knowledge

1. Define 'current'.
2. Give the equation for resistance.
3. State what pulling the rope in the rope model is like in a circuit.

Answers: 1 Current is the charge flowing per second 2 Resistance = $\frac{p.d.}{current}$ 3 The p.d./battery

Lesson resources

Activity: *Series and parallel* (student sheet, support sheet, teacher and technician sheet)

Trigger interest

Show students the Christmas lights images on the Lesson presentation. Ask: *What is the difference between these two sets of lights? What will happen if a bulb breaks in each set of lights?* Share some responses. Explain that the first set has the lights in series but the second set has the lights in parallel – which is how they are usually made.

Exposition of main content

Series and parallel circuits Divide students into groups of five. Give each group a large sheet of paper with two circuit diagrams (as shown on the Lesson presentation), and a marker pen.

Ask students to write facts about each circuit next to the diagrams. Discuss ideas and describe the difference between series and parallel circuits; for example, a series circuit only has one loop but a parallel circuit has more than one loop.

Measuring current and p.d. in a circuit Ask: *Can you remember where ammeters and voltmeters need to be placed in a circuit to measure current and p.d.?* Ask a volunteer to draw an ammeter in the series circuit so it measures the current through both lamps. Discuss whether the position chosen is correct. Ask another volunteer to draw the positions of three voltmeters, to measure the p.d. across the cell and each lamp. Ask other students to comment on these positions or suggest improvements. Discuss any possible misconceptions, such as that the current is bigger nearer the cell.

Main activity

Activity: Series and parallel (15 mins) Ask students to complete Activity: *Series and parallel*, where they investigate circuit rules for series and parallel circuits by carrying out mini-experiments set out around the room. Students visit each circuit and write down their measurements and observations.

Review and reflect

Discuss students' results and use large diagrams of the four mini-experiments to write the readings of each meter. Ask students to suggest patterns in what happens to the current and p.d. in each type of circuit. Ask students to copy and complete the rules table on the Lesson presentation.

Homework

Students draw a spider diagram based on what they have learnt in this chapter so far, for example, static electricity, current, p.d., resistance, series, and parallel circuits.

1.7 Magnets and magnetic fields

Theme: Electricity and magnetism
Physics NC links
- non-contact forces: forces between magnets
- magnetic poles, attraction and repulsion
- magnetic fields by plotting with compass, representation by field lines
- Earth's magnetism, compass and navigation

Sub-theme: Magnetism
Working scientifically NC link
- make and record observations and measurements using a range of methods for different investigations; and suggest possible improvements

Learning objective	Learning outcomes		
	Developing	Secure	Extending
Give the definition of a magnetic field	Identify a region where a magnetic field is present	**Give the definition of a magnetic field**	Compare and contrast electric, magnetic, and gravitational fields
Describe how to investigate and represent the shape of a magnetic field	Give one way to observe magnetic fields	**Describe how to investigate and represent the shape of a magnetic field**	Plan an investigation to observe how magnetic fields interact
Describe the Earth's magnetic field	Identify the north and south poles of the Earth	**Describe the Earth's magnetic field**	Explain how a compass works.

Tier 2 vocabulary	Tier 3 vocabulary	SB in-text question answers
magnetic field, magnetic material, *north pole, south pole*	magnetic field line	**A** A magnetic material will be attracted to a magnet, but cannot repel it **B** There is a force on a magnetic material in a magnetic field, but on a mass in a gravitational field **C** Aluminium is not a magnetic material/the filings would not align with the field

Lesson plan

Reactivate knowledge

1. Name the poles of a magnet.
2. State which of these would be attracted to a magnet: iron or glass.
3. Define 'gravitational field'.

Answers: **1** North and south **2** Iron **3** A region where a mass experiences a force

Lesson resources

Practical: *Drawing magnetic fields* (student sheet, support sheet, teacher and technician sheet)

Chapter 1: Electricity and magnetism

Trigger interest

Use a *'hot potato'* activity to assess prior knowledge.

Show students the 'levitating paperclip' set up and the ferrofluid image on the Lesson presentation.

Ask students to work in pairs as parts of a larger group of 8–10. Give each pair a piece of paper with a heading related to magnetism (for example, 'levitating paperclip', 'magnetic materials', or 'magnetic poles').

Give students 30 seconds to write down key ideas related to their heading before passing the paper to the next pair of students. Students read the key ideas and add their own. Once each piece of paper has been passed around the group, discuss ideas as a whole class. Discuss any possible misconceptions, such as that all metals are magnetic.

Exposition of main content

Demonstrating magnetic fields Demonstrate the magnetic field around a bar magnet using iron filings. Ask students to predict what will happen to the iron filings when they are sprinkled around the bar magnet. Ask: *What do the iron filings show? Why do they show this pattern? Would the same happen if you sprinkled sugar around the magnet?* Discuss the similarities and differences between magnetic fields, electric fields, and gravitational fields.

Main activity

Practical: Drawing magnetic fields (20 mins)
Discuss that although iron filings show the pattern of the magnetic field, they do not show it very clearly and do not show the direction of the magnetic field lines. Show students how to use a compass to begin plotting the magnetic field lines around the bar magnet and explain that the compass points in the direction of the field lines around the magnet.

Ask students to complete Practical: *Drawing magnetic fields*.

Students can peer-mark each other's diagrams. They should include one thing that was done well and one improvement that could be made, based on the success criteria on the Lesson presentation.

Review and reflect

Show students the images on the Lesson presentation and ask them to suggest a link. Hang a bar magnet by a fine thread so that it is not moving. Ask students to predict what will happen if you push or turn the magnet and to explain their answer.

Homework

Students investigate three uses of magnets around the home or in daily life and write a short paragraph explaining why they are used.

1.8 Electromagnets

Theme: Electricity and magnetism

Physics NC link
- the magnetic effect of a current, electromagnets

Sub-themes: Electromagnetism, Magnetism

Working scientifically NC links
- make predictions using scientific knowledge and understanding
- make and record observations and measurements

	Learning outcomes		
Learning objective	**Developing**	**Secure**	**Extending**
Describe the magnetic field around a current-carrying wire	Identify the magnetic field around a wire	**Describe the magnetic field around a current-carrying wire**	Compare the magnetic field of a current-carrying wire and a permanent bar magnet
Describe how to make an electromagnet	List the equipment needed to make an electromagnet	**Describe how to make an electromagnet**	Explain how to test the strength of an electromagnet
Describe how to change the strength of an electromagnet	Identify factors that affect the strength of an electromagnet	**Describe how to change the strength of an electromagnet**	Explain why, by looking at diagrams, certain electromagnets have different field strengths

Tier 2 vocabulary	Tier 3 vocabulary
core, electromagnet	magnetise

SB in-text question answers

A The field lines get further apart **B** The field lines are straight lines close together **C** You could not turn it off because it would still be magnetic

Lesson plan

Reactivate knowledge

1. Define 'magnetic field'.
2. Name one way to investigate the shape of a magnetic field.
3. State how you know a field is strong.

Lesson resources

Activity: *Changing the strength of electromagnets* (student sheet, support sheet, teacher and technician sheet)

Answers: 1 A region where a magnetic material experiences a force 2 Using iron filings or a plotting compass 3 The field lines are close together

Chapter 1: Electricity and magnetism

Trigger interest

Show students the images on the Lesson presentation of a bar magnet, an electromagnet used in a bell, and an electromagnet used in a scrap yard. Ask students to 'think pair share': *What are the similarities between these images? What are the differences?* Discuss any possible misconceptions, such as that all silver-coloured items are attracted to a magnet or that larger magnets are always stronger than smaller magnets.

Exposition of main content

Demonstrating the magnetic field around a wire and a coil of wire Ask students to predict what will happen to a compass when it is placed near a current-carrying wire. Use a compass to plot some field lines. This should show that there is a magnetic field around the wire and the magnetic field lines are circular. Show the image on the Lesson presentation. Ask: *The magnetic field lines are circular and become further apart as the distance from the wire increases; what does this tell us about the magnetic field?*

Explain to students that the magnetic field around just one wire is not very strong, so an electromagnet is made from lots of loops. Show students the magnetic field pattern around a coil of wire (a solenoid) and compare it with the field of a bar magnet.

Main activity

Practical: Changing the strength of electromagnets (20 mins) Ask students, in pairs, to complete Practical: *Changing the strength of electromagnets* (three mini-experiments). Students make a prediction about each variable before recording their results and drawing conclusions.

Review and reflect

Use the *'snowballing'* technique for students to share their observations and draw conclusions. Each pair joins with another pair, and then the group of four join with another group of four. At each stage, students discuss their results and how each variable affected the strength of the electromagnet. Students can also discuss any difficulties they encountered when carrying out the experiments. A spokesperson from each group of eight can then share their findings with the rest of the class.

Homework

Students can choose from various homework activities based on stars which increase in difficulty.

1.9 Using electromagnets

Theme: Electricity and magnetism
Physics NC link
- the magnetic effect of a current, electromagnets, DC motors (principles only)

Sub-theme: Electromagnetism
Working scientifically NC link
- ask questions based on observations of the real world, alongside prior knowledge and experience

Learning outcomes

Learning objective	Developing	Secure	Extending
Describe some uses of electromagnets	Give some uses of electromagnets	**Describe some uses of electromagnets**	Explain why the properties of electromagnets make them suitable for different uses
Compare permanent magnets and electromagnets	Identify examples of permanent magnets and electromagnets	**Compare permanent magnets and electromagnets**	Evaluate the use of permanent magnets and electromagnets for different purposes
Describe how a simple motor works	Identify simple motors in everyday life	**Describe how a simple motor works**	Explain how different factors can affect the speed of a motor

Tier 2 vocabulary	Tier 3 vocabulary	SB in-text question answers
switch	levitating, *relay*	**A** North and south **B** Neither are magnetic materials **C** Permanent magnets would not be strong enough

Lesson plan

Reactivate knowledge

1. Name three things you need to make an electromagnet.
2. Name two ways to make an electromagnet stronger.
3. Name three magnetic materials.

Answers: 1 Wire, battery, nail **2** Add more coils/use a bigger current/use a core **3** Iron/steel, nickel, cobalt

Lesson resources

Activity: *Researching the uses of electromagnets* (student sheet, support sheet, teacher and technician sheet)

Chapter 1: Electricity and magnetism

Trigger interest

Print the nine images on the Lesson presentation and stick them to the walls around the room. Add a large sheet of blank paper underneath each image. Ask students to walk around the room looking at the images. At each one, give them 30 seconds to write down what they know about the image, and any questions they may have about it. Discuss some of the ideas and questions.

Exposition of main content

Permanent magnets and electromagnets Ask: *Can you think of some uses of permanent magnets in your homes? Why are electromagnets not used in these examples?*

Demonstrate making a homopolar motor and/or show students a fully constructed Westminster motor. Describe how a motor needs both an electromagnet and a permanent magnet to be able to spin.

Ask students to suggest some examples of where motors are used and how the motor can be made to spin faster. If there is time (or another lesson), students could construct their own homopolar motor and investigate which variables affect how fast it spins.

Main activity

Activity: Researching the uses of electromagnets (25 mins) Ask students to work in groups of four to complete Activity: *Researching the uses of electromagnets*. Students research uses of electromagnets and create a poster or information leaflet.

Review and reflect

Ask students to describe their research to the rest of their group. Ask one member of each group to describe a use which they did not research to the rest of the class. Give students the opportunity to ask any questions that they may have about any of the uses.

Homework

Ask students to write five questions where the answer is one of the words from the list they are given.

P2 Chapter 1: Electricity and magnetism

Introduction to checkpoint intervention

This checkpoint intervention provides suggestions for a lesson to follow up the P2 1 Electricity and magnetism checkpoint assessment. Depending on the outcomes of the assessment, these suggestions could move a class towards secure, to target specific learning outcomes, or to consolidate knowledge for students achieving secure outcomes. Use students' outcomes from the checkpoint assessment to address general misconceptions from the content covered. Be prepared to re-cover content as required; three key concepts from the chapter are covered in more detail below.

Checkpoint secure learning outcomes

- Give the definition of an electric field
- Describe how to measure current in a simple circuit
- Calculate resistance using simple values of potential difference and current
- Describe the difference between series and parallel circuits
- Describe how to investigate and represent the shape of a magnetic field
- Describe how to change the strength of an electromagnet

Student reflection

Encourage students to reflect on whether there were any checkpoint questions they found difficult or straightforward, as well as their preparation for the checkpoint assessment, including how they revised, the time spent on revision, and what areas they could improve on. For more strategies, see the Metacognition chapter or the Metacognition in Key Stage 3 Science guide on Kerboodle.

Intervention activity: Calculate resistance using simple values of potential difference and current

Most students can identify that the current in a component depends on its resistance and the potential difference (p.d.) across it. Some struggle to link these in the correct equation and substitute values to calculate resistance. This activity give students practice in calculating resistance.

Calculating resistance

The 'I do, we do, you do' method will improve students' confidence and ability to calculate resistance on their own. Write the first of four 'calculating resistance' questions on the board. Model the method you would use to answer it:

1. Underline the quantities and corresponding numbers in the question, and write them underneath the question; for example: current = 1.5 A; p.d. = 7.5 V; resistance = ?
2. Write down the equation for resistance.
3. Substitute the values of current and p.d. into the equation.
4. Calculate the answer and write it with the correct unit.

For the second question, model the answer but ask students to suggest what to do for each step. For the third question, discuss each step and ask students to complete steps on a mini-whiteboard; feedback on any errors. For the fourth question, ask students to work individually. Model the correct answer on the board for students to mark their work. Discuss any errors.

A further activity could involve students working in pairs: they both write a question and then answer each other's question. Students working at the extending level could write questions that require the resistance equation to be rearranged to calculate current or p.d.

Intervention activity: Describe the difference between series and parallel circuits

Most students can identify series and parallel circuits, but many struggle to compare the current and potential differences in these circuits. Students used the rope model in lessons; in this activity, they will use a different model.

Modelling circuits

Students use the 'sweet delivery' model to demonstrate what happens in a series circuit. Student A holds a pot of sweets while two other students, B and C, hold empty pots and stand in a loop with A. Other students individually carry sweets from the pot and deposit them between B and C so that they return to A to collect more sweets and repeat the process. Student D stands in the circuit, but takes no sweets and counts how many sweets pass them in a chosen time. Ask students to identify what each part of the model represents in an electrical circuit (A = the cell/battery; B and C = a lamp/resistor; Group carrying sweets = current; D = an ammeter; Sweets = energy transferred from the cell to the lamp/resistor). You can then ask students to suggest how they could change the model to represent a parallel circuit.

Draw series and parallel circuits on the board. Ask students to compare them by completing the table with these words:

divides between branches	divides across components	more than one
same across each branch	same through each component	one

	Series circuit	Parallel circuit
Number of loops		
Current		
p.d.		

Intervention activity: Describe how to investigate and represent the shape of a magnetic field

Students often struggle with the concept of magnetic fields as they cannot see them. This activity helps by revisiting how to draw magnetic fields.

Plotting a magnetic field

Show students a bar magnet and compass. Provide a list of instructions, in the wrong order, of how to use the compass to plot the magnetic field. Ask students to rearrange them. Try some of the incorrect answers suggested to show why they don't work.

Students then play a memory game. Put a diagram of the magnetic field around a bar magnet on the board. Give students 20 seconds to memorise it before removing it from the board, and then 30 seconds to reproduce the diagram. Ask them to swap diagrams with a partner and comment on how well it was drawn based on success criteria (for example, N and S poles labelled, magnetic field lines drawn correctly, direction of field shown correctly).

Repeat for two repelling magnets and two attracting magnets.

P2 Chapter 2: Energy

Introduction to chapter

This chapter introduces students to energy resources, stores, and transfers. Students will look at how electricity is generated by renewable and non-renewable energy resources. They will be introduced to stores of energy and methods of transfer between stores, in particular, by particles, radiation, and forces. Students will also study the links between energy, work done, and power, and will have the opportunity to develop their mathematical skills to real-life scenarios when calculating work done, power, and the cost of using domestic appliances.

Core concepts
- Energy resources
- Energy stores and transfers
- Work done, energy, and power

GCSE links
- Energy changes in a system involving heating, doing work using forces, or doing work using an electric current: calculating the stored energies and energy changes involved
- Calculating work done as force × distance
- Power as the rate of transfer of energy
- Conservation of energy in a closed system, dissipation
- Calculating energy efficiency for any energy transfers
- Renewable and non-renewable energy sources used on Earth, changes in how these are used

Prerequisite knowledge
- Observe that some materials change state when they are heated or cooled, and measure or research the temperature at which this happens in degrees Celsius (°C) (KS2)

Common learning misconceptions

- Energy is a thing and object or something that is tangible
- Energy transfers are always 100% efficient
- 'Heat' is a substance which can flow from place to place
- An object at rest has no energy
- Energy and force are interchangeable terms
- Energy, such as food or fuel, gets used up / energy can be made
- Devices use up energy
- Energy is confined to some particular origin, e.g. food, the electric company
- 'Heat' rises (as opposed to hot substances rising)
- Thermal conductors and insulators are opposites, not part of a continuum
- Hot objects can cool down without something else around them getting hot
- Energy is only transferred upwards by heating
- Cold can be transferred
- Energy disappears in many energy transfers
- When you heat a substance, particles get hotter
- Energy is fuel
- Work is synonymous with labour or a job, and not to do with forces
- Power and energy are the same thing
- Heat and temperature are the same thing

Chapter 2: Energy

Teaching preparation

Key maths skill

Substituting values into an equation to calculate work done, power, and the cost of using domestic appliances Students apply their Year 7 knowledge of equations to help calculate work done, power, and the cost of using domestic appliances. You may need to remind them of the best way to set out questions involving equations; that is, write the equation out in full, substitute the values in, then calculate the final answer.

Key maths skill

Changing the subject of an equation Students working to an extended level will change the subject of the equations introduced in this chapter.

Key vocabulary

Scientific terms This chapter has many key terms that students may have encountered in everyday life but have specific meanings in science, such as 'work done' and 'power'. Energy is a difficult concept to teach because it is an abstract idea that is difficult to define. Energy and transfers of energy are taught in terms of stores instead of types or forms. We cannot observe energy or measure amounts of energy directly, but we can look at how objects have gained or lost energy.

Encourage students to make their own glossary of key terms which they can add to throughout the topic and refer to when answering questions.

Key working scientifically skills

Using simple gears and levers Students use simple gears and levers to investigate how forces transfer energy between stores. They will practise different working scientifically skills, such as evaluating risks, making predictions using scientific knowledge and understanding, recording measurements in a table, and identifying trends and patterns in their results.

2.1 Food and fuels

Theme: Energy

Physics NC link
- comparing energy values of different foods (from labels) (kJ)

Sub-themes: Energy resources, Energy stores

Working scientifically NC link
- present reasoned explanations, including explaining data in relation to predictions and hypotheses

Learning objective	Learning outcomes		
	Developing	Secure	Extending
Compare the energy values of foods and fuels	Identify foods with high and low energy values	**Compare the energy values of foods and fuels**	Predict energy values based on different proportions of food groups
Compare the energy requirements of different activities	Identify different situations or activities which need greater intakes of energy	**Compare the energy requirements of different activities**	Explain the diets of different groups of people, relating this to their energy needs

Tier 2 vocabulary	Tier 3 vocabulary	SB in-text question answers
energy, fuel, joule	kilojoule	**A** 200 000 J **B** 400 kJ **C** 60 kJ

Lesson plan

Reactivate knowledge

1. Name a fuel that you burn.
2. Name a fuel that you put in a car.
3. State which of these activities is more tiring – sitting or walking.

Answers: 1 E.g., coal, wood 2 Petrol / diesel 3 Walking

Lesson resources

Activity: *Energy in food and fuels, and in activities* (student sheet, support sheet, teacher and technician sheet)

Students should know that humans need to eat foods with the right types and amounts of nutrition. They may also know about the content of a healthy human diet.

Trigger interest

Ask students: *What did you have for breakfast? Why is it important to eat breakfast?* Show the class an apple and a plate of chips on the Lesson presentation. Ask: *What are the differences between these foods?*

Guide discussion towards 'energy' being mentioned. You could demonstrate setting sugar alight to show that it is a store of energy (see https://science.cleapss.org.uk/resource-info/sra033-powder-flash.aspx).

Exposition of main content

Energy values of food and fuels Show students the images of different foods and fuels on the Lesson presentation. Ask what the images have in common. Show the image of a food label. Ask students: *Can you think of any other quantities that can be measured in two or more different units? Why do foods have this information on the labels? Why is the amount of energy stated per 100 g?* Discuss possible misconceptions, such as: Energy is only found in living things; fruit and vegetables don't contain energy; energy is a fuel.

Energy for different activities Ask students to *think pair share*: *How much energy from food should a person have on average per day?* Discuss students' suggestions until you agree that it depends on many factors such as gender, age, job, activities carried out. Show students examples of people with different energy requirements on the Lesson presentation.

Main activity

Activity: Energy in foods and fuels (15 mins) Give students a list of foods and fuels such as soups, crisps, ready meals, coal, oil and so on. Ask students to work in pairs and predict the order of the foods and fuels in increasing energy per 100 g. Put the labels of these foods and fuels around the room. Students record the energy per 100 g of each food and fuel and put them in order of increasing energy.

Activity: Energy for activities (5 mins) Students compare the energy requirements of different activities by putting them in rank order. They can also convert the energy values in joules into kilojoules so that they can have a better understanding of which foods would provide the required energy for these activities.

Review and reflect

Ask students to form small groups and compare the order they put the foods and fuels in. Ask students to discuss if they were surprised with any of the energy values. Each group can then share their ideas with the rest of the class.

Homework

Ask students to write down the meals that they would eat in a day with the energy provided by each food and compare this to the total amount of energy they require.

2.2 Energy resources

Theme: Energy

Physics NC link
- fuels and energy resources

Sub-themes: Energy resources, Energy stores

Working scientifically NC link
- ask questions based on observations of the real world, alongside prior knowledge and experience

Learning objective	Learning outcomes		
	Developing	Secure	Extending
Describe how fossil fuels are formed	Name three fossil fuels	**Describe how fossil fuels are formed**	Compare the differences between fossil fuels
Describe the difference between a renewable and a non-renewable energy resource	Identify renewable and non-renewable energy resources	**Describe the difference between a renewable and a non-renewable energy resource**	Compare the long-term use of renewable and non-renewable energy resources
Describe how electricity is generated with renewable and non-renewable resources	Label the parts of a power station	**Describe how electricity is generated with renewable and non-renewable resources**	Evaluate the suitability of different energy resources for different locations

Tier 2 vocabulary	Tier 3 vocabulary
energy resource, fossil fuel, non-renewable, renewable	nuclear power station, thermal power station, uranium

SB in-text question answers
A Coal is formed from trees; oil is formed from sea creatures; both take millions of years to form **B** You need water for cooling and to make steam in a power station **C** Both use a generator; wind turbines turn a generator directly, but biomass is burnt to produce steam to turn a turbine and generator

Lesson plan

Reactivate knowledge

1 Name the unit of energy.
2 Convert 2000 J to kJ.
3 Name two fuels.

Answers: **1** Joules **2** 2 kJ **3** Any two from: coal, oil, gas, wood

Lesson resources

Activity: *Energy resources* (student sheet, support sheet, homework sheet, teacher and technician sheet)

Students should have prior knowledge from Key Stage 2 about how fossils are formed when things that have lived are trapped within rock.

Trigger interest

Show students the images on the Lesson presentation and ask: *Where does the energy come from?* Guide discussion towards 'energy resources' being suggested. Ask students to write down a fact they already know about an energy resource on a sticky note and stick it onto the board. Discuss some of these facts but don't say if they are correct. Explain that they will be learning more about these resources so you will return to the sticky note facts at the end of the lesson.

Exposition of main content

Renewable and non-renewable energy resources
Show students samples of different resources, such as wood, oil, coal, a solar cell, and the images on the Lesson presentation. Ask students to suggest two groups that the samples and images could be divided into. Discuss the groups suggested.

Fossil fuels and power stations Ask students to *think pair share*: *What are fossil fuels and how are they formed?* Share students' ideas.

Use the Lesson presentation image to discuss how fossil fuels are used to produce electricity; discuss advantages and disadvantages of using fossil fuels. Ask: *How is this different from how a wind turbine generates electricity?*

Discuss any misconceptions that arise, such as: Fossil fuels must be renewable because they are formed from the remains of dead plants and animals; fossil fuels will last forever as they are still being formed.

Main activity

Activity: Energy resources (25 mins) Ask students to complete Activity: *Energy resources*. Working in pairs and as part of a larger group, they research and write an extended response about an energy resource.

Ask them to spend a few minutes in their pairs planning what they will need to include in their answer before showing them ideas on the Lesson presentation. Give each pair of students one energy resource to focus their answer on. Students use the resources around the room to research their energy resource, plan their response by writing down relevant notes, and then write an extended response to the question.

Review and reflect

Students join together in their groups so that each energy resource has been covered in that group. Students read out their answers and other students in the group give positive feedback and suggestions for improvements. If time, students could peer-review each other's answers based on success criteria.

Revisit the sticky notes from the start of the lesson and ask students if they agree or disagree with some of the statements.

Homework

Students complete Homework: *Energy resources*.

2.3 Energy adds up

Theme: Energy

Physics NC links

- other processes that involve energy transfer: changing motion, dropping an object, completing an electrical circuit, stretching a spring, metabolism of food, burning fuels
- energy as a quantity that can be quantified and calculated; the total energy has the same value before and after a change
- comparing the starting with the final conditions of a system and describing increases and decreases in the amounts of energy associated with movements, temperatures, changes in positions in a field, in elastic distortions, and in chemical compositions
- using physical processes and mechanisms, rather than energy, to explain the intermediate steps that bring about such changes

Sub-themes: Energy stores, Energy transfer

Working scientifically NC link

- make and record observations

Learning objective	Learning outcomes		
	Developing	Secure	Extending
Describe the energy stores involved in everyday transfers	Name a range of everyday energy stores	**Describe the energy stores involved in everyday transfers**	Describe the energy stores in unfamiliar energy transfers
Describe the ways of transferring energy between stores	Give ways in which energy can be transferred between stores	**Describe the ways of transferring energy between stores**	Describe how energy is transferred in unfamiliar scenarios
Use the law of conservation of energy in energy analysis	Describe ways energy can be dissipated	**Use the law of conservation of energy in energy analysis**	Apply the law of conservation of energy to an unfamiliar scenario

Tier 2 vocabulary	Tier 3 vocabulary	SB in-text question answers
dissipated, electromagnetic, nuclear, thermal	chemical store, energy store, gravitational, kinetic, law of conservation of energy, potential	**A** Money can be transferred, and there is always the same total amount of money at the end as there is at the beginning **B** Any situation where an electrical appliance is used **C** When energy is transferred to the thermal store of the surroundings not to the water

P2 Chapter 2: Energy

Lesson plan

Reactivate knowledge

1. Name two non-renewable energy resources.
2. State how long coal takes to form.
3. State the main advantage of using fossil fuels to generate electricity.

Answers: **1** Two from coal, oil, gas **2** It takes millions of years to form **3** It's very reliable

Lesson resources

Activity: *Energy adds up* (student sheet, support sheet, teacher and technician sheet)

Trigger interest

Ask: *If you brought money to school, how much will you have left if you do not spend any?*

Explain that today's lesson is about energy and, like money, energy cannot just disappear and you cannot end up with more than you had at the start. This is the law of conservation of energy.

Show students the image of Angel Falls on the Lesson presentation. Tell students that the temperature of the water at the bottom of the waterfall is higher than at the top. Ask: *Why?* Discuss responses.

Exposition of main content

Energy is a difficult concept. Ask: *What does the word 'energy' mean to you? How could you use the word 'energy' in a sentence?* Discuss answers.

Energy stores Discuss the list of energy stores on the Lesson presentation. Discuss any misconceptions, such as: Light, sound, and electricity are stores of energy; an object at rest has no energy; energy is a fuel.

Energy transfers Explain that energy can be transferred between stores. Demonstrate this using glass beakers to represent energy stores and a coloured liquid to represent energy. Ask students to *think pair share*: *How can this model be used to represent the transfer of energy between stores and the law of conservation of energy?* Guide discussion to the idea that the liquid (energy) starts in one beaker (store) and can be transferred to other beakers (stores) but the total amount of liquid (energy) is conserved.

Use the examples on the Lesson presentation to describe the ways or pathways that energy can be transferred. If there's time, you could use a model steam engine connected to a dynamo and bulb and describe the energy stores and transfers.

Main activity

Activity: Energy adds up (25 mins) Ask students to complete Activity: *Energy adds up*. They identify energy stores before and after an energy transfer and carry out a series of activities.

Review and reflect

Ask students to peer-mark each other's answers. Discuss any common mistakes that students made.

Refer back to the Angel Falls image and question. Can students now explain why the temperature of the water is higher at the bottom of the waterfall?

Homework

Ask students to make flashcards with energy stores on one side and examples of that store on the other side.

193

2.4 Energy and temperature

Theme: Energy
Physics NC links

- the total energy has the same value before and after a change
- comparing the starting with the final conditions of a system and describing increases and decreases in the amounts of energy associated with movements, temperatures, changes in positions in a field, in elastic distortions, and in chemical compositions
- using physical processes and mechanisms, rather than energy, to explain the intermediate steps that bring about such changes

Sub-theme: Energy and temperature
Working scientifically NC links

- make and record observations
- make predictions using scientific knowledge and understanding

Learning objective	Learning outcomes		
	Developing	Secure	Extending
Describe the difference between energy and temperature in terms of the particles in a substance	Give the units of temperature and energy	Describe the difference between energy and temperature in terms of the particles in a substance	Explain why heating a material can cause the temperature to increase in terms of particle motion
Describe the factors that affect the change in temperature of a substance	Give some factors that can affect the temperature increase of a substance	Describe the factors that affect the change in temperature of a substance	Calculate the energy required to increase the temperature of different substances
Explain what is meant by equilibrium in terms of energy and temperature	Identify scenarios in which equilibrium has been reached	Explain what is meant by equilibrium in terms of energy and temperature	Predict the effect of different factors on the position of equilibrium

Tier 2 vocabulary	Tier 3 vocabulary
equilibrium	

SB in-text question answers

A If you had put your hand in hot water, and then put it in the warm water it would feel cold **B** There are a lot more particles in the bath, even if they are not moving as fast **C** The average speed of the particles will decrease

Lesson plan

Reactivate knowledge

1. Name the unit of energy.
2. Name a unit of temperature we usually use.
3. Describe what is meant by an 'energy store'.

Lesson resources

Activity: *Energy and temperature* (student sheet, support sheet, teacher and technician sheet)

Answers: 1 Joules **2** Degrees Celsius, °C **3** Ways in which energy can be calculated

Trigger interest

Show the image of the volcano on the Lesson presentation. Ask: *Why do rocks melt?* Students should suggest that the rocks get very hot. Explain that a lot of energy is needed to heat the rock up to a high enough temperature (about 1200 °C).

Exposition of main content

The words 'energy' and 'temperature' are often mixed up. This lesson will help students learn why and how they are different.

Activity: Energy and temperature: Ask students to carry out Activity: *Energy and temperature*. Ask for volunteers to stick their cards on the board in the order they have chosen. Discuss why they have chosen this order.

Hot sparks: Show students the image of the sparkler on the Lesson presentation and ask students to *think pair share*: Why don't the sparks from a sparkler burn you?* Encourage students to think about the difference between energy and temperature.

Energy and temperature: Use the information on the Lesson presentation to describe the difference between energy and temperature. Compare the units of energy and temperature.

Main activity

Demonstration: Thermal equilibrium (20 mins)
Place a test tube of hot water into an insulated beaker of cold water. Measure the temperature of both. Ask students to predict the temperature of the water in the test tube and in the beaker after 15 minutes. Write some suggestions on the board.

While waiting for the 15 minutes to elapse, ask students to look at the images on the Lesson presentation and think about what happens to the objects in terms of thermal energy transfer.

After 15 minutes, compare the demonstration results with students' predictions. Discuss their ideas about energy transfer, and discuss any misconceptions, such as: The cold from an object travels to the hotter object.

Demonstration: What affects temperature rise? (10 mins) Heat up beakers of water and oil behind a safety screen to compare how much the temperature increases if different heating methods or amounts of each liquid are used. Ask: *Which beaker will have the biggest increase in temperature? Why? What factors affect the increase in temperature of a substance?* Share students' ideas and then compare with the actual results.

Activity: Energy and temperature (5 mins) Ask students to answer questions on what they have learnt this lesson.

Review and reflect

Ask students to write down three things that they have learnt during the lesson and then share this with their partner. Each pair can then share one of their ideas with the rest of the class.

Homework

Ask students to research and write down three facts about the hottest and coldest places on Earth.

2.5 Energy transfer: particles

Theme: Energy

Physics NC link
- the total energy has the same value before and after a change

Sub-themes: Energy and temperature, Energy transfer

Working scientifically NC links
- make and record observations
- interpret observations and data, including identifying patterns and using observations, measurements, and data to draw conclusions

Learning objective	Learning outcomes		
	Developing	Secure	Extending
Describe how energy is transferred by particles during conduction	Identify scenarios in which conduction occurs	Describe how energy is transferred by particles during conduction	Explain, using the particle model, why conduction occurs at different rates in different substances
Describe how energy is transferred by particles during convection	Identify scenarios in which convection occurs	Describe how energy is transferred by particles during convection	Explain how convection occurs in unfamiliar scenarios
Explain how an insulator can reduce energy transfer	Give some everyday examples of conductors and insulators	Explain how an insulator can reduce energy transfer	Compare conductors and insulators using the particle model

Tier 2 vocabulary	Tier 3 vocabulary
conduction, conductor, insulator, radiation	convection, convection current

SB in-text question answers
A Aluminium **B** Good **C** At the bottom

Lesson plan

Reactivate knowledge

1 State whether particles in a liquid move faster or more slowly as you heat it.
2 Define 'insulator' in terms of circuits.
3 Name a non-metal that conducts electricity.

Lesson resources

Activity: *Energy transfer: particles* (student sheet, support sheet, Information sheet, teacher and technician sheet)

Answers: 1 Faster **2** A material that does not allow a current to pass through easily **3** Graphite

Trigger interest

Hold a burning splint. Ask: *The burning end of the splint is at about 1000 °C, so how is it possible to hold the other end?* Then heat the water at the top of a test tube which has ice at the bottom. Ask: *How is it possible to heat the water in the test tube so that the ice does not melt but the water at the top of the tube boils?* Ask students to *think pair share* their ideas about both questions. Discuss students' ideas and write some on the board – but do not say if they are correct at this stage.

Exposition of main content

Conduction Explain that one method of transferring energy by particles between stores is conduction. Show the image of the saucepan on the Lesson presentation. Ask: *Why is the saucepan made of metal but the handle is made of plastic?* Guide discussion towards the terms 'conductor' and 'insulator'.

Show the images of conduction in a non-metal and in a metal on the Lesson presentation. Ask volunteers to be 'pupil particles' to model how thermal energy is transferred through the non-metal and the metal by the particles. Emphasise that it is the collisions between free electrons and atoms (not atoms with other atoms) that cause rapid energy transfer. The model can also be used to show that liquids and gases are poor conductors because the particles are far apart. Ask students to draw labelled diagrams to describe conduction in a non-metal and in a metal, using the Student Book Chapter 2.5 to help. Discuss any misconceptions, such as: The particles themselves get hotter.

Demonstrating convection Demonstrate convection taking place using, e.g., heating the circular holes from a hole punch in water, heating potassium permanganate crystals in water, the coal mine shaft demonstration. Ask students to describe what they can see and explain why convection takes place using the image on the Lesson presentation. Discuss other situations in everyday life where something is heated by convection.

Discuss any misconceptions, such as: The particles themselves become less dense or lighter.

Main activity

Activity: Investigating conduction (15 mins) In pairs, students use different equipment to measure energy transfers and compare how well materials act as thermal conductors in this experiment.

Review and reflect

Ask students to work in groups of four to discuss their observations from the main activity. Ask each group to suggest common features of conductors and common features of insulators.

Revisit the two questions from Trigger interest and ask students to reflect on their earlier ideas and suggest improvements.

Students can then complete the information sheet to describe convection.

Homework

Ask students to write one multiple-choice question about conduction and one multiple-choice question about convection. For each question, there should be one correct answer and three incorrect answers.

2.6 Energy transfer: radiation

Theme: Energy

Physics NC links
- the total energy has the same value before and after a change
- other processes that involve energy transfer: burning fuels
- temperature difference between 2 objects leading to energy transfer from the hotter to the cooler one, through radiation

Sub-themes: Electromagnetic waves, Energy and temperature, Energy transfer

Working scientifically NC links
- make and record observations
- interpret observations and data, including identifying patterns and using observations, measurements, and data to draw conclusions
- identify independent, dependent, and control variables

Learning objective	Learning outcomes		
	Developing	Secure	Extending
Give the definition of radiation	Describe the difference between temperature and radiation	**Give the definition of radiation**	Explain the difference between radiation and temperature
Give the waves of the electromagnetic spectrum	Identify waves that are part of the electromagnetic spectrum	**Give the waves of the electromagnetic spectrum**	Explain how the properties of different waves relate to their uses
Compare energy transfer by conduction, convection, and radiation	Identify everyday examples of conduction, convection, and radiation	**Compare energy transfer by conduction, convection, and radiation**	Justify the energy transfer in unfamiliar scenarios

Tier 2 vocabulary	Tier 3 vocabulary
radiation	electromagnetic spectrum, infrared radiation, thermal imaging camera

SB in-text question answers

A The Sun; a light bulb **B** A cup of hot tea
C Dark colours

Lesson plan

Reactivate knowledge

1 Name the radiation that the eye detects.
2 State what happens when light hits a mirror.
3 Name the states of matter that convection happens in.

Answers: 1 Light **2** Reflects **3** Gases and liquids

Lesson resources

Practical: *Which colour objects are the best emitters?* (student sheet, support sheet, teacher and technician sheet)

Trigger interest

Show students the images on the Lesson presentation. Ask students to *think pair share*: *What can you see in the images? What do the images have in common? Why can't you usually see the footprints you leave behind?* Discuss students' ideas.

Exposition of main content

Radiation Show students the image of coal burning on the Lesson presentation. Ask: *Which types of radiation does the burning coal give out?* Show the image of the Sun on the Lesson presentation and discuss how visible light, infra-red, and ultraviolet are part of a family of waves known as the electromagnetic spectrum. Discuss how different frequency waves have different uses. Ask students to match the names of the waves to the images on the Lesson presentation. Discuss the fact that, in general, the higher frequency waves are more dangerous.

Absorbing and reflecting infrared radiation Show students the thermal image of the house on the Lesson presentation and ask: *How is this image useful to people?* You could give students pieces of heat-sensitive paper to investigate this further.

Demonstration: Falling corks Demonstrate how different colours absorb different amounts of infrared radiation using two squares of aluminium – one shiny, the other painted dull black – heated at equal distances from a flame. A cork is stuck to the back of each plate with Vaseline. Ask students to predict which cork will fall off first.

Discuss where students have noticed that dark colours absorb more radiation or where white, shiny surfaces are used to reflect radiation.

Emitting infrared radiation Explain that thermal energy cannot be transferred through space by conduction and convection because space is a vacuum (no particles). Energy can be transferred through space by radiation as particles are not needed, but the type and amount of radiation emitted by an object can vary.

Main activity

Practical: Which colour objects are the best emitters? (20 mins) Discuss what factors might affect how much radiation is emitted. Ask students to complete Practical: *Which colour objects are the best emitters?* They measure the temperature drop of different-coloured cans and determine which colour is the best emitter of radiation. They identify variables, draw a conclusion, and then answer questions comparing conduction, convection, and radiation. Discuss that the lids are used in this practical not only for safety, but also to stop radiation from escaping.

Review and reflect

What's the question? Show students key words or phrases on the Lesson presentation from the topic so far and ask them to write a question on a mini-whiteboard where one of the key words or phrases is the answer. Students can then ask each other their questions.

Homework

Ask students to design a house that loses as little thermal energy as possible. This could be a written description or a labelled diagram.

Students should include ideas about insulators, conduction, convection, and radiation.

2.7 Energy transfer: forces

Theme: Energy
Physics NC links
- the total energy has the same value before and after a change
- simple machines give bigger force but at the expense of smaller movement (and vice versa): product of force and displacement unchanged
- work done

Sub-theme: Power and work
Working scientifically NC links
- make and record observations
- interpret observations and data, including identifying patterns and using observations, measurements, and data to draw conclusions

Learning objective	Learning outcomes		
	Developing	Secure	Extending
Give the definition of work	Identify the meaning of the term 'work'	**Give the definition of work**	Explain why no work is done when an object moves in a circle
Calculate work done	Give the factors that will affect work done	**Calculate work done**	Change the subject of the work done equation to calculate force or distance
Apply the law of conservation of energy to simple machines	Describe a simple machine	**Apply the law of conservation of energy to simple machines**	Explain how a force multiplier works

Tier 2 vocabulary	Tier 3 vocabulary
lever, simple machine, *work*	newtonmeter

SB in-text question answers
A You are not exerting a force over a distance
B When you apply a force with your hand, you get a bigger force acting on the lid
C Work = force × distance = 80 N × 1 m = 80 J

Lesson plan

Reactivate knowledge

1 Name the unit of force.
2 Define 'weight'.
3 State the law of conservation of energy.

Lesson resources

Practical: *Energy transfer: forces* (student sheet, support sheet, teacher and technician sheet)

Answers: 1 Newtons **2** Force of the Earth on an object **3** Energy cannot be created or destroyed, only transferred between stores

Students should have prior knowledge from Key Stage 2 that some mechanisms, including levers, pulleys, and gears, allow a smaller force to have a greater effect.

Chapter 2: Energy

Trigger interest

Show students the image on the Lesson presentation of the winding road. Ask: *Why do roads in the mountains wind backwards and forwards and not go straight up the mountain?* Discuss students' ideas.

Exposition of main content

What is work? Show students the images on the Lesson presentation. Ask students to *think pair share*: *In which images are people doing work?* Students will probably have different ideas about what work means. Explain what 'work' means in science.

Calculating work done Introduce the equation to calculate work done and go through Calculation 1 on the Lesson presentation. Ask students to do Calculations 2 and 3 (on the Lesson presentation) using mini-whiteboards to show their workings so you can pick up on any misunderstandings.

Using simple machines Show the images on the Lesson presentation, and set up a pulley and gears system. Ask students to *think pair share*: *What do these images and equipment have in common? How would you use them?* Guide discussion to the idea that they are all simple machines that make a job easier to do.

Main activity

Activity: Energy transfer: forces (20 mins) Students carry out two short practical activities using gears and levers.

After students have completed this activity, ask them to share what they have learnt about using simple machines. Students should be aware that a simple machine reduces the force that is needed to do a job. Remind students of the law of conservation of energy – you cannot create energy, so the amount of energy transferred when using a simple machine is the same as without the machine. This means that if the force is smaller, the distance moved in the direction of the force must be bigger.

Review and reflect

Revisit the question from Trigger interest. Ask students if they can improve their answers from earlier using ideas about work and forces.

Show students the image on the Lesson presentation and ask if they can use the idea of the ramp as a simple machine to explain why the mountain roads are winding.

Homework

Ask students to list three simple machines that they have seen and describe what they are used for.

2.8 Energy and power

Theme: Energy
Physics NC links
- comparing power ratings of appliances in watts (W, kW)
- domestic fuel bills, fuel use and costs

Sub-theme: Power and work
Working scientifically NC links
- make and record observations
- interpret observations and data, including identifying patterns
- make predictions using scientific knowledge and understanding

Learning objective	Learning outcomes		
	Developing	Secure	Extending
Describe the difference between energy and power	Give the definition of power	Describe the difference between energy and power	Explain how power can vary in unfamiliar situations
Calculate power and energy	Identify the units of work done, energy transferred, and power	Calculate power and energy	Change the subject of the power equation to calculate time
Calculate the cost of using domestic appliances	Give the link between kilowatts and kilowatt hours	Calculate the cost of using domestic appliances	Change the subject of the kilowatt hour equation to calculate time, power, or cost

Tier 2 vocabulary	Tier 3 vocabulary
watt	kilowatt, kilowatt hour, power rating

SB in-text question answers

A Energy = power × time = 800 W × 10 s = 8000 J
B Energy units are joules; on an electricity bill you use kWh

Lesson plan

Reactivate knowledge

1. Give the equation for calculating work.
2. Name the unit of work.
3. Give the number of joules in a kilojoule.

Answers: **1** Work = force × distance **2** Joules **3** 1000

Lesson resources (k)

Activity: *Power ratings* (student sheet, support sheet, teacher and technician sheet)

Trigger interest

Show students the images on the Lesson presentation. Ask students to *think pair share*: Why do some microwave ovens cook popcorn faster than others? Why do some electric heaters warm up a room faster than others? Why do some hairdryer settings dry your hair faster than others? Share some students' ideas and agree that different appliances have different power ratings, measured in watts (W) or kilowatts (kW).

Exposition of main content

Power ratings Ask students: *What is the difference between energy and power? How are power and energy linked?* Discuss misconceptions, such as: Power and force are the same thing.

Calculating energy, work, and power Introduce students to the equations that can be used to calculate energy, work, and power. Work through the two examples on the Lesson presentation.

Tell students that this is how they should set out their answers whenever they complete similar calculations.

The cost of energy After working through Example 2, explain that electricity companies use the unit of kilowatt hours instead of joules to calculate your bill. Work through the calculation on the Lesson presentation, showing how power is measured in kW and time is measured in hours.

Main activity

Activity: Power ratings (15 mins) Ask students to complete Activity: *Power ratings*. They predict the order of the power ratings of different appliances. Give students the power rating of a washing machine (e.g., 1700 W) so that they have something to compare the appliances with. Explain that power can also be measured in kilowatts and show students how to convert kW into W. Students examine each appliance to find out its power rating and record it with the correct unit in a table.

They then compare their observations with their prediction and discuss any unexpected results.

Activity: Calculating power, energy, and cost (10 mins) Students work their way around the questions calculating the power of, or energy transferred by, different appliances.

Review and reflect

Ask students to peer mark their partner's answers. Encourage students to use different-coloured pens to make changes or improvements. Volunteers can work through some of the answers on the board, with other students giving feedback at each stage.

Homework

Ask students to choose five appliances in their house and put them in order of cost to run, based on their power ratings and time they are switched on for.

P2 Chapter 2: Energy

Introduction to checkpoint intervention

This checkpoint intervention provides suggestions for a lesson to follow up the P2 2 Energy checkpoint assessment. Depending on the outcomes of the assessment, these suggestions could move a class towards secure, to target specific learning outcomes, or to consolidate knowledge for students achieving secure outcomes. Use students' outcomes from the checkpoint assessment to address general misconceptions from the content covered. Be prepared to re-cover content as required; three key concepts from the chapter are covered in more detail below.

Checkpoint secure learning outcomes

- Describe the difference between a renewable and a non-renewable energy resource
- Describe the difference between energy and temperature in terms of the particles in a substance
- Describe how energy is transferred by particles during convection
- Give the definition of radiation
- Apply the conservation of energy to simple machines
- Calculate the cost of using domestic appliances

Student reflection

Encourage students to reflect on whether there were any checkpoint questions they found difficult or straightforward, as well as their preparation for the checkpoint assessment, including how they revised, the time spent on revision, and what areas they could improve on. For more strategies, see the Metacognition chapter or the Metacognition in Key Stage 3 Science guide on Kerboodle.

Intervention activity: Describe how energy is transferred by particles during convection

Most students can identify situations where thermal energy (heat) is transferred by particles during convection, but many struggle to describe the process due to misconceptions, such as:

- heat is a substance which can flow from one place to another
- heat rises (as opposed to hot substances rising)
- when a substance is heated, the particles get hotter and lighter.

In this activity, students first model convection using 'pupil particles', then write model answers and compare them with others'.

Describing convection

Ask one group of students to stand by the heater in the classroom and another group to stand at the other end of the room. (This represents air particles near the ceiling.) Both groups model the behaviour of air particles when the heater is switched off. Then tell students that the heater is switched on. How does the behaviour of the gas particles change, and why? Other students can make suggestions to help the 'pupil particles' model the air particles' motion. Discuss the movement of both groups of particles and link to their comparative energy. Draw a diagram of the room with a heater and ask students to use their knowledge from the pupil particles model to identify where the hot and cold air would be. Ask students to describe what has happened to the air particles near the heater and draw out ideas of the particles gaining energy, moving faster, and spreading out. Then ask about the density of the air at different places. Draw an arrow to show how the less dense air will rise and the denser air will sink.

Split the class in half. Ask one half to work in pairs to describe how a room is heated by convection using a heater. Ask the other half to work in pairs to describe how the heating element in a kettle heats the water by convection. Students can use the diagram on the board to help; some may copy it and add labels to help with their descriptions. Students then join with a pair from the other half of the class and discuss their descriptions. Discuss some answers as a whole class to check any misunderstandings.

Intervention activity: Apply the conservation of energy to simple machines

Most students can use the law of conservation of energy in energy analyses, but many struggle to apply this to simple machines that act as force multipliers. Students often have the misconception that force multipliers *increase* the energy that you get out of a system. This activity revisits how force multipliers work.

Simple machines as force multipliers

Carry out demonstrations to show how force multipliers work. The aim is to show that if, for example, the output force needs to be bigger than the input force, the input force moves through a bigger distance than the output force. So, in each case, the work done is *the same* and energy is *conserved*. Use a diagram of the lever or pulley system, with suitable values, to show that the work done is the same.

Ask students to apply this to some questions:

1. Jack is using a lever to lift a box. The box is 50 cm from the lever's pivot. First, Jack pushes down on the other end of the lever, 1.0 m from the pivot, but he cannot lift the box.

   Jack then pushes down at a distance of 2.0 m from the pivot. Explain why Jack can now lift the box and why energy is conserved.

2. Explain why a long-armed stapler can staple more sheets than a short-armed stapler.

Intervention activity: Calculate the cost of using domestic appliances

Most students will can substitute values into equations to calculate energy and power. But some find it difficult to use the equations to calculate the *cost* of using an appliance; they particularly struggle to choose the correct units. In this activity, students practise calculating the cost of using an appliance.

Calculating the cost

The 'I do, we do, you do' method will improve students' confidence and ability to calculate the cost of using an appliance on their own.

Write the first of four 'calculating the cost' questions on the board. Model the method you would use to answer the question:

1. Underline the quantities and corresponding numbers in the question, and write them underneath the question; for example: power = 500 W; time = 30 minutes; energy transferred = ?
2. Convert quantities into the correct units.
3. Write down the equation for energy transferred.
4. Substitute the values of power and time into the equation.
5. Calculate the answer and write it down with the correct unit.
6. Use the energy transferred and the cost per kWh to calculate the cost of using the appliance.

For the second question, model the answer but ask students to suggest what to do for each step. For the third question, discuss each step and ask students to complete steps on a mini-whiteboard; feedback on any errors. For the fourth question, ask students to work individually. Model the correct answer on the board for students to mark their work. Discuss any errors.

A further activity could involve students working in pairs: they both write a question and then answer each other's question. Students working at the extending level could write questions that require the equation to be rearranged to calculate time or power.

P2 Chapter 3: Motion and pressure

Introduction to chapter

This chapter introduces students to speed, pressure, and turning forces. Students will look at how motion can be described using distance–time graphs. They will be introduced to pressure in gases, in liquids, and on solids. Students will also study situations in which a force has a turning effect.

Students will have the opportunity to develop their mathematical skills by using equations to calculate speed and pressure.

Core concepts
- Speed and distance–time graphs
- Pressure
- Turning forces

Prerequisite knowledge
- Recognise that some mechanisms, including levers, pulleys and gears, allow a smaller force to have a greater effect (KS2)

GCSE links
- Interpreting quantitatively graphs of distance, time, and speed
- Pressure in fluids acts in all directions: variation in Earth's atmosphere with height, with depth for liquids, up-thrust force (qualitative)
- Links between pressure and temperature of a gas at constant volume, related to the motion of its particles (qualitative)

Common learning misconceptions

- Pressure and force mean the same thing
- Pressure arises from moving liquids or gases
- Moving fluids cause higher pressures
- Pressure in liquids and gases can be stronger in one direction than another
- Objects float in water because they are light and sink because they are heavy
- Gas pressure is caused by collisions between gas particles
- Air does not exert a force because it is too light
- Pressure only acts downwards

Teaching preparation

Key maths skill

Substituting values into an equation to calculate speed, pressure, and the moment of a force Students apply their Year 7 knowledge of equations to help calculate speed, pressure, and the moment of a force. You may need to remind them of the best way to set out questions involving equations; that is, write the equation out in full, substitute the values in, then calculate the final answer.

Key maths skill

Changing the subject of an equation Students working to an extended level will change the subject of the equations introduced in this chapter.

Key maths skill

Drawing and interpreting data graphically Students need the following maths skills to draw and interpret distance–time graphs:

- drawing and labelling a pair of coordinate axes
- plotting points and joining them accurately with straight lines
- reading the scales on the axes.

Students will determine average speed by finding the change in distance over a period of time and carrying out a suitable division. They should be able to label and describe an object's motion using a distance–time graph.

Key vocabulary

Scientific terms This chapter has some key terms that students may have encountered in everyday life but have specific meanings in science, such as 'moments'. Students need to be able to define terms such as 'pressure' and 'atmospheric pressure'. Encourage them to make their own glossary of key terms which they can add to throughout the topic and refer to when answering questions.

Key working scientifically skills

Volume and temperature Students watch demonstrations to see how volume and temperature affect gas pressure, and how depth affects liquid pressure. They also investigate why some objects float and some objects sink.

Students will practise different working scientifically skills, such as presenting observations and data (including graphs), paying attention to objectivity and concern for accuracy, precision, repeatability, and reproducibility, making predictions using scientific knowledge, and understanding and planning the most appropriate type of scientific enquiries to test predictions.

3.1 Speed

Theme: Forces and motion
Physics NC links

- speed and the quantitative relationship between average speed, distance and time (speed = distance ÷ time)
- relative motion: trains and cars passing one another

Sub-theme: Motion
Working scientifically NC links

- apply mathematical concepts and calculate results
- present observations and data using appropriate methods, including tables and graphs
- pay attention to objectivity and concern for accuracy and precision

Learning objective	Learning outcomes		
	Developing	Secure	Extending
Calculate average speed	Identify the correct units for speed, distance, and time	**Calculate average speed**	Change the subject of the speed equation to calculate distance and time
Describe the difference between average and instantaneous speed	Identify examples of instantaneous and average speed	**Describe the difference between average and instantaneous speed**	Compare the average and instantaneous speeds on different sections of the same journey
Describe examples of relative motion	Identify situations in which relative motion is seen	**Describe examples of relative motion**	Compare relative motion of objects in an unfamiliar situation

Tier 2 vocabulary	Tier 3 vocabulary
average speed, relative motion	instantaneous speed, metres per second

SB in-text question answers

A m/s B Just before it hits the ground C 80 km/h

Lesson plan

Reactivate knowledge

1. Give the unit of distance we use in science.
2. Give the unit of time we use in science.
3. Give the steps for writing out a calculation.

Answers: 1 Metres, m **2** Seconds, s **3** Write the equation, put the numbers in the equation, calculate the answer, write the unit

Lesson resources

Activity: *Speed* (student sheet, support sheet, teacher and technician sheet)

Chapter 3: Motion and pressure

Trigger interest

Show students the images on the Lesson presentation of a car, a cheetah, and a person going downhill on a bike. Ask students to *think pair share*: Which object has the fastest speed? What does speed mean? Why is it important that we can work out the speed of an object? Discuss students' answers and explain that speed is a measure of how far something can travel in a particular time and can be measured in different units.

Exposition of main content

Instantaneous and average speed Show students the image of a speedometer on the Lesson presentation and the student statements. Ask students to *think pair share*: Which student do you agree with? Discuss the ideas of instantaneous speed and average speed. Show students the equations for speed and average speed and the example of calculating speed.

Relative motion Ask: *Have you ever been travelling in a car on the motorway when a motorbike overtakes you? If the motorbike overtaking you is travelling at 113 km/h (70mph) and you are travelling at 105 km/h (65 mph), why does it seem like the motorbike is travelling much slower than 113 km/h?* Explain that relative motion means how fast one object is travelling compared to another. Discuss the examples on the Lesson presentation.

Main activity

Activity: Speed (20 mins) Ask students to complete Activity: *Speed*. They work in pairs to time each other moving a set distance in different ways, calculate their average speeds, and then answer some questions.

Review and reflect

Ask students to peer-mark their questions and use different coloured pens to make comments and improvements.

Ask students, in their pairs, to use mini-whiteboards and compete to be the quickest to match up the data on the Lesson presentation. Students must be able to show how they worked each speed out!

Homework

Ask students to research the average speed of different activities and objects.

3.2 Motion graphs

Theme: Forces and motion
Physics NC link
- the representation of a journey on a distance–time graph

Sub-theme: Motion
Working scientifically NC links
- apply mathematical concepts and calculate results
- present observations and data using appropriate methods, including graphs

Learning objective	Learning outcomes		
	Developing	Secure	Extending
Describe motion using a distance–time graph	Label a distance–time graph with descriptions of an object's motion	**Describe motion using a distance–time graph**	Explain why a distance–time graph matches a specific journey
Use data from a distance–time graph to calculate average speed	Identify areas of different speeds from a distance–time graph	**Use data from a distance–time graph to calculate average speed**	Calculate instantaneous speed on a distance–time graph

Tier 2 vocabulary	Tier 3 vocabulary
distance–time graph	

SB in-text question answers

A The slopes do not change **B** A straight line that is shallower than the line for the car **C** Instantaneous

Lesson plan

Reactivate knowledge

1 Give the equation for speed.
2 State the difference between instantaneous and average speed.
3 Estimate walking speed in m/s.

Lesson resources

Activity: *Motion graphs* (student sheet, support sheet, teacher and technician sheet)

Answers: 1 Speed = distance ÷ time **2** Instantaneous speed = speed at a certain time, average speed = total distance ÷ total time **3** 1–2 m/s

Trigger interest

Ask students: *Describe your journey to school. What was your average speed?* Explain that you can tell the story of a journey and work out your speed using a distance–time graph.

Exposition of main content

Distance–time graphs: walking to the shop Show students the simple distance–time graph on the Lesson presentation of a person walking to a shop to buy something. Ask if they can describe the journey.

Distance–time graphs: cycling Show students the image of the distance–time graph for a cyclist on the Lesson presentation. Ask students to work in pairs and use mini-whiteboards to match each section of the journey with the descriptions.

Distance–time graphs: running Show students the graph for runners P and Q on the Lesson presentation.

Ask: *What is the difference in the motion of runner P and runner Q?* Explain that the slope (gradient) of the graph represents the speed. Work through the calculations to find the average speed of the runners.

Ask students: *What would the graph look like if the runners accelerated?*

Distance–time graphs: accelerating Show students the graph showing acceleration in Figure 7 of the Student Book. The slope changes gradually, not suddenly. Instantaneous speed at a certain time can be worked out by drawing a tangent to the curve at that time and calculating the gradient of the tangent.

Main activity

Activity: Motion graphs (20 mins) Ask students to complete Activity: *Motion graphs*. They plot a graph of a bus journey to school and answer questions to describe the journey.

Review and reflect

Ask students to match the distance–time graphs on the Lesson presentation to the descriptions. There is also a distance–time graph animation on Kerboodle.

Homework

Ask students to write a story about a real or imaginary journey and draw a distance–time graph for the journey.

3.3 Pressure in gases

Theme: Forces and motion
Physics NC link
- atmospheric pressure decreases with increase of height, as weight of air above decreases with height

Sub-theme: Pressure
Working scientifically NC link
- interpret observations and data, including identifying patterns and using observations, measurements, and data to draw conclusions

Learning objective	Learning outcomes		
	Developing	Secure	Extending
Describe how volume and temperature affect gas pressure	Identify factors that affect gas pressure	**Describe how volume and temperature affect gas pressure**	Explain how changing particular factors affects gas pressure
Give the definition of atmospheric pressure	Give the cause of atmospheric pressure	**Give the definition of atmospheric pressure**	Compare the atmospheric pressure of different planets
Describe how atmospheric pressure changes with height	Identify altitudes and different locations at which atmospheric pressure will be higher or lower	**Describe how atmospheric pressure changes with height**	Explain why changing altitude affects atmospheric pressure using the particle model

Tier 2 vocabulary	Tier 3 vocabulary
atmospheric pressure, *compressed*, gas pressure, density	

SB in-text question answers

A It expands/gets bigger **B** It increases **C** The mass of 1 m³ of gas is bigger at the bottom of the mountain than it is at the top

Lesson plan

Reactivate knowledge

1. Name the force that slows down objects moving through the air.
2. Define 'unbalanced force'.
3. Write down what happens to the speed of gas molecules as you heat the gas.

Lesson resources

Activity: *Pressure in gases* (student sheet, support sheet, teacher and technician sheet)

Answers: 1 Air resistance/drag **2** The forces do not cancel out **3** They speed up

Students are likely to know about the properties of the states of matter in terms of the particle model, including gas pressure.

Chapter 3: Motion and pressure

Trigger interest

Blowing up a balloon Start to blow up a balloon and ask: *What will happen if I blow into it too much? Why will it happen?* Encourage students to use ideas about particles. Write ideas on the board but do not say if they are correct at this stage as you will return to it later.

Collapsing can Demonstrate the collapsing can. Discuss what happens to the water in the can when it is heated. Ask: *Why does the can collapse?* Write ideas on the board for discussion.

Exposition of main content

Pressure in gases Show students the balloon on the Lesson presentation; ask: *What causes gas pressure?* Discuss students' ideas before providing an explanation. Discuss any misconceptions, such as: Gas pressure is caused by collisions between gas particles.

Air pressure Ask volunteers to help with the air pressure demonstrations outlined in the teacher and technician sheet. For each demonstration, ask: *Can you describe what is happening?* Explain that air pressure is important as it explains, for example, weather patterns and how aeroplanes can fly. Ask: *What causes air pressure? Why don't we feel the air pushing on us? Is atmospheric pressure the same everywhere?* Discuss any misconceptions, such as: Air does not exert a force because it is too light; pressure only acts downwards.

Main activity

Activity: Pressure and temperature (20 mins) Show students the two balloons described in the teacher and technician sheet. Ask students to *think pair share*: *Why is the balloon from the freezer smaller than the balloon at room temperature?* Show a video of a balloon being put into liquid nitrogen and ask the same question. Write ideas on the board. Encourage students to comment and add to the ideas. Use the diagram on the Lesson presentation to explain how pressure and temperature are linked.

Pressure and volume Demonstrate the effect of increasing the pressure on the volume of a small balloon in a sealed syringe. Ask: *Why does the balloon get smaller?* Use the diagram on the Lesson presentation to explain how pressure and temperature are linked.

Review and reflect

Revisit the **Trigger interest** questions. Ask students to improve their answers. Show the 'magic egg' demonstration. Ask students to write a simple explanation individually, then in pairs, and then in groups of four, before creating one final explanation and sharing it with the class.

Homework

Ask students to explain – using words and/or diagrams – why a packet of crisps expands when you take it onto an aeroplane.

3.4 Pressure in liquids

Theme: Forces and motion
Physics NC link
- pressure in liquids increasing with depth; upthrust effects, floating and sinking

Sub-theme: Pressure
Working scientifically NC links
- ask questions and develop a line of enquiry based on observations of the real world, alongside prior knowledge and experience
- make predictions using scientific knowledge and understanding

Learning objective	Learning outcomes		
	Developing	Secure	Extending
Describe how liquids exert a pressure in all directions	Describe how particles cause pressure	**Describe how liquids exert a pressure in all directions**	Apply knowledge of liquid pressure to unfamiliar situations
Describe how liquid pressure changes with depth	Identify areas in which liquid pressure is greater	**Describe how liquid pressure changes with depth**	Explain why liquid pressure changes with depth using the particle model
Explain why some everyday objects float and some sink	Identify objects that will float or sink	**Explain why some everyday objects float and some sink**	Compare floating and sinking in unfamiliar liquids

Tier 2 vocabulary	Tier 3 vocabulary
incompressible, liquid pressure, upthrust	

SB in-text question answers

A 90 degrees **B** There is little space between the particles in a liquid, so it cannot be compressed. There is a lot of space between particles in a gas, so it can be compressed. **C** The supertanker has a large area in contact with the water.

Lesson plan

Reactivate knowledge

1 State what produces gas pressure.
2 State what happens to atmospheric pressure as you go down a mountain.
3 Define 'upthrust'.

Answers: **1** Collisions between gas particles and a surface **2** It increases/gets bigger **3** The upwards force of water or air on an object

Lesson resources

Activity: *Floating and sinking* (student sheet, support sheet, teacher and technician sheet)

Chapter 3: Motion and pressure

Trigger interest

Show students a polystyrene cup and ask: *How can you use water to squash the cup without touching it?* Share some students' answers and discuss why water exerts a pressure and why a submarine isn't squashed at the bottom of the sea.

Exposition of main content

Pressure in liquids Ask: *What happens when you try to compress a sealed syringe with air inside, or one with water inside?* Ask a volunteer to try. Ask students to *think pair share*: *Why can you compress a gas but not a liquid?* Encourage students to use ideas about particles in their answers.

Floating and sinking Show students a sample of different objects such as those on the Lesson presentation. Ask: *Can you explain which of these objects will float in water and which will sink?* Students are likely to explain floating in terms of density. Discuss misconceptions, such as: Heavy things sink and light things float. Show students the image on the Lesson presentation to explain upthrust.

Main activity

Demonstration: Liquid pressure (10 mins) Show students two same-sized plastic bottles: one with a number of holes near the bottom at the same depth, the other with three holes vertically down one side. Block the holes and fill the bottles with water. Ask students to predict what will happen when the holes are unblocked. Ask: *What does this tell you about pressure in liquids?* Use the images on the Lesson presentation to explain.

Activity: Floating and sinking (15-mins) Working in pairs, students investigate how to make a lump of modelling clay float, then explain their observations.

Review and reflect

Discuss students' observations from Activity: *Floating and sinking* to check their understanding of why objects float and sink. Ask: *How is it possible for a very heavy oil tanker to float?*

Homework

Ask students use the internet to (make and) explain how a Cartesian diver works.

3.5 Pressure on solids

Theme: Forces and motion
Physics NC link
- pressure measured by ratio of force over area – acting normal to any surface

Sub-theme: Pressure
Working scientifically NC links
- ask questions and develop a line of enquiry based on observations of the real world, alongside prior knowledge and experience
- make predictions using scientific knowledge and understanding
- plan the most appropriate types of scientific enquiries to test predictions

Learning objective	Learning outcomes		
	Developing	Secure	Extending
Give the definition of pressure, and give the direction that it acts in	Identify situations in which pressure is acting on a solid	**Give the definition of pressure, and give the direction that it acts in**	Describe the relationship between pressure and force and between pressure and area
Calculate pressure	Identify the units of pressure, force, and area	**Calculate pressure**	Change the subject of the pressure equation to calculate force or area
Describe situations where high and low pressures are useful	Identify situations in which pressure is higher or lower	**Describe situations where high and low pressures are useful**	Explain the effect of changing area or force on pressure

Tier 2 vocabulary	Tier 3 vocabulary
pressure	newtons per metre squared, pascal

SB in-text question answers

A It is the same; they are all at right angles/90 degrees **B** N/m^2, N/cm^2, Pascals (Pa) **C** Wide straps have a big area, so the weight is spread over a larger area, making a smaller pressure

Lesson plan

Reactivate knowledge

1. State the direction of gas and liquid pressure on a surface.
2. State the unit of force.
3. State two units of area.

Lesson resources

Activity: *Pressure on solids* (student sheet, support sheet, teacher and technician sheet)

Answers: 1 At right angles, 90 degrees to the surface **2** Newtons, N **3** Centimetres squared, cm^2, metres squared, m^2

Chapter 3: Motion and pressure

Trigger interest

Show students the image on the Lesson presentation and ask: *What causes these footprints to be made?* Discuss students' ideas and explain that a person has exerted pressure on the surface. Show students a balloon popping when pressed against one drawing pin but show that it does not pop when pressed against several pins at the same time. Ask students to *think pair share* why the balloon does not pop – but do not tell them the correct answer at this stage. Discuss misconceptions, such as: Pressure only acts downwards.

Exposition of main content

Calculating pressure Ask students to *think pair share*: *Suggest how more/less pressure can be exerted so that the footprints are deeper/shallower. The legs on a table make dents in the carpet. What can you do to stop this happening?*

Guide discussion towards the equation to calculate pressure. Work through the examples on the Lesson presentation.

High and low pressure Show students the images on the Lesson presentation and ask: *Why do some of the objects have a large area in contact with the surface and some have a small area?* Encourage students to use ideas about force/weight and pressure in their answers.

Main activity

Activity: Pressure on solids (25 mins) In pairs, students predict if the pressure they exert on the ground is greater when they stand on one foot or on both feet. Students plan the method for their investigation (and, if time, carry it out) and answer questions about pressure. Be aware that student may be uncomfortable weighing themselves in front of others.

Review and reflect

Discuss students' observations from Activity: *Pressure on solids* to check their understanding. Students peer review their investigation plan using the success criteria on the Lesson presentation.

Homework

Students explain why a car will sink into the mud when driving across a muddy field but a tractor will not.

3.6 Turning forces

Theme: Forces and motion
Physics NC link
- moment as the turning effect of a force

Sub-theme: Rotation
Working scientifically NC links
- interpret observations and data, including identifying patterns and using observations, measurements, and data to draw conclusions
- pay attention to objectivity and concern for repeatability and reproducibility

Learning objective	Learning outcomes		
	Developing	Secure	Extending
Give the definition of the moment of a force	Identify scenarios in which there will be the turning effect of a force	**Give the definition of the moment of a force**	Explain turning effects of forces in unfamiliar situations
Calculate the moment of a force	Give the units of moment, distance from pivot, and force	**Calculate the moment of a force**	Change the subject of the moment equation to calculate a force or the distance from a pivot
Apply the law of moments	Identify situations in which moments are balanced or unbalanced	**Apply the law of moments**	Apply the law of moments to unfamiliar situations

Tier 2 vocabulary	Tier 3 vocabulary
centre of gravity, centre of mass, *pivot*	law of moments, *moment*, newton metres

SB in-text question answers

A Work is force × distance moved in the direction of the force; a moment is force × distance moved perpendicular to the force **B** The large apple exerts a bigger force so has to be placed at a smaller distance from the pivot to balance a smaller force at a larger distance **C** The point of the pencil, which acts as the pivot, is very narrow. It is difficult to position the pencil's centre of gravity, halfway up the pencil shaft, above the pivot. Usually, the centre of gravity is left or right of the pivot, so the pencil falls

Lesson plan

Reactivate knowledge

1 State the equation for work.
2 State where handles are in relation to hinges: close together/far apart.
3 State the difference between 'balanced' and 'unbalanced' forces.

Answers: 1 Work = force × distance in the direction of the force **2** Far apart **3** Balanced = no net force, unbalanced = net force

Lesson resources

Activity: *Turning forces* (student sheet, support sheet, teacher and technician sheet)

Trigger interest

Show the images on the Lesson presentation and ask students to *think pair share*: *Why does the tightrope walker use a long pole? Why is a screwdriver being used to open the tin lid?* Challenge a volunteer to push the classroom door shut using one finger close to the hinges and to compare it to pushing the door shut using one finger near the handle. Discuss the student's observations and introduce the idea of a pivot and a moment (the turning effect of a force).

Exposition of main content

Calculating moments Show students examples of levers, such as using a screwdriver to lift the lid of a paint pot. Explain that they are 'force multipliers' – a larger force acts than is supplied. Ask students to suggest two ways in which the force on the paint pot lid can be increased. Guide discussion to the conclusion that the longer the lever, and the further the effort force acts from the pivot, the greater the force on the paint pot lid. This can be demonstrated using, for example, screwdrivers of different lengths to lift the paint pot lid. Discuss any misconceptions, such as: A bigger turning effect occurs when the force is near to the pivot. Introduce the equation for the moment of a force and work through the example on the Lesson presentation.

Unstable objects Challenge volunteers to stand up straight next to a wall, with their heels, back, and head against the wall. Follow the instructions on the Lesson presentation. Ask students to suggest reasons for their observations. Write some ideas on the board without saying if they are correct at this stage. Encourage students to comment on each other's ideas.

Challenge another volunteer to decide if it is easier to topple a marker pen stood on its end, or a Bunsen burner stood upright. Ask students if they can explain why.

Centre of gravity Use students' ideas to introduce the term 'centre of gravity' (mass) and its position with respect to the pivot for a stable and an unstable object.

Main activity

Activity: Turning forces (25 mins) Introduce the terms 'clockwise moments' and 'anticlockwise moments'. Demonstrate how to set up the equipment for Activity: *Turning forces*. Explain that students are going to work in pairs to investigate the law of moments. Ask them to complete Activity: *Turning forces*.

Review and reflect

Ask pairs of students to discuss their observations about the law of moments. Then ask them to join with another pair, and then another four students, and to draw a final conclusion. Share conclusions with the class. Ask students to identify if their results are reproducible and explain why.

Homework

Ask students to make a revision resource about Chapter 3, such as a knowledge organiser, flash cards, or a PowerPoint presentation.

Chapter 3: Motion and pressure

P2

Introduction to checkpoint intervention

This checkpoint intervention provides suggestions for a lesson to follow up the P2 3 Motion and pressure checkpoint assessment. Depending on the outcomes of the assessment, these suggestions could move a class towards secure, to target specific learning outcomes, or to consolidate knowledge for students achieving secure outcomes. Use students' outcomes from the checkpoint assessment to address general misconceptions from the content covered. Be prepared to re-cover content as required; three key concepts from the chapter are covered in more detail below.

Checkpoint secure learning outcomes

- Calculate average speed
- Describe motion using a distance–time graph
- Describe how atmospheric pressure changes with height
- Explain why some everyday objects float and some sink
- Describe situations where high and low pressures are useful
- Apply the law of moments

Student reflection

Encourage students to reflect on whether there were any checkpoint questions they found difficult or straightforward, as well as their preparation for the checkpoint assessment, including how they revised, the time spent on revision, and what areas they could improve on. For more strategies, see the Metacognition chapter or the Metacognition in Key Stage 3 Science guide on Kerboodle.

Intervention activity: Describe motion using a distance–time graph

Most students can interpret and label some parts of a distance–time graph but some struggle to link speed to distance and time. This activity consolidates what lines of different gradients on a distance–time graph mean.

Distance–time graphs

Sketch a distance–time graph on the board. It should have sections, labelled A to D, to show an object:

- not moving
- moving at a constant speed away from the starting position
- moving at a faster constant speed away from the starting position
- moving at a constant speed for the return journey to the starting position.

Ask students to look at how the distance changes over each section and relate this to the object motion. Discuss any misconceptions that arise.

Sketch on the board, one at a time, four graphs each with just two sections. Ask students to write a description of the motion for each section on a mini-whiteboard (you could write descriptions on the board for students to choose from). Then describe simple motions and ask students to draw the matching distance–time graph on the mini-whiteboards.

P2 Chapter 3: Motion and pressure

Intervention activity: Describe situations where high and low pressures are useful

Many students confuse the words 'pressure', 'force', and 'weight' so struggle to describe why low or high pressure is useful in different situations.

Display this exam-style question:

Explain why people in countries with lots of snow wear snowshoes when walking.

Ask students to suggest why snowshoes are worn. Write ideas on the board for other students to comment on. Encourage students to process their thoughts:

- Establish if high or low pressure is needed and why (in this case, low pressure is needed so that the person does not sink into the snow).
- Think about the pressure equation and how this can help you to determine how to achieve a lower pressure (low force and/or high area).
- Decide which method has been used in this example (shoes with a large surface area in contact with the ground).

With the help of students, write a model answer to the exam-style question.

Discuss other examples of situations where high or low pressure is useful, e.g., a sharp knife. Then, ask students to work in pairs. Each student should explain a different situation, then swap answers and mark each other's work based on these criteria:

- Identify if high or low pressure is needed. (1 mark)
- Explain why this pressure is needed. (1 mark)
- Refer to the pressure equation. (1 mark)
- State if it is the (small/large) area and/or (small/large) force that determines if the pressure is high or low. (1 mark)

Intervention activity: Apply the law of moments

Most students understand the concept of a force's turning effect and intuitively know how to balance a seesaw, but many struggle to apply the law of moments correctly in mathematical problems.

Set up a plank of wood (at least 2 m long) on a brick as the pivot. Place an object on one end of the plank 0.5 m from the pivot. Ask students to suggest how the plank and a selection of weights can determine the weight of the object and then add weights to the other end of the plank (at the same distance from the pivot) until it balances. Discuss why the plank balances in terms of moments and write out the calculations on the board. Move the weights closer to the pivot. Discuss why the plank no longer balances (using the idea of moments) and use calculations to explain what happens.

The 'I do, we do, you do' method will improve students' confidence and ability to apply the law of moments.

Draw the diagram and write the first of four questions on the board where either a missing force or distance needs to be calculated. Model the method you would use to answer the question:

1 Underline the quantities and corresponding numbers in the question, and write them underneath the question; for example: anticlockwise force = 2.5 N; anticlockwise distance from pivot = 15 cm; clockwise force = 7.5 N; clockwise distance from pivot = ?

2 Write down the equation for moment of a force.

3 Substitute the relevant numbers into the equations to calculate clockwise moment and anticlockwise moment.

4 Apply the law of moments for equilibrium: clockwise moment = anticlockwise moment.

5 Rearrange the equation to calculate the missing quantity.

For the second question, model the answer but ask students to suggest what to do for each step. For the third question, discuss each step and ask students to complete steps on a mini whiteboard; feedback on any errors. For the fourth question, ask students to work individually. Model the correct answer on the board for students to mark their work. Discuss any errors.

Answers

Answers to Maths, Working scientifically, and Literacy activities and chapter openers are supplied on Kerboodle.

Working scientifically

WS2.1 Planning investigations 2

1. Accurate data – close to the true value; precise data – repeat measurements with a small spread; hazard – something that could hurt you or anybody else; risk – how likely it is you could hurt yourself *(3 marks for all correct; 2 marks for 2 correct; 1 mark for 1 correct)*
2. Repeatable – similar results/small spread/precise data when you repeat an investigation [1 mark]; reproducible – similar results when different people carry out the same investigation, or when you repeat an investigation using a different method or equipment [1 mark]
3. For example: hazard – boiling water [1 mark], risk – scalding [1 mark], control measure – leave to cool before moving [1 mark]; hazard – lit Bunsen burner [1 mark], risk – hair catching fire [1 mark], control measure – tie hair back [1 mark]

WS2.2 Presenting data 2

1. Mean – add up values, and divide by number of values; mode – identify the value that occurs most; median – place numbers from smallest to biggest, and find the middle one [2 marks for all correct; 1 mark for 1 correct]
2. Blue 72° [1 mark], brown 108° [1 mark], green 126° [1 mark], hazel 54° [1 mark]
3. Mean = 146.8cm, median = 155cm, mode = 122cm [1 mark for each correct answer]

   The mean is affected by outliers (the three shorter students). [1 mark] The mode finds the most common height, which is low in this example. [1 mark] The median is the best measure, as it ignores the outliers. [1 mark]

WS2.3 Analysing and evaluating 2

1. Best fit [1 mark], linear [1 mark], directly proportional [1 mark], secondary [1 mark]
2. Repeat an experiment (several times) [1 mark], use a wider range [1 mark], use secondary data [1 mark]
3. At 20 m bungee length, extension = 10 m [1 mark]; at 40 m bungee length, extension = 20m [1 mark] (or equivalent data), showing that a doubling of the independent variable [1 mark] causes a doubling of the dependent variable [1 mark]

WS2.4 Communicating scientific information

1. Make it clear [1 mark], correct [1 mark], coherent [1 mark], and concise [1 mark]
2. Any four from: When you write for a journal you need to use scientific vocabulary correctly [1 mark], use formal language [1 mark], and set out evidence that supports any conclusions drawn [1 mark]. When you are writing for the public you need to explain scientific vocabulary [1 mark], write less formally [1 mark], and use examples [1 mark].
3. Example answers [6 marks]: Leaflet that shows appropriate vocabulary, explains scientific terms, uses short words, uses short sentences, and uses illustrations or diagrams. Description or list of the strategies used that reflects the content of the leaflet. This ensures the child's interest is kept and they are able to understand the information being presented as it is broken down into small, manageable chunks.

WS2.5 Using evidence and sources

1. Peer reviewed [1 mark], reliable [1 mark], biased [1 mark], funding [1 mark]
2. a) It was published in a journal [1 mark], and so was peer reviewed before publication [1 mark]
   b) Any five from: the journalist may not personally believe in global warming [1 mark]; the journalist may believe climate change only has natural causes [1 mark]; the journalist may not want to reduce their own use of fossil fuels [1 mark]; the journalist may see the claims as a threat to their existing lifestyle [1 mark]; they may believe the claims are exaggerated [1 mark]; claims of climate change may harm the financial interests of their newspaper/employer [1 mark]; the claims challenged established scientific thinking, and so need further evidence to be collected before being fully accepted [1 mark]
3. Any four from: if the funder of the research also produces the product being researched, they may ask the scientists to focus on possible positive effects [1 mark]; the company may risk losing money if the research does not produce positive effects [1 mark]; the scientists may worry about losing their jobs if they do not focus on the positive effects [1 mark]; any negative effects may be ignored or overlooked [1 mark]; named possible negative effect e.g. high salt content [1 mark]; the research has been published by the company, and so has not been peer reviewed [1 mark]; these reasons make the research unreliable [1 mark]

Answers

WS2.6 Development of scientific understanding

1. Explanation [1 mark], evidence [1 mark], method [1 mark], law [1 mark], model [1 mark]
2. Any two from: if their experiment does not give the expected results [1 mark]; if new evidence is discovered through new technology/different experiments [1 mark]; another scientist has a different idea that explains a concept more accurately [1 mark]
3. Any three from (accept other reasonable suggestions): Ptolemy was a respected scientist [1 mark]; the geocentric model had been in place for 1500 years [1 mark]; the model went against established scientific thinking [1 mark]; Copernicus was not a well-known scientist [1 mark]; Copernicus's work might have undermined the work of other eminent scientists [1 mark]; Copernicus's model did not always accurately predict planetary positions, so there might be a different explanation [1 mark]

Biology Chapter 1: Health and lifestyle

Chapter 1.1: Nutrients

1. carbohydrates – provide energy vitamins and minerals – remain healthy
   lipids – energy store and insulation water – needed in cells and bodily fluids
   protein – growth and repair fibre – provide bulk to food [6 marks]
2. Any two from: provides you with a store of energy/keeps you warm by providing a layer of insulation under your skin/protects your organs from damage [2 marks]
3. a) Carbohydrates provide energy [1 mark] through the process of respiration in cells [1 mark]
   b) Adds bulk to food [1 mark] so food is pushed along the gut / out of the body more easily [1 mark]

Chapter 1.2: Food tests

1. starch – turns blue-black; sugar – turns orange-red; lipids – makes paper translucent; protein – turns purple [4 marks]
2. a) Crush cereal with a pestle and mortar, add a few drops of water [2 marks]
   b) Benedict's solution [1 mark]
3. Benedict's solution [1 mark] as cakes contain sugar [1 mark], ethanol [1 mark] as cakes contain butter / margarine / oil [1 mark].

Chapter 1.3: Unhealthy diet

1. Energy, joules/kilojoules, obese, heart disease /stroke / diabetes / some cancers, tired [5 marks]
2. a) 11 000 kJ – 9000 kJ = 2000 kJ [2 marks]
   b) Difference in energy requirement = 15 000 kJ – 10 000 kJ = 5000 kJ
   Percentage increase from original job = 5000 kJ ÷ 10 000 kJ × 100 = 50% [4 marks]
3. Estimate within the range >9000J and <13 000J [1 mark] Reasoning: teacher will be on their feet for much of the day so will use more energy than an office worker [1 mark] but are not doing manual work so will use less than a construction worker [1 mark]

Chapter 1.4: Digestive systems

1. stomach – food is mixed with acid and digestive juices
   small intestine – small molecules of nutrients are absorbed into the bloodstream
   large intestine – water is absorbed back into the body
   rectum – faeces are stored here until they pass out of the body mouth – food is chewed and mixed with saliva [4 marks]
2. large food molecules like carbohydrates / proteins / fats [1 mark] are broken down into smaller molecules [1 mark] like sugar/ amino acids / fatty acids and glycerol [1 mark]
3. Any 4 from: walls covered with villi [1 mark], increasing the surface area [1 mark] for more nutrients to be absorbed [1 mark] lots of blood capillaries [1 mark] to transport absorbed nutrient molecules [1 mark]

Chapter 1.5: Bacteria and enzymes in digestion

1. carbohydrates, carbohydrase, amino acids, protease, fatty acids and glycerol, lipase [6 marks]
2. a) Large intestine [1 mark]
   b) Fibre [1 mark]
   c) Produce vitamins / named vitamin which we use [1 mark]
3. Any 4 from: they speed up digestion [1 mark], breaking down large molecules into small molecules [1 mark] so they can be absorbed into the bloodstream [1 mark]; enzymes do not get used up [1 mark], as they are catalysts [1 mark]

Chapter 1.6: Drugs

1. chemicals, recreational, medicinal, addiction, withdrawal symptoms [5 marks]
2. Any three from:
   Medicinal drugs are used in medicine, benefit health, treat symptoms, or cure an illness. Examples include paracetamol and antibiotics. Recreational drugs are used for enjoyment, may help a person relax or give them more energy, have no health benefit, are harmful in some cases, and many are illegal. Examples include heroin, cocaine, cannabis, and ecstasy. [2 marks]
3. Examples of possible answers – award up to 2 marks for impact, and up to 2 marks for linked explanations:
   Increased crime e.g. violence – due to aggressive behaviour / stealing – to get money for drugs
   Increased medical care / costs - to treat withdrawal symptoms / medical issues linked to drug taking
   More police time required – to deal with linked crimes / to prevent availability of drugs

Chapter 1.7: Alcohol

1. ethanol, depressant, nervous, liver [4 marks]
2. a) (alcoholic drink is consumed); ethanol is absorbed into your bloodstream [1 mark]; it then travels to your brain [1 mark], where it affects your nervous system [1 mark].
   b) drinking (large amounts) of alcohol over a long time [1 mark] causes scarring / cirrhosis [1 mark]
3. Alcohol passes through to baby's bloodstream. [1 mark] It affects development of organs/brain/nervous system. [1 mark] This increases the risk of (award a further 2 marks for 2 named conditions): miscarriage, Fetal Alcohol Syndrome (FAS), stillbirth, premature birth, or low-weight babies.

Chapter 1.8: Smoking

1. Tar – contains chemicals which cause cancer. Nicotine – addictive and makes the heart beat faster. Carbon monoxide – reduces the amount of oxygen the blood can carry. [2 marks for all 3 correct, 1 mark for 1 correct]
2. Two from: Increased risk of a miscarriage, cause low-birth-weight babies, affects fetal development. Carbon monoxide in cigarette smoke stops oxygen binding to haemoglobin, so less oxygen reaches baby.
3. a) To remove mucus [1 mark], as cilia that would normally do this are paralysed by smoking. [1 mark]
   b) Mucus flows into the lungs [1 mark] containing microorganisms (which can cause infection). [1 mark]

Chapter 1 Summary Answers

1. Proteins – used for growth and repair [1 mark]
   Vitamins and minerals – needed in small amounts to keep you healthy [1 mark]
   Carbohydrates – provide energy [1 mark]
   Lipids – provide a store of energy and are used to insulate the body. [1 mark]
2. a) Gullet/oesophagus. [1 mark]
   b) Nutrients are absorbed into the blood. [1 mark]
   c) U [1 mark]
   d) Large food molecules are broken down [1 mark] into smaller food molecules (which can be absorbed). [1 mark]
3. Carbohydrates – for energy, lipids – for energy/insulation/organ protection, proteins – for growth/repair, vitamins and minerals – needed in small amounts to maintain health, water – needed in cells / body fluids, fibre – to add bulk to food/prevent constipation. [Award up to 2 marks for naming relevant functions, and up to 2 marks for linked descriptions]
4. a) Pestle and mortar. [1 mark]
   b) Any two from: wear eye protection, wash hands immediately if chemicals come into contact with skin, wear gloves, keep alcohol away from naked flame. [2 marks]
   c) Add copper sulfate solution and sodium hydroxide solution to the food solution (biuret). If the solution turns purple, protein is present. [3 marks]
5. a) Medicinal drugs have a medical benefit to health, recreational drugs are taken for enjoyment. [2 marks]
   b) Drugs alter chemical reactions in the body. [1 mark]
   c) Stimulants speed up the nervous system, for example, caffeine, nicotine, ecstasy, cocaine. Depressants slow down the nervous system, for example, alcohol, cannabis, heroin. [2 marks]
6. a) Enzymes break large molecules down into smaller molecules. [1 mark]
   b) Enzymes speed up reactions without being used up. [2 marks]
   c) Any four from: Both are broken down from large molecules into smaller ones. Both are broken down by enzymes. Both are broken down in the stomach and small intestine. Carbohydrate is broken down by carbohydrase whereas protein is broken down by protease. Carbohydrates are broken down into sugar molecules whereas protein is broken down into amino acids. Carbohydrates are also broken down/digested in the mouth. [4 marks]
7. Students should be marked on the use of good English, organisation of information, spelling and grammar, and correct use of specialist scientific terms. The best answers will provide a full explanation of issues with conception and fetal development [6 marks maximum].

Answers

Examples of correct scientific points:
Alcohol can reduce fertility in men and women.
Alcohol can reduce the number of sperm a man produces, reducing the chances of the egg being fertilised.
When people drink alcoholic drinks, ethanol is absorbed into the blood stream.
The ethanol can have damaging effects on the development of the organs and nervous system of the foetus.
This is because substances are passed from the bloodstream of the mother to the foetus through the placenta.
This can cause Foetal Alcohol Syndrome (FAS), which affects the way the brain develops.
Other complications can include miscarriage, still birth, and low baby weights/premature birth.

8. If you eat too much/more energy than you need, you will become overweight [1 mark] as the body stores additional fat over the skin. [1 mark] Overweight/obese people have an increased risk of heart disease/strokes/diabetes/some cancers/arthritis [1 mark] explanation of disease e.g., as blood vessels become blocked/increased body mass damages joints. [1 mark]
If you eat too little/less energy than you need, you will become underweight. [1 mark] Underweight people often suffer from a poor immune system/lack energy to do things, [1 mark] and may suffer from a lack of vitamins or minerals. [1 mark; alternatively, award 1 mark for a correctly named deficiency]

Biology Chapter 2: Biological processes

Chapter 2.1: Photosynthesis

1. algae, producers, photosynthesis, carbon dioxide, glucose, light [6 marks]
2. a) Yes because sunlight is available. [1 mark]
   b) No because no sunlight is available. [1 mark]
   c) No because there is no sunlight. There are no chloroplasts in the root hair cells. [2 marks]
3. Producers / plants use the process of photosynthesis to produces glucose [1 mark]. This provides energy for plants to grow [1 mark]. Animals cannot make their own food [1 mark]. Animals therefore eat plants / producers to gain energy. [1 mark]

Chapter 2.2: Leaves

1. Stomata – allow gases to diffuse into and out of the leaf
   waxy layer – reduces amount of water evaporating
   guard cells – open and close stomata
   veins – transport water to cells in leaf (Award 3 marks if all correct, 2 marks if 2 correct and 1 mark for 1 correct)
2. Water diffuses into the root / root hair cells [1 mark] is transported through the plant in the water vessels [1 mark] evaporates out of leaves [1 mark]
3. Thin – to allow carbon dioxide to diffuse into the leaf [1 mark] large surface area - to absorb as much (sun) light as possible [1 mark]. Both factors allow the plant to maximise the rate of photosynthesis [1 mark]

Chapter 2.3: Plant minerals

1. Minerals, nitrates, roots, vessels [4 marks]
2. To replace missing minerals from the soil / provide additional minerals [1 mark] to ensure a crop does not have a mineral deficiency / has all the minerals it needs for healthy growth [1 mark]
3. Nitrates make amino acids [1 mark] amino acids join together to make proteins [1 mark] proteins needed to grow new leaves / shoots / for repair [1 mark]

Chapter 2.4: Aerobic respiration

1. mitochondria, respiration, glucose, energy, water [5 marks]
2. Aerobic respiration occurs in the mitochondria. Mitochondria are found in cells. Oxygen reacts with glucose. It releases carbon dioxide and water, together with energy. [4 marks]
3. Any four from: Inhaling fills alveoli (in the lungs) with oxygen [1 mark]; the oxygen diffuses into the bloodstream [1 mark]. Oxygen is carried by red blood cells / binds to haemoglobin [1 mark] and is transported in the bloodstream to cells [1 mark]. Glucose is taken in through food [1 mark]; the food is digested [1 mark] and glucose absorbed through the wall of the small intestine [1 mark]. Glucose is carried to cells in the blood (plasma) [1 mark].

Chapter 2.5: Anaerobic respiration

1. anaerobic, oxygen, energy, lactic acid, cramp, [5 marks]
2. Any three from:
   Anaerobic respiration occurs without oxygen, aerobic respiration requires oxygen [1 mark]
   Anaerobic respiration produces lactic acid, aerobic respiration does not [1 mark]
   Anaerobic respiration produces less energy per glucose molecule. [1 mark]
   Aerobic respiration produces water, anaerobic respiration does not [1 mark]
3. Aerobic respiration transfers more energy per glucose molecule [1 mark], so is more efficient / requires less food to be eaten [1 mark] anaerobic respiration produces lactic acid [1 mark] which causes painful cramps / makes moving difficult [1 mark]

225

Chapter 2 Summary Answers

1. a) (Aerobic) respiration. [1 mark]
   b) Mitochondria. [1 mark]
   c) Oxygen, carbon dioxide. [2 marks]
2. a) Producer. [1 mark]
   b) Chloroplasts. [1 mark]
   c) Oxygen [1 mark]
   d) Add iodine, [1 mark] turns blue-black. [1 mark]
3. a) Nitrates/phosphates. [1 mark]
   b) Manure/fertiliser. [1 mark]
   c) To make chlorophyll [1 mark] which absorbs light [1 mark] for photosynthesis. [1 mark]
4. a) B, D, A, C [3 marks]
   b) Yellow-brown → Blue/black. [2 marks]
   c) For example, for respiration/to build cell walls. [1 mark]
5. a) Oxygen [1 mark]
   b) Carbon dioxide and water [2 marks]
   c) Allow carbon dioxide into the leaf [1 mark] and allow oxygen out of the leaf [1 mark]
   d) Bubbles would stop [1 mark] as photosynthesis would stop [1 mark], because there is no light. [1 mark]
6. Students should be marked on the use of good English, organisation of information, spelling and grammar, and correct use of specialist scientific terms. The best answers will provide a full explanation of the adaptations for photosynthesis. [maximum 6 marks]

   Examples of correct scientific points:
   Fermentation is a type of anaerobic respiration.
   Fermentation occurs in some microorganisms/yeast.
   These microorganisms respire in the absence of oxygen.
   Energy is transferred from glucose.
   glucose → ethanol + carbon dioxide (+ energy)
   The ethanol product can be used in alcoholic drink production.
   The carbon dioxide product is used in bread production/to make dough rise.
7. Students should be marked on the use of good English, organisation of information, spelling and grammar, and correct use of specialist scientific terms. The best answers will provide a full explanation of fermentation, with the process explained in a logical order. [6 marks maximum]

   Examples of correct scientific points:
   Leaves contain chlorophyll, which traps light.
   Leaves are thin, which allows gases to diffuse in and out of the leaf easily.
   Leaves have a large surface area to absorb as much light as possible.
   Leaves have veins/xylem to transport water to cells.
   Leaves have a palisade layer/cells with more chloroplasts near the top of the leaf, to maximise the absorption of sunlight.
   Leaves have stomata to allow carbon dioxide into (and oxygen out of) the leaf.

Biology Chapter 3: Ecosystems and adaptation

Chapter 3.1: Food chains and webs

1. 1 food chain – diagram showing the transfer of energy between organisms
   food web – diagram showing linked food chains
   predator – animal that eats another animal
   prey – animal that is eaten (3 marks for all correct, 2 marks for 2 correct, 1 mark for 1 correct)
2. a) giraffe/impala/zebra [1 mark]
   b) acacia tree/grass [1 mark]
   c) acacia tree [1 mark]
   d) Credit any suitable answer. For example,
      grass → impala → leopard → lion
      [1 mark for correct order of organisms, 1 mark for arrows in correct direction]
3. Any four from: As energy is transferred along a chain, some is transferred to the surroundings / by heating, some energy is lost in waste products, and not all of an organism is eaten; therefore at each level of the food chain less energy is transferred to the organism in the next level; this means there is not enough energy available to support higher levels within a food chain. [4 marks]

Chapter 3.2: Disruption to food chains and webs

1. food, shelter (first 2 can be in either order)
   interdependence, bioaccumulation [4 marks]
2. a) The way in which organisms depend on each other [1 mark] to survive / grow / reproduce [1 mark]
   b) Rabbit population would increase [1 mark] as it has no predators/it will not get eaten. [1 mark]
3. The hawk / fox population may decrease [1 mark] as they have reduced food supplies. [1 mark]
   The caterpillar population may increase [1 mark] as they have fewer predators. [1 mark]

Chapter 3.3: Ecosystems

1. ecosystem – living organisms in a particular area, and the habitat they live in
   community – plants and animals found in a particular habitat
   habitat – place where a plant or animal lives
   (Award 2 marks for all, 1 mark for one)
2. Bees and birds have different niches / they eat different things [1 mark]. Bees require nectar from flowers, whereas birds live off insects living on the leaves. [1 mark]
3. A niche is the place or role that an organism has in a habitat. [1 mark] Award up to 3 additional marks for examples with associated explanations:
   e.g. Not every organism lives in the same part of the tree. Microorganisms at the base of the tree break down old leaves; this gives the tree further nutrients to absorb for growth.

Insects live in the tree trunk; the insect larvae are food for birds that may live in the canopy.
Squirrels and bees live in the canopy; the activities of each organism do not conflict each other, and so different organisms can co-exist.
Bees gather pollen and nectar when the tree is in blossom, while squirrels gather acorns as food.

Chapter 3.4: Competition

1. compete, resources, mates, light [4 marks]
2. When there are lots of prey, the population of predators increases.
The large predator population will cause the prey population to decrease.
There is now not enough food for all the predators so the predator population decreases.
The prey population will now increase as less are being eaten.
The cycle starts again.
[3 marks]
3. Any four from Initially, the population of European ladybirds will increase significantly [1 mark] because they can feed on aphids and other ladybird species. [1 mark] Eventually their food supply will decrease [1 mark] so the seven-spotted ladybird population will decrease [1 mark] this allows the population of aphids to increase [1 mark] as less are eaten [1 mark] The cycle then starts again.

Chapter 3.5: Adapting to change

1. Characteristics, camouflaged, survival (3 marks)
2. Any three from: waxy layer, spines instead of leaves, large root system, stems which can store water. (3 marks)
3. Any four from: Grow leaves in the spring when light / temperature is high [1 mark] to enable / maximise photosynthesis [1 mark]; lose leaves in the winter to save energy [1 mark]; leaves provide a layer of warmth / protection at the base of the tree [1 mark] / nutrients can be reused [1 mark].

Chapter 3 Summary Answers

1. a) Arctic. [1 mark]
   b) White fur – camouflage. [1 mark]
      Thick fur – insulation. [1 mark]
      Large feet – to stop the bear sinking into snow. [1 mark]
      Sharp claws and teeth – to catch and eat prey. [1 mark]
2. a) Shelter/food. [1 mark]
   b) Different to (a), for example: food/shelter/mates. [1 mark]
   c) Light. [1 mark]
3. a) Corn → mouse → owl. [1 mark]
   b) Corn. [1 mark]
   c) Producers have energy transferred from glucose they make. Consumers have energy transferred from the organisms they eat. [2 marks]
   d) Mice population would increase [1 mark] as there are no owls to eat them. [1 mark]

4. a) The spider population would increase as there are no predators/nothing would eat them. [2 marks]
   b) The grasshopper population would decrease as shrews and spiders would need to eat more of them to survive. [2 marks]
   c) Mice and shrews occupy different niches because they eat different foods. [2 marks]
   d) Any three from: toxic chemical builds up in the food chain. Owls eat many other organisms so owls receive a higher dose of the toxic chemical. High levels can cause death to an organism. Correct use of term bioaccumulation. [4 marks]
5. Students should be marked on the use of good English, organisation of information, spelling and grammar, and correct use of specialist scientific terms. The best answers will provide a correct food chain and a complete explanation of the insecticide's effects laid out in a logical order. [6 marks maximum]
   Examples of correct scientific points:
   Plankton → fish → fish-eating birds
   Insecticide runs into river.
   Taken up by plankton.
   DDT accumulates in fish when they eat the plankton.
   One fish eats lots of plankton, but not enough to cause death.
   DDT accumulates in birds when they eat the fish.
   One bird eats many fish.
   DDT level is now so high/concentrated that it causes death in the bird.
6. Students should be marked on the use of good English, organisation of information, spelling and grammar, and correct use of specialist scientific terms. The best answers will provide at least two named examples with relevant adaptations. [6 marks maximum, award 1 mark for each named example and up to 2 marks for explaining relevant adaptations]
   Examples of correct named organisms and adaptations:
   Snowshoe hair changes fur colour [1 mark] it grows white fur in winter to blend in with the snow [1 mark] grows red/brown fur in summer for camouflage against the earth. [1 mark]
   Birds/named bird, e.g, swallows [1 mark] migrate and fly to warmer places in the winter [1 mark] for a better food supply/less harsh environmental conditions. [1 mark]

Biology Chapter 4: Inheritance

Chapter 4.1: Variation

1. species, characteristics, variation, environmental, inherited [5 marks]
2. a) Environmental: tattoo, scar. [1 mark] Inherited: blood group, eye colour. [1 mark] Both: body mass, intelligence [1 mark]
   b) A person chooses to style their hair in a particular way [1 mark] it is not determined by the genetic material they inherit [1 mark]

3. Identical twins have the same genetic material [1 mark] so they have the inherited characteristics [1 mark]. Any differences between the twins must therefore be caused by environmental factors. [1 mark]

Chapter 4.2: Continuous and discontinuous

1. discontinuous, continuous, bar chart, histogram [4 marks]
2. Continuous:, maximum sprinting speed, average leaf size. Discontinuous: hair colour, shoe size. [4 marks]
3. a) Most people are of an average height, around 150 cm. Few people are very short, below 135 cm. Few people are very tall, above 170 cm. [3 marks]
   b) Height is affected by both inherited and environmental factors. If your parents are tall, you are also likely to be tall (inherited). However, growth can be affected by environmental factors, for example, malnourishment. [3 marks]

Chapter 4.3: Inheritance

1. DNA, chromosome, gene
2. a) gene, chromosome, DNA, nucleus, cell [2 marks]
   b) Sperm contains chromosomes from the father [1 mark] egg cell contains chromosomes from the mother [1 mark] nuclei join during fertilisation [1 mark] so embryo / baby produced has genetic material from both parents [1 mark]
3. Any four from: Chromosomes occur in pairs [1 mark] one of the chromosomes in the pair is inherited from the mother and one from the father [1 mark], during every fertilisation [1 mark] a different combination of chromosomes is inherited [1 mark], so some characteristics will be the same if the same chromosome is inherited [1 mark], but others may be different if a different characteristic is inherited [1 mark]

Chapter 4.4: Natural selection

1. Evolved, millions, fossils, remains, stone [5 marks]
2. Organisms which have adaptations suited to their habitat survive for longer. This means they produce more offspring. Offspring are likely to inherit their parents' advantageous characteristics. Therefore more offspring with the advantageous characteristics survive, continuing the process. [3 marks]
3. Any four from: Before the Industrial Revolution, pale moths were more successful as they were camouflaged from predators on pale tree bark. [1 mark] Therefore most of the peppered moth population was pale. [1 mark] The Industrial Revolution caused trees to become blackened. [1 mark] Pale moths became less camouflaged / successful. [1 mark] Dark moths became more camouflaged / successful. [1 mark] Therefore dark moths reproduced more than pale moths / The population of dark moths increased rapidly. [1 mark] Therefore a greater proportion of peppered moths were dark in colour [1 mark].

Chapter 4.5: Extinction

1. extinct, anywhere, environment, predators, research [5 marks]
2. Gene banks store genetic samples from many different species. These samples can be used for research. These samples can be used to create new individuals. [3 marks]
3. Any four from: A change to an organism's habitat can cause individuals to die / they are less well adapted [1 mark] e.g. climate change / introduction of a disease [1 mark] This could lead to more competition for food / food sources become more scarce / disease may kill organisms. [1 mark]. Fewer / no offspring are produced as a result [1 mark]. Population of the species decreases [1 mark]. Extinction occurs when all individuals of a species, throughout the world, have died [1 mark]

Chapter 4 Summary Answers

1. a) Nucleus. [1 mark]
   b) Watson, [1 mark] Franklin. [1 mark]
2. a) Differences in a characteristic within a species. [1 mark]
   b) Bathroom/Newton scales. [1 mark]
   c) A characteristic/body mass value that can take any value within a range. [1 mark]
   d) Histogram. [1 mark]
3. a) DNA. [1 mark]
   b) A chromosome is a long strand of DNA. A gene is a (short) section of DNA. Chromosomes contain many genes and each gene codes for a single characteristic. [2 marks]
   c) Half of chromosomes come from the mother and half from the father. Genetic material is transferred from mother via the egg and from father via sperm. Sperm and egg's genetic material combine during fertilisation. Embryo/fertilised egg contain pairs of chromosomes/46 chromosomes. [4 marks]
4. a) Fossils (of dinosaur skeletons). [1 mark]
   b) No organisms of that species are alive anywhere in the world. [1 mark]
   c) The introduction of new predators can mean more organisms in a species are eaten than number of offspring produced. Destruction of habitat can mean loss of shelter for organisms, which leads to the death of individuals through exposure. Credit any other sensible suggestions of causes of extinction with a relevant explanation. [4 marks]
   d) Gene banks store genetic samples, for example, seeds/eggs/sperm/tissue. Samples from gene bank can be used to create new organisms in the future. Samples can also be used for research. [3 marks]
5. a) 70%. [1 mark]
   b) discontinuous, the characteristic can only result in one of two values. [2 marks]
   c) For example, tattoo/body piercing/scar. [1 mark]
6. Students should be marked on the use of good English, organisation of information, spelling and grammar, and correct use of specialist scientific terms. The best

answers will provide a full overview of the process of natural selection in a logical order. [6 marks maximum]
Examples of correct scientific points:
Organisms evolve through natural selection slowly over time.
Organisms in a species show variation – this is caused by differences in their genes.
The organisms with the characteristics that are best adapted to the environment survive and reproduce. Less well adapted organisms die.
This process is known as 'survival of the fittest'.
Genes from successful organisms are passed to the offspring in the next generation.
This means the offspring are likely to possess the characteristics that made their parents successful.
This process is then repeated many times.
Over a long period of time this can lead to the development of a new species.

7. Students should be marked on the use of good English, organisation of information, spelling and grammar, and correct use of specialist scientific terms. The best answers will provide a full overview of the process of inheritance and the environment in a logical order. [6 marks maximum]
Examples of correct scientific points:
Variation is the difference in characteristics within a species.
Inherited variation depends on the genetic material/characteristics inherited from parents.
This is passed on when the egg and sperm cell combine/during fertilization
Environmental variation is caused by the effects of a person's surroundings and/or lifestyle.
Many inherited characteristics can be altered through environmental factors.
Named examples e.g., hair colour, body mass, height, or leaf size.
Explained example e.g., you may inherit the genetic characteristics to be tall but if you eat a poor diet your growth rate may be reduced.

Chemistry Chapter 1: The Periodic Table

Chapter 1.1: Three elements

1. Copper – shiny, easy to hammer into thin sheets, good conductor of thermal energy ; sulfur – brittle, does not conduct electricity [5]
2. copper – electric cables because copper is a good conductor of electricity; germanium – fibre optic cables because germanium can change the direction of light. [4]
3. copper and germanium are shiny, but sulfur is not; copper is a good conductor of electricity, germanium and sulfur are brittle, but gold is not. [4]

Chapter 1.2: Metals and non-metals 1

1. Properties, without [2]
2. metals – copper, magnesium, zinc; non-metals – chlorine, oxygen, sulfur [6]
3. metals are good conductors of electricity and thermal energy , but most non-metals are not; metals are shiny but non-metals are not; metals have high densities but non-metals have low densities; metals are malleable and ductile but non-metals are brittle; metals are sonorous but non-metals are not; metals have high melting point but non-metals have low melting points. [6]

Chapter 1.3: Metals and non-metals 2

1. non-metal oxides – acidic, gas at 20 °C; metal oxides – basic, solid at 20 °C [4]
2. the chemical properties of a substance describe its chemical reactions [1]
3. the product of the reaction of sodium with oxygen is a basic solid, but the product of the reaction of sulfur and oxygen is an acidic gas. [2]

Chapter 1.4: Groups and periods

1. Groups, periods [2]
2. Density increases from top to bottom of the group [1]
3. In both periods, the melting point increases from left to right for the first four elements, and the melting point of the other elements are low. [2]

Chapter 1.5: The elements of Group 1

1. Conduct, low, softer
2. a) [diagram of chromatography setup: chromatography paper, pencil, beaker, green spot from felt tip pen, pencil line, water]
   b) Hardness decreases going down the group.
   c) 0.4 Mohs
3. Hydrogen; all other elements in the group react with water to make hydrogen gas

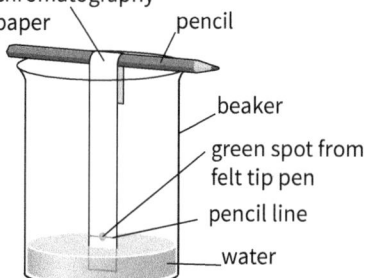

Chapter 1.6: The elements of Group 7

1. Halogens, right, non-metals, chloride, less
2. Chlorine – green gas; bromine – orange liquid; iodine – grey solid
3. In Group 7, melting point increases from fluorine (-220 °C) at the top of the group to iodine (114 °C) at the bottom of the group. But in Group 1, melting point decreases from lithium (180 °C) at the top of the group to rubidium (39 °C) at the bottom of the group. Argon's melting point is between −248 °C and −158 °C.

Chapter 1.7: The elements of Group 0

1. Non-metals, colourless, low, gas, unreactive [5]
2. Helium has a lower density than air [1]
3. Melting point increases from helium (-270 °C) at the top of the group to xenon (-112 °C) at the bottom of the group.

Chapter 1 Summary Answers

1. a) From top to bottom of the group, melting point increases. [2 marks]
   b) About 1750 °C. [2 marks]
2. a) One from: low melting point, dull. [1 mark]
   b) Non-metal [1 mark] since its properties are consistent with those of a typical non-metal. [1 mark]
   c) Y. [1 mark]
3. a) One of the products of the reaction is formed in the gas state. [1 mark]
   b) Solution formed is alkaline. [1 mark]
   c) Sodium + water → sodium hydroxide + hydrogen [3 marks – 1 for correct reactants, 1 for correct reactants, 1 for arrow drawn correctly]
   d) i) One of the products is hydrogen. [1 mark]
      ii) Reaction of potassium with water is more vigorous. [1 mark]
   e) Reactions get more vigorous from top to bottom of the group (from lithium to potassium). [1 mark]
4. From left to right of the period (sodium to chlorine), relative size decreases. [1 mark]
5. a) Two from: fluorine, chlorine, bromine, iodine, astatine. [2 marks]
   b) Do not conduct electricity [1 mark], poor conductors of heat. [1 mark]
   c) i) Bromine. [1 mark]
      ii) Increases from top to bottom of the group. [1 mark]
      iii) any answer between −219 and −8 °C [1 mark]

Chemistry Chapter 2: Separation techniques

Chapter 2.1: Pure substances

1. A [1]
2. Pure [1] because melting point is fixed [1]
3. In science – one substance only, with identical particles; in everyday life – something that has not be processed (or similar definition)

Chapter 2.2: Mixtures

1. True – C; corrected version of A – A mixture is made up of different substances that are not joined together; corrected version of B – you can change the amounts of substance in a mixture

2. For example: mixture – its substances are not joined together, compound – the atoms of its elements are joined together strongly; mixture – usually easy to separate, compound – need to do chemical reactions to separate into its elements.
3. For example: vaccine – preventing disease; paint – make things colourful

Chapter 2.3: Solutions

1. Solution, solute, solvent, water, salt [5 marks]
2. Sugar particles separate from each other and are surrounded by water particles. The sugar and water particles mix randomly and move around, sliding over each other. [4 marks]
3. 75 g – 4 g = 71 g [2 marks]

Chapter 2.4: Solubility

1. An insoluble substance does not dissolve; a soluble substance dissolves in a solvent; solubility increases with temperature for most solutes; solubility is the mass of substance that dissolves in 100 g of water. [4 marks]
2. Line graph, with temperature on labelled x-axis and solubility on labelled y-axis. The graph shows that the solubility of zinc bromide increases with temperature. [4 marks]
3. Solubility of lead nitrate increases evenly from about 36 g/100 g of water at 0 °C to about 95 g/100 g of water at 60 °C. The solubility of cerium(III) sulfate decreases with temperature, from about 18 g/100 g of water at 0 °C to about 3 g/100 g of water at 30 °C. The solubility of cerium(III) sulfate does not change between 40 °C and 100 °C. [4 marks]

Chapter 2.5: Filtration

1. From top – insoluble filtrate; liquid residue. [2 marks]
2. The material traps solid bits of dirt and liquid oil passes through the gaps between the fibres. [2 marks]
3. Insoluble solid from liquid, for example sand and water; small pieces of solid from gases, for example face masks that separates viruses from air; insoluble solid from a solution, for example coffee solution from ground-up coffee beans. [4 marks]

Chapter 2.6: Evaporation and distillation

1. Heat/warm the solution. Water evaporates, leaving salt behind. [2 marks]
2. When one liquid reaches its boiling point, it evaporates. The gas then rises into the condenser and condenses back into a liquid. [4 marks]
3. (a) – evaporation, because the substance needed (copper chloride crystals) is the solute; distillation, because the substance needed (propanone) is the solvent; distillation, because the substance needed (ethanol) is the solvent [3 marks]

Chapter 2.7: Chromatography

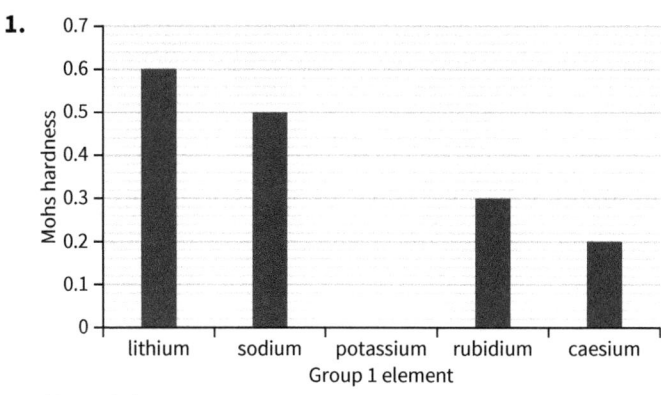

1.

[Bar chart showing Mohs hardness of Group 1 elements: lithium 0.6, sodium 0.5, potassium 0, rubidium 0.3, caesium 0.2]

(6 marks)

2. Spinach, because the pattern of the spots matches the pattern of spots in figure 3 [2 marks]
3. Some dyes in the mixture mix with water better than others. All the dyes are attracted to the paper, but some are attracted more strongly than others. In one minute, a dye that is attracted more strongly to the water than to the paper moves further than a dye that is attracted more strongly to the paper. [2 marks]

Chapter 2 Summary Answers

1. B, D, F, A, C, E [4 marks]
2. a) Mass of salt. [1 mark]
   b) Whether or not the ball floats. [1 mark]
   c) For example, temperature/mass of golf ball. [1 mark]
   d) 100 g + 10 g = 110 g [2 marks – 2 for correct answer, 1 if working is correct but answer is incorrect]
   e) 20 g [1 mark]
   f) 20 g × 2 = 40 g [1 mark]
   Mass of water is doubled, so mass of salt must be doubled. [1 mark]
3. a) [Graph of mass of sodium nitrate that dissolves in 100 g of water vs temperature in °C]

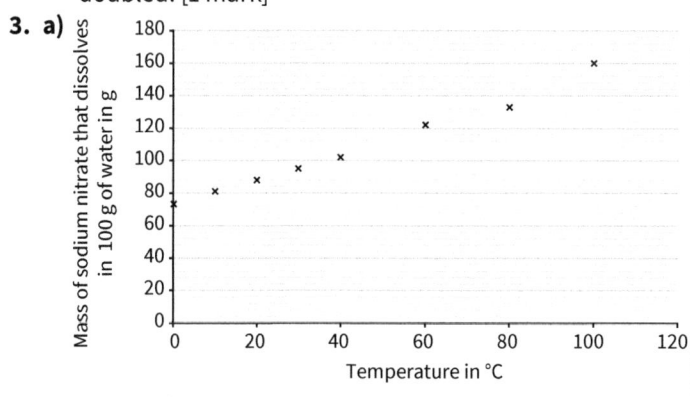

   [1 mark for each correctly labelled axis, 1 mark for each sensibly labelled scale, 1 mark for correctly plotting all the points]
   b) [1 mark for correctly drawn line of best fit]
   c) As temperature increases, so the mass of sodium nitrate that dissolves also increases. [1 mark]

Chemistry Chapter 3: Metals and other materials

Chapter 3.1: Metals and acids

1. salt, hydrogen, lead, magnesium, gold [5 marks]
2. Calcium + hydrochloric acid → calcium chloride + hydrogen [3 marks]
3. Products – calcium nitrate and hydrogen [2 marks]
   Word equation – calcium + nitric acid → calcium nitrate + hydrogen [3 marks]

Chapter 3.2: Metals and oxygen

1. magnesium/zinc, oxides, copper, gold.
2. zinc + oxygen → zinc oxide
3. reacts very vigorously with oxygen, product is lithium oxide

Chapter 3.3: The reactivity series

1. C [1 mark]
2. lithium hydroxide and hydrogen [2 marks]
3. nickel is between iron and lead – nickel reacts with hydrochloric acid, but lead does not; iron reacts with water and air, but nickel does not [2 marks]

Chapter 3.4: Metals displacement reactions

Summary questions

1. zinc [1 mark]
2. a, c, d [3 marks]
3. zinc + copper chloride → zinc chloride + copper [2 marks]
   Zinc + lead oxide → zinc oxide + lead [2 marks]
   Magnesium + iron chloride → magnesium chloride + iron [2 marks]

Chapter 3.5: Extracting metals

1. separate the metal compound from the compounds it is mixed with in the rock; use chemical reactions to extract the metal from its compound [2 marks]
2. 6% × 400 kg = 24 kg
3. magnesium is above carbon in the reactivity series. Carbon can only be used to extract metals that are below it in the reactivity series.

Chapter 3.6: Ceramics

1. Hard, brittle, electrical insulator, high melting point [4 marks]
2. B and D, because they have high hardness values, and very high melting points [2 marks]
3. There are very strong forces between the atoms in the structure, and a great amount of energy is needed to break these strong forces. [2 marks]

Chapter 3.7: Polymers

1. flexible and strong [2 marks]
2. a) low density [1 mark]
   b) poor conductor of thermal energy [1 mark],
3. PVC is harder than nylon, and has a greater density. Nylon is stronger when pulled than PVC. [3 marks]

Chapter 3.8: Composites

1. low density, does not rust, can be moulded to any shape [3 marks]
2. concrete withstands pushing forces, steel withstands pulling forces [2 marks]
3. fibreglass is 5 times stronger when pulled. [1 mark]

Chapter 3 Summary Answers

1. Brittle, electrical insulator, hard, high melting point, stiff. [5 marks]
2. a) A mixture of materials, each with different properties. [1 mark]
   b) Concrete and steel/iron. [2 marks]
   c) It can withstand high squashing forces and high stretching forces. [1 mark]
3. Calcium – bubble vigorously; copper – no change; potassium – moves on surface of water and purple flame. [2 marks]
4. a) Two from: same temperature, same volume of acid, acid of same concentration. [2 marks]
   b) Wear eye protection [1 mark] because the acid may be harm eyes. [1 mark]
   c) Zinc [1 mark] - of the three metals, it is highest in reactivity series. [1 mark]
   d) Hydrogen. [1 mark]
5. a) magnesium + oxygen → magnesium **oxide** [1 mark]
   b) sodium + water → sodium hydroxide + **hydrogen** [1 mark]
   c) zinc + hydrochloric acid → zinc **chloride** + hydrogen [1 mark]
   d) iron + **oxygen** → iron oxide [1 mark]
   e) potassium + **water** → potassium hydroxide + hydrogen [1 mark]
   f) calcium + **hydrochloric** acid → calcium chloride + hydrogen [1 mark]
   g) zinc + copper oxide → zinc oxide + **copper** [1 mark]
   h) magnesium + iron oxide → magnesium **oxide** + iron [1 mark]
6. a) X and Z [1 mark] because in each case, the metal on its own is more reactive/higher in the reactivity series than the metal in the compound. [1 mark]
   b) One from:
   iron + copper oxide → iron oxide + copper
   iron + lead oxide → iron oxide + lead
   [3 marks – 1 for correct reactants, 1 for correct products, 1 for correctly drawn arrow]
7. a) i) The metal. [1 mark]
   ii) Two from – volume of acid, concentration of acid, temperature, amount of metal, size of pieces of metal. [2 marks]
   iii) So that the investigation is fair. [1 mark]
   b) Pour the same amount of acid into each test tube [1 mark] and add the same amount of metal to each test tube. [1 mark] The metal that bubbles most vigorously is the most reactive. [1 mark]
   c)

metal	observations
iron	
magnesium	
zinc	

   d) To see if the order of reactivity for the three metals is the same for the different acid. [1 mark]

Chemistry Chapter 4: The Earth

Chapter 4.1: The Earth and its atmosphere

1. crust, mantle, outer core, inner core [4 marks]
2. gas, nitrogen, oxygen, carbon dioxide, carbon dioxide [5 marks]
3. The crust cannot flow, but the outer core can flow; both the crust and inner core cannot be compressed [3 marks]

Chapter 4.2: Sedimentary rocks

1. porous (air or water can get into the gaps between the grains); soft (easy to scratch); can withstand strong pushing forces. [3 marks]
2. weathering breaks rock into smaller pieces; erosion breaks rock into smaller pieces and moves them from the original rock; transport moves sediments far from the original rock; deposition is the settling of sediments; compaction involves the weight of sediment above making sediments below stick together [5 marks]
3. advantage – strong or can withstand strong pushing forces; disadvantage – easy to scratch or damaged by acidic rain [3 marks]

Chapter 4.3: Igneous and metamorphic rocks

1. Igneous, igneous, metamorphic, metamorphic, non-porous, hard. [6 marks]
2. They are hard and durable, so are not damaged when people walk on them [3 marks]
3. Igneous rock – liquid rock freezes to form crystals; metamorphic rock also consists of crystals, but they were formed by the action of pressure on an existing rock, or by the action of heat (without melting) on an existing rock [3 marks]

Answers

Chapter 4.4: The rock cycle

1. (a) melting (b) cooling (c) compaction or cementation [5 marks]
2. Fossils in limestone that formed on the seafloor have been found on Mount Everest. This shows that the rock that is now the mountain must have moved upwards [2 marks]
3. Metamorphic to sedimentary – metamorphic rock weathered, sediments transported and deposited, action of compaction or cementation forms sedimentary rock. Sedimentary to igneous – sedimentary rock is heated and becomes hot enough to melt, liquid rock cools to make igneous rock [6 marks]

Chapter 4.5: The carbon cycle

1. respiration, combustion, photosynthesis, dissolving, sedimentary, coal [6 marks]
2. For example from a fossil fuel (store) to the atmosphere (store) by combustion (process). Then from the atmosphere to the ocean (store) by dissolving (process). Then from the ocean to sedimentary rock (store) by deposition (process) [7 marks]
3. Combustion is a chemical reaction, but dissolving is a physical change; combustion adds carbon dioxide to the atmosphere, but dissolving removes carbon dioxide from the atmosphere [4 marks]

Chapter 4.6: Global heating

1. Greenhouse effect, global heating [2 marks]
2. Makes Earth warm enough for life, allows water to be in the liquid state [2 marks]
3. For example: Between 1900 and 1925, the global average air temperature was between 13.5 °C and 14.0 °C. The global average temperature has increased since the 1950s, when it was between 13.75 and 14.0 to 2000, when it was about 14.3 °C [5 marks]

Chapter 4.7: Climate change

1. Fossil fuels, global heating, climate change *[3 marks]*
2. For example, melting ice caps/glaciers cause flooding; climate change results in extinctions and makes it harder to grow food [3 marks]
3. For example: make walking/cycling safer or improve public transport so that people travel by car less – this works because travel by most cars results in the emission of carbon dioxide; insulate houses – this works because less fuel is needed for heating; grow more food locally – this works because fewer lorries are needed to transport food, so lorries use less fuel. [6 marks]

Chapter 4.8: Recycling

1. collecting old glass bottles, melting the glass, and making new bottles; collecting and melting poly(propene) bottle tops, and using them to make poly(propene) rope [2 marks]
2. aluminium objects are collected, shredded and melted; the liquid is poured into an ingot and cooled until it freezes; the ingot is warmed and rolled into thin sheets, the sheets are made into new aluminium objects [7 marks]
3. Advantages – natural resources will last longer, needs less energy than using new materials, reduces waste and pollution; disadvantages – some people do not like sorting their rubbish, collecting lorries use fuel and make pollution; a statement giving an overall judgement [6 marks]

Chapter 4 Summary Answers

1. Igneous, metamorphic, sedimentary. [3 marks]
2. From left: oxygen, nitrogen. [2 marks]
3. a) From top: crust, mantle, outer core, inner core. [4 marks]
   b) From top: solid, solid, solid, liquid. [4 marks]
4. a) Hand lens. [1 mark]
   b) A [1 mark]
   c) No [1 mark]
   d) B or C [1 mark]
   e) A [1 mark]
   f) A [1 mark]
   g) B or C [1 mark]
5. a) C [1 mark]
   b) A [1 mark]
   c) Liquid rock/magma/lava cooled and froze/solidified. [2 marks]
   d) Surrounding rocks have eroded, [1 mark] but granite has not. [1 mark]
   e) Was heated by the magma that formed the granite [1] and of the three sedimentary rocks, rock B is the only limestone. [1 mark]

Physics Chapter 1: Electricity and magnetism

Chapter 1.1: Charging up

1. positive, negative, electrons, repel, attract, field [6 marks]
2. Electrons are transferred between the balloon and the jumper. The balloon is charged, but the wall is neutral. The charge of the balloon repels like charges from the surface of the wall. [3 marks]
3. Any 2 similarities + any two differences, maximum [4 marks]
   Example answers:
   Gravitational and electric fields produce forces.
   You cannot see or feel a gravitational or electric field.
   They produce non-contact forces.
   Gravitational fields are produced by masses. Electric fields are produced by charges.
   Gravitational fields produce forces that only attract. Electric fields produce forces that attract and repel.

Chapter 1.2: Circuits and current

1. charge, second, electrons, ammeter, amps, A [6 marks]
2. a) Series circuit with battery of cells, motor, and switch. Students should annotate the switch, and explain how this can be switched on and off to control the circuit. [2 marks]
   b) The electrons move/a current flows. [1 mark]
3. a) Have two people pulling the rope [1 mark]
   One pulls one way, and the other pulls in the opposite direction [1 mark]
   The rope does not move, so no current flows/the lamp goes out [1 mark]
   b) have a third person who grabs the rope and stops it [1 mark]
   when you open the switch the current doesn't flow [1 mark]

Chapter 1.3: Potential difference

1. push, energy, voltmeter, rating, rating [5 marks]
2. The buzzer would sound louder, because the three cells transfer more energy than the two [2 marks]
3. Example answers (4 marks maximum)
4. a) The current is like the amount of rope passing a point per second (do not allow current is the rope), the battery is like the person pulling the rope.
   b) You can add a person watching how much rope goes past per second, you cannot measure the pull or the energy transferred.

Chapter 1.4: Resistance

1. easy/hard, potential difference, current (either order), electrons, energy, conductors, insulators [7 marks]
2. resistance = $\frac{\text{potential difference}}{\text{current}} = \frac{12V}{0.4A} = 30\,\Omega$ [2 marks]

   resistance = $\frac{\text{potential difference}}{\text{current}} = \frac{12V}{0.1A} = 120\,\Omega$ [2 marks]
3. a) there are no charges free to move [1 mark]
   b) the charges are now free to move. [1 mark]

Chapter 1.5: Changing the subject

1. relationship, subject, dividing [3 marks]
2. a) W = mg dividing both sides by g, m = W/g [2 marks]
   b) W = mg, dividing both sides by m, g = W/m [2 marks]
3. The extension depends on the force and spring constant. A bigger force means bigger extension, and a bigger spring constant means a smaller extension. So x = F/K.

Chapter 1.6: Series and parallel

1. one, more than one, parallel, series [4 marks]
2. Resistance = p.d./current, if the current is bigger the resistance will be smaller. [2 marks]

3. a) Current = p.d./resistance = 6V/10 W = 0.6A
   b) 6V
   c) The ammeter reading would decrease to 0.3A
   The voltmeter reading would decrease to 3V.

Chapter 1.7: Magnets and magnetic fields

1. north, south, repel, attract, force, filings, compass [7 marks]
2. A compass needle always points in a north–south direction.
   The compass needle lines up in the Earth's magnetic field (which does not change). [2 marks]
3. a) There is an force on the ball bearing because it is a magnetic material in a magnet field.
   The force due to each magnet is equal is size but opposite in direction so they cancel out. [2 marks]
   b) The force due to the magnet on the left would be bigger the point would move towards the magnet on the right to compensate [2 marks]

Chapter 1.8: Electromagnets

1. current, magnetic field, more, bigger, magnetic field [5 marks]
2. Wind a wire around the nail.
   Attach the ends of the wires to the battery using the leads and crocodile clips. [2 marks]
3. Example answer, 4 marks maximum
   There is a magnetic field around a wire carrying a current.
   The field is stronger if there are more loops of wire because the fields add together.
   The magnetic material inside the coil becomes magnetised when you put it in a magnetic field.
   This increases the strength of the electromagnet.

Chapter 1.9: Using electromagnets

1. trains, relay, spins, cannot [4 marks]
2. a) A simple motor contains a coil of wire and two permanent magnets.
   A current flows in the coil of wire.
   The coil becomes an electromagnet.
   The forces between the coil and the permanent magnets make it spin. [4 marks]
3. Example answer, 4 marks total:
   An electromagnet is on the two walls.
   A magnetic material is on the doors.
   The magnetic material on the doors is attracted to it so the doors stay open while a current flows.
   When the fire alarm sounds, the current to the electromagnet is cut, so the magnetic material on the doors is no longer attracted to it.
   The doors close.

Chapter 1 Summary Answers

1. a) Electrons. [1 mark]
   b) Attract. [1 mark]
   c) Charge. [1 mark]
2. a) S on the left, N on the right. [1 mark]
   b) A – attract [1 mark]
      B – repel [1 mark]
   c) One from: you can turn it on and off, you can make it much stronger. [1 mark]
3. a) Wire, a nail/metal rod, battery. [3 marks]
   b) Increase, decrease, decrease. [3 marks]
4. a) Credit suitable parallel circuits with two cells on one branch, with a bulb and a switch on two other branches. [2 marks]
   b) Parallel. [1 mark]
   c) X, Y, X and Y [3 marks]
   d) Attach an ammeter between the bulbs and the switches. [2 marks]
5. a) Circuit diagram as described. [2 marks]
   b) The push of the battery/energy transferred in a component. [1 mark]
   c) The potential difference that the lamp is designed to work at. [1 mark]
   d) resistance = $\dfrac{\text{p.d.}}{\text{current}} = \dfrac{6\text{ V}}{0.4\text{ A}} = 15\ \Omega$ [2 marks]
   e) current = $\dfrac{\text{p.d.}}{\text{resistance}} = \dfrac{6\text{ V}}{10\ \Omega} = 0.6\text{A}$ [2 marks]
6. Students should be marked on the use of good English, organisation of information, spelling and grammar, and correct use of specialist scientific terms. The best answers will explain in detail how the rod becomes charged and is able to attract the small pieces of paper. [6 marks maximum]
   Examples of correct scientific points:
   Both the rod and cloth contain atoms.
   Atoms contain electrons, protons, and neutrons.
   Electrons are negatively charged.
   Protons are positively charged.
   When you rub the rod, electrons move from the cloth to the rod (or vice versa).
   The rod becomes negatively charged/cloth becomes positively charged (or vice versa, as above).
   The rod repels the electrons on the top of the pieces of paper.
   The top of the pieces of paper become positively charged.
   The paper is attracted to the rod.

Physics Chapter 2: Energy

Chapter 2.1: Food and fuels

1. food, fuels, joules, breathing, growing [6 marks]
2. There are 1000kJ in 100g of chips, so there are 2000kJ in 200g of chips
   Cycling uses 26kJ per minute so you need to cycle for 2000kJ/26kJ/minute = 77 minutes [1 mark]
3. Example answers [4 marks]:
   Identifies the time that he/she spends doing activities.
   Calculates the energy for each activity by multiplying the time by the energy per minute.
   Works out the mass of apple and chips that would be needed for the daily activities.
   Comments on the contrast in mass between apples and chips.

Chapter 2.2: Energy resources

1. non-renewable, fossil fuel, renewable [3 marks]
2. Burning gas heats water to produce steam. Steam drives a turbine. The turbine drives a generator. The generator generates electricity. [4 marks]
3. In thermal power stations water is converted to steam
   Steam drives turbines, which drive generators
   Water is used in hydroelectric, wave and tidal energy resources
   Water drives a turbine, which drives a generator.

Chapter 2.3: Energy adds up

1. created, destroyed, chemical, thermal, cannot [5 marks]
2. a) The battery has chemical energy. [2 marks]
   b) Chemical energy transferred to thermal energy by electricity and light. [2 marks]
3. [4 marks]. Example answer, OWTTE

	Before	After
What we have	More wood, oxygen, Cold sausages	Less wood, oxygen, Cooked sausages
Thinking about energy	There is more energy in the chemical store associated with the wood (and oxygen).	There is more energy in the thermal store associated with the sausages. There is less energy in the chemical store associated with the wood and oxygen. There is more energy in the thermal store associated with the air.

Chapter 2.4: Energy and temperature

1. temperature, thermometer, temperature, energy, solids, equilibrium [6 marks]
2. a cup of water at 30 °C, a saucepan of water at 30 °C, a saucepan of water at 50 °C [1 mark]
3. [4 marks]. Example answers:
   The hotter the tray the more particles vibrate. When you take the tray out of the oven energy moves from the thermal store of the tray to the thermal store of the air. The air heats up/particles move faster. The tray reaches the same temperature as the air and the particles in the tray vibrate less.

Chapter 2.5: Energy transfer: particles

1. conduction, temperature, convection, move, slowly [6 marks]
2. a) The particles in a solid are close together, so can pass on the vibration; the particles in a gas or in a liquid are too far apart. [2 marks]
   b) The particles in a gas or in a liquid can move; the particles in a solid cannot. Convection involves the movement of particles to transfer energy. [2 marks]
3. [4 marks]. Example answers:
   The metal element heats the water near it, and the hot water becomes less dense.
   Hot water floats up
   Cooler (denser) water sinks to replace it.
   A convection current forms, and the water circulates until all the water is hot.

Chapter 2.6: Energy transfer: radiation

1. sources, radiation, temperature, microwaves, visible, X-rays, medium, vacuum [8 marks]
2. a) White surfaces reflect infrared radiation so the houses will absorb less and stay cooler. [1 mark]
   b) To reflect infrared back into the flask [1 mark]
3. Venn diagram/visual summary example answers [6 marks]:
   Conduction/ convection overlap – both need particles
   Convection/ radiation overlap- happen in liquids/gases
   Conduction/ radiation overlap – happens in some solids
   All three overlap – types of energy transfer. [4 marks]

Chapter 2.7: Energy transfer: forces

1. force, distance, machine, lever, force, gear, conservation, energy [8 marks]
2. a) lever [1 mark]
   b) work done = force × distance = 200 N × 0.25 m = 50 J [2 marks]
3. Climbing Mount Everest: Work done = force × distance
   = 600 N × 10 000 m = 6 000 000 J
   Climbing upstairs to bed: Work done = force × distance
   = 600 N × 2.5 m = 1500 J
   Comparing the two: 6 000 000 J ÷ 1500 J = 4000
   so climbing Mount Everest requires 4000 times the work. [4 marks]

Chapter 2.8: Energy and power

1. joules, watts, second, kWh, lower, less [6 marks]
2. a) energy = power × time = 10kW × 1.5hours = 15kWh
   b) Cost = 15kWh × 10p/kWh = 150p, or £1.50. [2 marks]
3. [4 marks] Example answer:
   The energy that you pay for in kWh depends on the power and the time that you use it for.
   If the power is bigger the time will be shorter
   So the number of kWh would be the same
   The cost per kWh is the same, so it costs the same.

Chapter 2 Summary Answers

1. Wind, solar, geothermal. [1 mark]
2. a) C [1 mark]
   b) kW, watts, kilowatts, W. [1 mark]
3. a) Purple solid dissolves, purple-coloured water moves up across the top of the water and then down. The Bunsen burner heats the water around the solid, and the purple colour diffuses throughout the water in a convection current. [3 marks]
   b) Water is heated by the Bunsen burner, so the water molecules move faster. [1 mark] The water expands/becomes less dense. [1 mark] Hot water floats, and is replaced by cold water. [1 mark] Energy from burning gas is transferred to water which moves around the beaker. [1 mark]
   c) Infrared. [1 mark]
4. a) 100 mins. [1 mark]
   b) Smaller as you would use more energy when walking quickly so would take less time. [2 marks]
5. a) Gravitational potential. [1 mark]
   b) i) Energy is conserved/cannot be lost. [1 mark]
      ii) Some energy is transferred/dissipated to the thermal store as the ball falls through the air. [1 mark]
   c) There is a force (of gravity) acting on the ball. [2 marks]
6. a) Gravity. [1 mark]
   b) 300 N × 1m = 300 J [3 marks - 2 for calculation, 1 for unit]
   c) The time it took to lift. [1 mark]
   d) Power = energy/time, so divide answer to part (b) by the time it took in seconds. [1 mark]
7. Energy = 8000 kJ = 8000 000J [1 mark]
   Time = 1 day = 24 × 60 × 60 s = 86 400s [1 mark]
   Power = energy/time
   = 8000 000J/86400s [1 mark]
   = 93W (=92.59) [1 mark]
   Yes, it would be even brighter than 60W. [1 mark]
8. Students should be marked on the use of good English, organisation of information, spelling and grammar, and correct use of specialist scientific terms. The best answers will explain in detail how insulation reduces energy bills. [6 marks maximum]
   Examples of correct scientific points:
   Energy is transferred from a warm house to the cold air outside.
   Energy is transferred by conduction, convection, and radiation.
   To keep a house at the same temperature it needs to be heated.
   A lot of insulators trap air.
   Air is a poor conductor.
   Insulators reduce the rate of transfer of energy to the surroundings.
   The rate at which you need to heat the house to maintain the temperature decreases.
   A lower power heater is needed/heating is required for less time.

This reduces the number of kWh of energy used.
This will cost less money.

Physics Chapter 3: Motion and pressure

Chapter 3.1: Speed

1. distance, time, total distance, total time, instant, relative [6 marks]
2. Average speed = total distance ÷ total time
   = 100 m ÷ 12.5 s = 8 m/s [2 marks]
3. Their relative motion is 70 km/h either towards each other, if they haven't passed yet, or away from each other if they have already passed. [2 marks]
4. a) speed = distance/time
      Speed × time = distance × time/time
      Speed × time/speed = distance/speed
      Time = distance/speed [2 marks]
   b) distance = 6km, = 6000m
      time = 6000m/330m/s
      = 18 seconds
      Time = 5000m/300 000 000m/s
      = 0.00002s.

Chapter 3.2: Motion graphs

1. distance, time, slope, stationary, increasing [5 marks]
2. a) distance = 4000 m – 2400 m = 1600 m
      time = 45 min – 35 min = 10 min = 10 × 60 = 600 s
      speed = distance ÷ time = 1600 m ÷ 600 s = 2.67 m/s [4 marks]
   b) 0 m/s [1 mark]
3. 4 marks. Example answers:
   a) Both graphs start at a distance of zero and finish at a distance of 3 km.
      because the students travel the same total distance
   b) The slope of the graph for the car is steeper than that for the person walking
      The car travels faster than the person.

Chapter 3.3: Pressure in gases

1. collide with, bigger, smaller, smaller, fewer [4 marks]
2. a) There is less oxygen as you go up a mountain because gas pressure is reduced. The density of oxygen is low. [2 marks]
   b) It would take up too much space if it were not compressed. The oxygen pressure will be very high if the gas is compressed. [2 marks]
3. a) The pressure decreases
      The particles are not colliding with the sides of the can so much because the steam has condensed to water
   b) The atmospheric (water) pressure outside the can is higher than the pressure inside.
      The atmospheric pressure from the outside exerts a force on all sides of the can and it collapses

Chapter 3.4: Pressure in liquids

1. all, increases, weight, bigger, upthrust [5 marks]
2. a) Water pressure from the bottom creates the force upthrust. The clay boat floats because the upthrust balances out the weight of the boat. [2 marks]
   b) The area is much smaller, the difference between the force pushing down and the force pushing up is not enough for the upthrust to balance the weight. [2 marks]
3. a) it increases [1 mark]
   b) The difference in pressure between the top and the bottom of the ball produces a (upthrust) force that depends on the area of the ball in contact with the water When you let the ball go the upthrust is bigger than its weight so the ball moves up.

Chapter 3.5: Pressure on solids

1. force, area, big, small, N/m^2 [5 marks]
2. area of two hands = 150 cm^2 × 2 = 300 cm^2
   pressure = force ÷ area = 600 N ÷ 300 cm^2 = 2 N/cm^2 [3 marks]
3. a) force = pressure × area
      = 101 000 N/m^2 × 1.5m^2 [1 mark]
      = 151 500N (1 mark for number, 1 mark for unit)
   b) 151 500N/1000N per panda = 151 pandas [1 mark]
   c) The air is exerting a force in all directions, not just downwards. [1 mark]

Chapter 3.6: Turning forces

1. turning, force, distance, equilibrium, law, weight, gravity [7 marks]
2. moment = force × distance
      = 5 N × 0.75 m [1 mark]
      = 3.75 Nm (1 mark for answer, 1 mark for unit)
3. a) the girl would have to move closer to the pivot [1 mark]
      The boy's moment has been reduced because the distance to the pivot is smaller [1 mark]
      So she would need to reduce her moment to maintain equilibrium [1 mark]
   b) There are now two clockwise moments on the see-saw [1 mark]
      she would need to move further from the pivot [1 mark]
      so that there is a bigger anticlockwise moment to balance it [1 mark]

Chapter 3 Summary Answers

1. m/s, mph, km/s [3 marks]
2. B [1 mark]
3. a) i) B [1 mark]
      ii) D [1 mark]
   b) Speed = distance/time [1 mark]
      = 300 m/60 s [1 mark]
      = 5 m/s [1 mark]
   c) bigger. [1 mark]

4. a) 90°. [1 mark]
   b) There is a difference in pressure between the top and bottom of the balloon [1 mark] and (force = pressure × area), so there is a buoyancy force/upthrust on the balloon. [1 mark]
   c) If the balloon is smaller the difference in pressure and area are smaller, [1 mark] so the force would be smaller. [1 mark]
5. a) P = F/A [1 mark]
   = 700 N/200 cm³ [1 mark]
   = 3.5 [1] N/cm³ [1 mark]
   b) It will halve [1 mark], since the area is double, so the pressure is half. [1 mark]
   c) The area of their feet is smaller. [1 mark]
6. a) Clockwise moment = force × distance = 1.5 N × 0.3 m [1 mark] = 0.45 Nm [1 mark]
   b) Anticlockwise moment = 0.45 Nm = force (exerted by muscle) × 0.03 m [1 mark]
   Force exerted by muscle = 0.45 Nm ÷ 0.03 m = 15 N [1 mark]
   c) The force is bigger because anticlockwise moment = clockwise moment (for the system to remain balanced). [1 mark] The distance from the pivot is much less. [1 mark]
7. Students should be marked on the use of good English, organisation of information, spelling and grammar, and correct use of specialist scientific terms. The best answers will explain in detail how a bag of crisps appears to expand at a higher altitude. [6 marks maximum]
   Examples of correct scientific points:
   The bag of crisps contains air.
   Air molecules collide with the inside of the bag.
   Air molecules in the atmosphere collide with the outside of the bag
   If the pressure is the same inside and outside the bag, the bag does not get bigger.
   Atmospheric pressure decreases with height, because gravity pulls the air molecules down.
   There are fewer collisions between air molecules and objects as you go higher.
   The air pressure inside the plane is less than the air pressure on the ground (inside the crisp packet), so the bag gets bigger.
8. a) There is no turning force [1 mark] because the weight of the plank acts through the shoulder. [1 mark]
   b) The weight produces a moment about the new pivot. [1 mark] The person will need to exert a moment in the opposite direction, [1 mark] so the moments are equal. [1 mark]

Index

A
acceleration 211
accurate data 9
acid rain 92, 93
acids and metals 124–5
adaptation 66
    how can animals live in a desert? 66
    how can plants live in a desert? 66–7
    how do animals cope with the seasons? 67
    how do organisms cope with environmental change? 67
    how do trees cope with the seasons? 67
    natural selection 78–9
addiction 35, 36
aerobic respiration 50
    how do glucose and oxygen get into cells? 51
    how does carbon dioxide leave the body? 51
    where does respiration happen? 50
alcohol 36
    alcoholics 36
    dangers of alcohol 37
    pregnancy 37
    units of alcohol 36–7
algae 44
aluminium, recycling 159
ammeters 168
amps 169
anaerobic respiration 52–3
anecdotal evidence 16
atmosphere 145
    atmospheric pressure 213
    carbon cycle 152–3
    greenhouse effect 154–5
atoms 166
attracting charges 166
audience *see* writing for an audience
average speed 209
averages 11

B
bar charts 10
batteries (cells) 168, 170
beer 53
bees 60
Benedict's solution 27
bias 17
bile 33
bioaccumulation 61
biodiversity 81
biuret solution 27
blood 31, 51
bread 53

C
camouflage 66
carbohydrase 33
carbohydrates 24
carbon 133
    carbon stores 153
    metal extraction 133
carbon dioxide 51
    carbon cycle 152–3
carbon monoxide 39
catalysts 32
categorical data 10
cells 50–1
    nucleus 76
cells (batteries) 168
cementation 147
centre of gravity (mass) 219
ceramics 134
    properties of ceramics 134–5
    uses of ceramics 135
    what gives ceramics their properties? 135
charge 166
    electric fields 167
    how do charged objects interact? 166–7
    how do objects become charged? 167
charts 10
chemical properties of elements 92–3
    Group 0 elements 101
    Group 1 elements 97
    Group 7 elements 99
chemical stores 192
chlorine 98
chlorophyll 45, 48
chloroplasts 46
chromatography 118
    chromatograms 118
    how does chromatography work? 118
    how is chromatography useful? 119
chromosomes 76
circuit symbols 169
climate change 156–7
combustion 152
communicating scientific information 14–15
    effective writing 14–15
    planning your communication 14
    purpose of communication 14
communities 62
compaction 147
competition 64–5
    best competitors 65
    environmental change 67
    predator–prey relationships 65
    what do animals compete for? 64
    what do plants compete for? 64
composites 138–9
    carbon-fibre-reinforced plastic 139
compounds 108–9
compressed gas 212
conclusions 13
concrete, reinforced 138–9
conduction 196
    comparing conduction, convection and radiation 199
conductors 173, 196
consumers 44, 58, 61
continuous data 10
continuous variation 74, 75
control measures 9
convection 196, 197
    comparing conduction, convection and radiation 199
    convection currents 197
cooling 195
copper 88–9, 128, 130
core (Earth) 144
cores (electromagnets) 181
crust (Earth) 144, 145

D
data 9
    analysing and evaluating data 12–13
    communicating scientific information 14–15
    data spread 9
    presenting data 10–11
    using evidence and sources 16–17
decomposers 59
defibrillators 170
deficiencies 29, 48–9
deforestation 156
density 213
dependent variables 9
deposition 147
depressants 36
depth 215
diet, balanced 24–5
diet, unhealthy 28
    overweight 29
    underweight 28
    vitamin and mineral deficiencies 29
digestion 30–1
    bacteria and digestion 32
    digestive juices 32–3
digestive system 30
    moving through the digestive system 31
    passing into the blood 31
    structures in the digestive system 30–1
directly proportional relationships 12
discontinuous variation 74, 75
discrete data 10
displacement reactions 130–1
    oxides 131
dissipation of energy 193
dissolving 110–11
    carbon cycle 153
    solvents 111
distance–time graphs 210–11
distillation 117
DNA 76, 77
drugs 34
    drug addiction 35
    medicinal drugs 34
    recreational drugs 34, 35
durability 148

E
Earth 19, 144
    atmosphere 145
    crust 144, 145
    greenhouse effect 154–5
    magnetic field 179, 181
    outer and inner core 144
    rock cycle 150–1
    structure of the Earth 144
ecosystems 62
    co-existing in an ecosystem 63
    niches 63
    quadrat samples 62
elastic stores 192
electric charge 166–7
electric current 168
    circuit symbols 169
    how do you measure current? 168–9
    modelling electric circuits 169, 171, 177
    parallel circuits 176–7
    potential difference (p.d.) 170–1, 177
    resistance 172–5
    series circuits 176–7
    what are the two types of circuit? 176
    what is current? 168
    where do charges come from? 168
electric field 167
electromagnetic spectrum 198
electromagnetic stores 192
electromagnets 180–1
    cores 181
    increasing strength 181
    lifting car 183
    maglev trains 182
    making a motor 183
    permanent magnet or electromagnet? 183
    sorting metals 183
    starting a car 182
    switching on dangerous equipment 182
electrons 166, 168
elements 88–9
    do all elements fit the pattern? 91
    Group 0 elements 100–1
    Group 1 96–7
    Group 7 elements 98–9
    groups and periods 94–5
    how are elements organised? 90
    metal or non-metal? 91
endangered species 81
energy 28, 188–9
    energy analysis 192

energy and power 202–3
energy and temperature 194–5
energy resources 190–1
energy stores 192
how do cells transfer energy? 50
law of conservation of energy 192
nutrients 28, 29, 188–9
saving energy 193
transferring energy between stores 193
why do things happen? 193
energy transfer 196
comparing conduction, convection and radiation 199
conductors 196
forces 200–1
insulating liquids and gases 197
insulators 196
radiation 196, 198–9
sound 197
what is convection? 197
environment 62
environmental change 67
environmental variation 73
enzymes 32–3
equations 174–5
equilibrium 195
erosion 147
ethanol 36
evaporation 116
evidence 16
evolution 78
how do organisms evolve? 78–9
peppered moths 79
extinction 80
how do organisms become extinct? 80–1

F
fermentation 53
fibre 24, 25
filtration (filtering) 114
filtrates 114
how does filtering work? 114–15
how is filtration useful? 115
separating a solution from an insoluble solid 115
floating 215
food chains 58
bioaccumulation 61
disruption 60–1
how many levels in a food chain? 59
food energy 28, 29, 188
how much energy do you need each day? 189
what is an 'energy balance'? 189
food tests 26
testing for lipids 26–7
testing for protein 27
testing for starch 26

testing for sugar 27
food webs 59
interdependence in food webs 60
forces 200
do you get something for nothing? 201
how do levers work? 201
how do machines make life easier? 201
moments 218–19
what is work? 200
what makes objects unstable? 219
why are mountain roads winding? 201
fossil fuels 190
fossil record 78, 80
fuels 188, 190

G
gas pressure 212
atmospheric pressure 213
compressed gas 212
temperature and volume 212
gases 197
greenhouse gases 155
noble gases 100–1
genes 76, 79
gene banks 81
germanium 89
global heating (global warming) 155
causes 155
climate change 156–7
greenhouse effect 154–5
impacts of global heating 157
glucose 50, 51
gold 127, 128
graphs 10, 210–11
analysing and evaluating data 12–13
gravitational potential stores 192
greenhouse effect 154–5
groups of the Periodic Table 94–5
Group 0 100–1
Group 1 96–7
Group 7 98–9
guard cells 47

H
habitats 62
desert 66–7
haemoglobin 51
halogens 98
hazards 9
heating 195
hibernation 67
histograms 10, 11
hydrochloric acid 124–5
hypotheses 8–9

I
igneous rocks 148
how igneous rocks are made 149

impure substances 107
incompressibility 214
independent variables 9
infrared radiation 198, 199
inheritance 76
chromosomes 76
discovering DNA 77
genes 76–7
how is genetic material inherited? 77
inherited variation 73
insecticides 61
insoluble substances 113
separating a solution from an insoluble solid 115
instantaneous speed 209
insulators 173, 196
insulating liquids and gases 197
interdependence 60
investigations 8–9
iodine 26

J
joules 188
journals 16

K
kilojoules 188
kilowatts 202
kilowatt hours 207
kinetic stores 192

L
lava 149
laws 18, 19
law of conservation of energy 192
law of moments 218–19
leaves 46
gas exchange 47
how does water get into a plant? 47
levers 201
lightning 168
line graphs 10
line of best fit 13
linear relationships 12
directly proportional relationships 12
lipase 33
lipids 24, 25, 26–7
liquid pressure 214
does pressure change with depth? 215
floating and sinking 215
lithium 96, 116

M
machines, simple 201
maglev trains 182
magma 149
magnesium 48, 126
magnesium oxide 126
magnetic fields 178

investigating shape of a magnetic field 178–9
magnetic field lines 178–9
shape of Earth's magnetic field 179
shape of magnetic field around a wire 180
magnets 178, 180
electromagnets 180–3
magnetic materials 178, 181
magnetising 181
permanent magnet or electromagnet? 183
malnourishment 28–9
mantle (Earth) 144
mean 11
median 11
medicinal drugs 34
metalloids 91
metals 88
comparing reactions with acids and oxygen 127
displacement reactions 130–1
extracting metals 132–3
Group 1 elements 96–7
how do metals react with oxygen? 93
physical properties 91
reaction with hydrochloric acid 124–5
reaction with oxygen 126–7
reaction with steam 129
reaction with water 128–9
sorting metals 183
metamorphic rocks 149
uses of metamorphic rock 149
metres per second (m/s) 208
microorganisms 53
migration 67
minerals 24, 25, 29
plants 48–9
mitochondria 50
mixtures 108–9
mode 11
models 18, 19
modelling electric circuits 169, 171, 177
moments 218–19
motion 209, 210–11
motors 169, 183

N
natural polymers 136–7
natural selection 78–9
negative charge 166
neutrality 167
neutrons 166
newton metres (Nm) 200, 216, 218
niches 63
nitrates 48
noble gases 100–1
uses of noble gases 101
where do noble gases come from? 101
non-metals 89

Index

Group 7 elements 98–9
　how do non-metals react with oxygen? 92–3
　physical properties 91
non-renewable resources 190
north poles 178, 179
nuclear power stations 191
nuclear stores 192
nucleus 76
nutrients 24–5
　food tests 26–7

O
obesity 29
observations 18
ohms 172
ores 132
　extracting metals from ores 133
　how much metal is in an ore? 133
oxides 126, 131
　which metal oxides react with carbon? 133
oxygen 51, 92–3
　oxygen debt 52
　reaction with metals 93, 126–7

P
palladium 94–5
parallel circuits 176–7
particles 196–7
pascals (Pa) 216
passive smoking 38
peer reviews 16
peppered moths 79
Periodic Table 90
　groups 94–5
　periods 95
phosphates 48
photosynthesis 44–5, 152
　testing a leaf for starch 45
　where does photosynthesis occur? 45
physical properties of elements 90–1
　Group 0 elements 100–1
　Group 1 elements 97
　Group 7 elements 99
pie charts 10
pivots 218
plants 47, 60, 64, 66–7
　flowering plants 60
　mineral deficiency 48–9
　mineral requirements 48
　why do farmers use fertilisers? 49
plasma 51
plastic
　carbon-fibre-reinforced plastic 139
　recycling plastics 159
pollination 60
polymers 136
　natural polymers 136–7
　synthetic polymers 137

populations 60, 65
　consumer population 61
　producer population 61
positive charge 166
potential difference (p.d.) 170
　measuring potential difference 170–1
　what is potential difference? 170
power 202–3
　calculating power 202
　difference between energy and power 202
　how powerful are you? 203
　power rating 202
　power stations 190–1
　what are you paying for? 202–3
precise data 9
predators 58, 67
predictions 8
　conclusions and limitations 13
pressure 216
　big and small pressure 217
　calculating pressure 216–17
　pressure in gases 212–13
　pressure in liquids 214–15
prey 58, 65
producers 44, 58, 61
properties of elements 88–93
protease 33
proteins 24, 25, 27
protons 166
pure substances 106–7
　identifying 107

R
radiation 196
　comparing conduction, convection and radiation 199
　how is energy transferred by radiation? 198
　what absorbs or reflects infrared? 199
　what emits infrared? 199
　what is radiation? 198
ramps 201
rating 171, 202
reactive elements 97
　reactivity series 129, 133
recreational drugs 34, 35
recycling 158–9
　advantages and disadvantages 159
　can you recycle anything? 159
relays 182
renewable resources 191
repeatable data 9
repelling charges 166
reproducible data 9
research 17
residues 114
resistance 172
　calculating resistance 172–3
　changing the subject of resistance equations 174–5
　conductors and insulators 173

　what happens inside a wire? 173
resources 158
respiration 50–3, 152
risk assessments 9
rock cycle 150
　how does the rock cycle recycle materials? 151
　uplift 151

S
salts 125
saturated solutions 112
scientific method 18
　development of our understanding of the Solar System 19
　development of scientific ideas over time 19
sea salt 116
seasonal changes 67
secondary data 13
sedimentary rocks 146
　how sedimentary rocks are made 146–7
　properties 146
　uses of sedimentary rocks 147
sediments 146
series circuits 176–7
sinking 215
smoking 38
　disease 39
　tobacco smoke 39
Solar System 19
solubility 112–13
　effect of temperature 113
　soluble substances 112–13
solutions 110–11
　distillation 117
　evaporation 116, 117
　saturated solutions 112
　separating a solution from an insoluble solid 115
　solutes 110–11
solvents 111
sound 197
sources 16–17
south poles 178, 179
species 72, 78, 80
speed 208
　acceleration 211
　calculating speed 208–9
　distance–time graphs 210–11
　instantaneous or average speed? 208–9
　relative motion 209
starch 26, 45
starvation 28
static electricity 166
steel 128, 132
stomata 47
sugar 27
sulfur 89
switches 168
synthetic polymers 137

T
temperature 113
　cooling 195
　difference between energy and temperature 194–5
　heating 195
　pressure 212
　what is temperature? 194
terminals 170
theories 18, 19
thermal imaging cameras 199
thermal power stations 190–1
thermal stores 192
thermometers 194
transport, sedimentary 147
troposphere 145
turning forces 218–19

U
unreactive elements 101, 127
　reactivity series 129, 133
uplift 151
upthrust 215
uranium 191

V
variables 9
variation 72
　continuous variation 74
　discontinuous variation 74
　how do humans vary? 72
　patterns of variation 75
　plotting continuous variation 75
　plotting discontinuous variation 75
　what causes variation? 73
villi 31
vitamins 24, 25, 29
voltage 171
voltmeters 170–1
volts 170
volume 212

W
water 24, 25
　how does water get into a plant? 47
　water as solvent 110–11
watts 202
weathering 146
wine 53
wires 173
withdrawal symptoms 35
work 200
writing for an audience 14–15
　writing for a scientific audience 15
　writing for different audiences 15

Y
yeast 53

OXFORD
UNIVERSITY PRESS

Great Clarendon Street, Oxford, OX2 6DP, United Kingdom

Oxford University Press is a department of the University of Oxford. It furthers the University's objective of excellence in research, scholarship, and education by publishing worldwide. Oxford is a registered trade mark of Oxford University Press in the UK and in certain other countries.

© Oxford University Press 2022

The moral rights of the authors have been asserted

First published in 2022

All rights reserved. No part of this publication may be reproduced, stored in a retrieval system, or transmitted, in any form or by any means, without the prior permission in writing of Oxford University Press, or as expressly permitted by law, by licence or under terms agreed with the appropriate reprographics rights organization. Enquiries concerning reproduction outside the scope of the above should be sent to the Rights Department, Oxford University Press, at the address above.

You must not circulate this work in any other form and you must impose this same condition on any acquirer

British Library Cataloguing in Publication Data
Data available

978-1-38-202110-4

978-1-38-202098-5 (ebook)

10 9 8 7 6 5 4 3 2 1

Paper used in the production of this book is a natural, recyclable product made from wood grown in sustainable forests.

The manufacturing process conforms to the environmental regulations of the country of origin.

Printed and bound by CPI group (UK) Ltd, Croydon, CR0 4YY

Acknowledgements
The authors would like to thank the following:

Jo Locke:
Many thanks to my girls Emily and Hermione for all their support, encouragement, and delicious cakes, and to Dave for providing endless cups of tea and helpful ideas. It has been an honour to write again with the original Activate team of Philippa Gardom Hulme and Helen Reynolds; I couldn't have done it without you.

Alyssa Fox-Charles:
Thanks to Billy and my ever-supporting family Judy, Nic, Gemma, and Josie for their encouragement, help, and never-ending belief in me, and OUP for allowing me this amazing opportunity.

Anna Harris:
Many thanks for my family for all their support and encouragement, and to Kate and Anna for their advice. Also to OUP, especially to Laura, for their patience and support through this project.

The publisher and authors would like to thank the following for permission to use photographs and other copyright material:

Cover by Michal Bednarski.

Artwork by Q2A Media

Although we have made every effort to trace and contact all copyright holders before publication this has not been possible in all cases. If notified, the publisher will rectify any errors or omissions at the earliest opportunity.

Links to third party websites are provided by Oxford in good faith and for information only. Oxford disclaims any responsibility for the materials contained in any third party website referenced in this work.